IMAGINAL BODY

Para-Jungian Reflections on Soul, Imagination and Death

Roberts Avens

UNIVERSITY
PRESS OF
AMERICA

Copyright © 1982 by

University Press of America, Inc.

P.O. Box 19101, Washington, D.C. 20036

Library of Congress Cataloging in Publication Data

Avens, Roberts, 1923-
  Imaginal body.

  Bibliography: p.
  1. Imagination--Addresses, essays, lectures. 2. Soul
--Addresses, essays, lectures. 3. Death--Addresses,
essays, lectures. 4. Jung, C. G. (Carl Gustav), 1875-
1961. 5. Hillman, James. I. Title.
BF408.A87 1982   150.19   81-43814
ISBN 0-8191-2411-7   AACR2
ISBN 0-8191-2412-5 (pbk.)

TABLE OF CONTENTS

PART TWO

PREFACE

Uno itinere non potest parvenire
at tam grande Secretum.
Q. Aurelius Symmachus, Rel. III
(Seek's ed. p. 282).

The title of this book, Imaginal Body, implicitly points to the terror we occasionally experience at the thought that we are incomplete, non-achieved beings. Paradoxically, however, this terror is often the result of an obverse view of ourselves as embodied spirits destined to reach a hypothetical perfection in an earthly or heavenly utopia. As the utopia recedes or becomes more and more incredible, we find ourselves overwhelmed by the realization that our presumed spirituality is a sham which must be discarded in favor of a "realistic" view of life. At its extreme, "realistic" thinking asserts that we are no more than a collection of structured, breathing offal, a "naked ape," separated from the umbilical chain, a lonely and "sick animal" (Nietzsche) thrown into a world that knows us not.

The idea of an "imaginal body" stands between these two extremes of spiritualism and materialism. It denotes, not an artificial combination or a crossbreed of two independent things called "spirit" and "matter," but a sui generis reality which is ontologically prior to and paradigmatic of the so called spiritual as well as material realities. It is also for this reason that the notion of "imaginal body," instead of eliminating our endemic sense of incompleteness, carries it over into "the Beyond" - conceived not as a different realm of being but as a differently experienced mode of being. In other terms, I shall maintain that incompleteness is inseparable from an imaginatively oriented life in all its manifestations (including dying) and that anything like "wholeness" or "immortality" may be envisaged only through a full realization of a certain "lack" at the very core of our being. The expression "imaginal body" (commonly known in esoteric and parapsychological literature as the subtle or astral body) refers, not to a spook or to some other "paranormal" entity, but to this body of ours of which a verse from the Buddhist Pali Canon says: "My friend, in this very body, six feet of it with its senses, thoughts, and feelings, is the world, the origin of the world, the ceasing of the world and the way of its cessation." The body is a microcosm, the essential alchemical vessel in which everything happens, including the "happening" called "I" or "me." For all practical purposes this body is also identical with "soul" or "psyche" according to the uses to which these words are put in the present text.

The adjective "imaginal" (rather than "imaginary") is meant to indicate as strongly as possible that imagination, as William Blake said, is "the true man." In our culture imagination is generally feared, degraded into a lower faculty or used in the sense of business acumen; only poets and such are granted the license to be professionally imaginative. The fear of imagination is comparable to agrophobia - the chronic dread of vast and open spaces; ultimately it is the fear of the body which in its microcosmic import reflects these infinite spaces. We fear imagination as we fear life itself and its inseverable conjunction with death.

In our view, imagination is stronger than death: it does not cease with the demise of the physical body. It is not that imagination as such is immortal: it only immortalizes or eternalizes by creating something subtle out of the banal and the commonplace, and that new creation is momentarily, i.e., as long as it lasts, eternal.

Thus the word "imagination" in the present context stands not only for a special faculty or organ of perception, cognitively valid in its own right, but for reality itself. In turn, "reality" for us means "psychic reality" whose "content" (the images) is indistinguishable from "form" (the psyche). In the final analysis, therefore, the object of psychological knowledge or apperception is no other than the psyche itself and its images. This will involve us in circular reasoning - nothing to be abhorred once we realize the implications of a microcosmical view of man. Circularity is a way to see through empirics to image, through the letter that "killeth" to the spirit that "quickeneth."

The viewpoint I have adopted is that of Jungian thought as re-visioned by archetypal psychology and its author and main protagonist James Hillman. Both Jung and Hillman, as well as other kindred spirits on whose insights I depend (Swedenborg, Blake, Corbin, Cassirer, even the late Heidegger), belong to the Platonic and Neo-Platonic tradition of Western philosophy. But Platonism, such as we find it in archetypal psychology, is modified in the direction of a radical pluralism in that the psyche is seen as a multi-centered, polymorphous and polytheistic reality - a multitude of forces and persons none of which is allowed to usurp lasting hegemony over the others.

Hillman's psychology represents a return to that forgotten religious entity known as the soul and its _logos_ - a _logos_ which operates in the poetic and metaphorical mode rather than "logically." The logic of the soul is based on the Platonic insight that the cosmos, no less than man, is a soul-permeated magnitude. From this universal kinship the ancient thinkers derived the postulate that like is apprehended by like. Probably it is best expressed in Plotinus (_Ennead_ I. 6. 9): "For one must come to the sight with a seeing power akin and like to what is seen. No eye ever saw the sun without becoming sun-like, nor can a soul see beauty without becoming beautiful."

The soul is essentially protean: it changes shape according to its desires, and its progression alternates with regression. There is sickness and pathology in this movement. But the soul also desires order and rationality, though never for their own sake. Whatever the soul desires is always for the sake of seeing through to an ever greater depth so that, from a psychological perspective, nothing can be literally true or literally ultimate, not even the soul itself if it is used as an excuse from further exploration and wandering. What I am saying may sound scandalous or even relativistic and nihilistic to a mind bent on the pursuit and possession of unshakable certainty. The only consolation I have to offer is that nihilism, let's say a la Nietzsche, like any other "ism," is not exempt from the insighting power of the soul. In this sense the soul is indeed a kind of "nihilizing" power in that it reduces all rigid and absolutizing positions to their archetypal ingredients, the images. But that also means freedom - the freedom to imagine many - not any - possibilities. Instead of a laissez-faire attitude we shall stick to something like "letting-be." Images must be allowed to speak for themselves, to tell their own stories because they have many wonderous stories to tell.

The book is an essay in visionary anthropology - a tentative effort to clear some ground for a more adequate conception of what it means to be human in a time when the word "humanism" is used as a convenient prop for promoting basically anti-humanistic and anti-life ideologies born out of fascination with science and technological achievement. There is a strange collusion between the call for "old spiritual values" and the aggressive demand for more mastery over nature. I do not want to identify this kind of confused thinking as something in the order of "abomination of desolation;" I do fear, however, that it threatens to obliterate everything that the word humanitas has so far encompassed. Is it possible for the soul to renounce itself? The trouble with the soul is that it poses more questions than it can ever answer. But then it may very well be that posing questions or rather the questing itself is peculiarily the psyche's way of answering the question about itself.

The first part of the book, dealing with soul, imagination and death, should be seen as a necessary introduction to the phenomenon of "subtle embodiment." Put simply: without imagination there is no soul, without soul the body does not dream and without dreams it dies. Thus an imaginal body is not only a dreaming body, but also such stuff as dreams are made on - a dream body. The second part is devoted to this gossamer entity in selected areas of Western thought, preceded by a discussion of the parapsychological viewpoint. The inclusion of parapsychology is justified on the grounds that it exemplifies how the question of the subtle body, approached scientifically, may indeed be "soluble" ("in the near future" of course!") but only at the price of the death of both body and spirit. - I hope that the many loose ends, ommissions and occasional commissions will not significantly detract from what I have set out to accomplish - to show that man, this "quintessence of dust," verily imagined, is nevertheless one of the most remarkable ghosts in the sublunar world of apparitional beings.

PART ONE

I: THE GHOST OF IMAGINATION

The Romantic Eyes

What is an image and imagining? The question, asked in this form, cannot be answered because it is wrongly posed; it assumes - gratuitously - that there is some definite mental content which can be unambiguously described and fixed for future reference. An additional difficulty with this type of question is due to an excessive concentration on the sense of sight. We naturally talk of "picturing" or of "visualizing," but there are also aural, tactual, and olfactory imagery (a blind man's imagery presumably would be entirely of these kinds). Furthermore, there are images that appear to be within our mind. When we close our eyes, we "see" with the mind's eye memories of past events, or imagine future situations and we daydream of vividly textual happenings beyond the confines of time and space. This "inner reality," however, to most people in our culture is not as credible as the "external reality;" at best, it is accepted as pleasantly irrelevant or dismissed as deceptive or even dangerous to the sense of stability which is felt to be indispensable for a normal existence. Most of the time we are convinced that the inner and outer worlds are separate and that their mixing is due principally to autistic, pathological or otherwise "abnormal" conditions. Undoubtedly, these and similar considerations have led many philosophers and psychologists to the conclusion that there is something unreal about imaginative activity. Jean-Paul Sartre has expressed this opinion by saying that "the image contains a certain nothingness. However lively, however affecting or strong an image may be, it is clear that its object is non-existent."[1]

It is possible, up to a certain point, to follow the physiolog-

1

ical process of image formation. We find here that the light or the energy impulses which are relayed to the visual areas of the brain, are almost simultaneously translated into meaningful shapes, called images. What the brain receives, however, is not a picture or a portrait of the outside reality, but only a constellation of physical signals which are not identical with the visual perception appearing in consciousness. During the process of transmission these signals are transformed into a new class of perceptions which cannot be associated with any known organ.

There seems to be no such thing as immaculate perception. Seeing is not registering but interpreting - an original reaction of the whole organism to the patterns of light stimulating the back of our eyes. Or, is it the case, as Plotinus suggests, that the eyes are themselves "sunlike?" Our conclusion at this stage must be that images, whatever else they are supposed to mean, are the original units of psychic functioning. The ability to imagine is a human prerogative, enabling us to delay instantaneous reaction to stimuli and to build up during this momentary pause something new - a world with human face which even in its grotesquely distorted manifestations cannot help being human. Like the artist who sees what he paints (instead of painting what he sees) we, too, ineluctably see what we desire to see. As Dick Diver in F. Scott Fitzgerald's Tender is the Night declares: "You have romantic eyes. Your eyes see only what they want to see." But we must carry this observation further by admitting just as candidly that, for example, a butcher too must be credited with romantic eyes when, looking at a bull, he sees beef steaks.

What all this amounts to is that, epistemologically speaking, "reality" cannot be adequately approached in terms of the exclusivistic either/or maxim. Rather, we are compelled, whenever things seem to get mixed up, to proceed on the principle of the paradoxical both/and or what the mythologist Joseph Campbell calls the logic of "indissociation." This logic, undaunted by the

2

protestations of the rationalist, states that A is B, and C is also B.[2] And we have to swim in it!

It is also salutary to remind ourselves that paradoxical thinking links us, the moderns, to our remotest ancestors - at least to the cave dwellers in France, Spain and Africa who lived during the Ice Age (60.000 to 10.000 B.C.). For these people every event and natural force was animated with inner vision and no absolute distinction was made between sleeping and waking, between visions and perceptions. To give just one example, among the Central Australian Aranda, all life on earth is seen as a projection or duplication of a mythical dream-time, called altjeringa. Altjeringa is a fabulous, primordial epoch of the ancestors, representing paradigmatic history which man has to follow and repeat in order to assure the continuity of the world, of life and of society. In Northeast Australia, an Unambal, while repainting the image of a totemic ancestor on the rock wall, says: "I am going to refresh and invigorate myself; I paint myself anew..."[3]

Gaston Bachelard, author of some of the most stimulating work on imagination, has expressed the same idea more elegantly: "Adam found Eve after a dream: that is why woman is so beautiful."[4] Apparently Adam's faculty of sight not only functioned better during the dream but was informed by the dream when he woke up. It was the dream that added force, clearness, and distinctness to his day-light perception of Eve, going, as it were, straight to the core of the Urphänomen that was this particular woman. According to Indo-Tibetan cosmology, "in the beginning" all men possessed this faculty to see through the habitual opaqueness of things. The devas had created man not only with better eyes but also with a body that was fluid, protean and diaphanous. In the ensuing combat between the devas and asuras, the latter tried to destroy this body by progressive petrification: it became fixed and its skeleton, overcome by the

3

petrifying process, was immobilized. Then the devas, turning evil into good, created joints after having fractured the bones, and they likewise opened the ways of the senses by piercing the skull, which threatened to imprison the seat of the mind. "Thus, says the Tibetan medicine man, the solidifying process stops before reaching its extreme limit and certain organs in man, such as eyes, still keep something of the nature of the uncorporeal states."[5]

Some Historical Antecedents

Historically, the most controversial question is that of the psyhological (also epistemological) role of images; specifically, it is the question of how images are related to thinking. The usual answer is that images represent objects in their absence. They are indirect mental represenations of the external form of things by what we remember and know about them. Experiences deposit images and these images are handled as though they were the originals themselves.

This crude view of imagination, known as the copy theory, suggests that the image is a complete, colorful and mechanical replica of some visible scene or object floating tangibly in the mind. Nothing essentially different is said by admitting that memory can take things out of their context and "imagine" absurd creatures such as centaurs, griffins, the trunk of a human body with a cat's head or goat's limbs, etc. In both instances we are offered a concept of imagination whose only creative function consists either in duplicating or in falsifying reality.

The representational view seems to carry linguistic sanction in that the Latin root of "image" is imago (related to imitari, to imitate) meaning an imitation, copy or likeness. Thus it seems natural to ascribe to imagination a mimetic function - a move which in recent history was made by the British phiolospher David Hume (1711-1776). Hume, who was determined to emulate

4

Newton by reducing phenomena of nature to the simplest and most universal causes, held that for any sense impression "there is a copy taken by the mind, which remains after the impression ceases."[6] These copies he called indiscriminately ideas or images. Ideas are assumed to be distinct from images (impressions, passions and emotions) only insofar as the latter are preceived more intensely and vividly than the former. Ideas are simply faint images, weaker versions of the original sensuous perceptions.

In Hume's sensationalist theory of mind, images are repro-duced and joined together by the principle of association - a process which has the effect of compelling us to believe that there are permanent and separable objects in the world. Yet, while thus providing us with a sense of security, imagination deceives us, for "nothing is more dangerous to reason than the flights of imagination."[7]

The psychological atomism, inaugurated by Hume, repre-sents a formula for what may be called associative or reproductive imagination. The great ancestor of this account of imagination in Western philosophy is Aristotle. Prima facie Aristotle seems to attribute to imagination a role that is unqualifiedly central. The perceptions of the five senses (aisthēta) are said to be the material of the intellectual faculty (noēta) only after they have been worked upon by the faculty of imagination (fantasia which is a kind of motion resulting from sensation). The thinking soul (dianotikē psychē) must make use of phantasms which are like sensations except that they are immaterial. Aristotle admits that fantasy of the simple perceptual type (aisthētikē) is found also in animals; man alone, however, has the power of deliberately producing a single fantasy from a number of phantasms of the perceptual type. In an often quoted sentence, he states: "The soul never thinks without a mental picture."[8]

In the last resort, Aristotle makes imagination directly

dependent upon sensation. In his view imagination cannot be a
sui generis faculty, for nothing comes to our conscious awareness
from imagination as such which is said to be "for the most part
false."[9] In this he anticipates Locke's celebrated formula: nihil
est in intellectu quod non ante fuerit in sensu (nothing is to be
found in the intellect that does not come from the senses).

It is not an exaggeration to suggest that Aristotle fore-
shadows not only eighteenth century empiricisim but also Western
materialism in all its more or less sublimated forms. The only
function, ascribed to imagination in both Aristotle and Hume, is
to tidy up the "blooming buzzing confusion" (James) of sense
experience. We must use images in order to apply concepts to
things, i.e., to see meanings in the objects before us and so to
render the world of pure sensation familiar and manageable.

In the history of Western philosophy it is Immanuel Kant
(1724-1804) who must be credited with elevating imagination to a
position of prominence among other faculties. Kant distinguished
between two kinds of imagination: the reproductive and the
productive or transcendental. The workings of the productive
(empirical) imagination are subject to the laws of association; as
in Hume, its function is merely to solidify the chaos of sensations
into an image. The transcendental or productive imagination
(Einbildungskraft) is an active, spontaneous power (Kraft)
within man to build (bilden) into synthetic unity (ein-) purely
sensory data and intellectual apprehension. Far from being
merely one more faculty alongside sense and thought, imagination
is the common source which permits both sensation and thought
to spring forth. He calls it "a grounding-power of the soul
which lies as the ground of all a priori knowledge."[10] This
would mean that imagination is not reducible to sense or to
thought; rather, it is a dynamic and self-generating process. In
words that seem to anticipate depth psychology, Kant says that
imagination is "a blind but indispensable function of the soul,

without which we should have no knowledge whatever, but of which we are scarcely conscious."[11]

Martin Heidegger, in his controversial study of Kant has suggested that in the end Kant retreated from his previous view of the primacy of imagination. His discovery that the foundational function of imagination points to a ground more basic than sense and thought - to an "abyss" - filled him with alarm. In the second edition of The Critique, imagination, "the indispensable function of the soul," emerges as a mere handmaid of reason. By reaffirming the supremacy of reason Kant reverts to the traditional path of rationalism and logo-centrism.[12]

Imagination, Perception, Hallucination

The relationship between imagination and perception is ridden with centuries of controversy during which imagination has been either overestimated (in Romanticism) or denigrated (in philosophical empiricism and psychological behaviorism). In all instances the crucial question has been how to distinguish imagination in a decisive way from other mental acts and to identify it as an activity in its own right and with its own existential status. One group of philosophers (Aristotle, Averroës, Aquinas, Descartes, Locke, Hume, Merleau-Ponty) have seen a necessary continuity between perception and imagination. Hume, who exemplifies this tradition, regards imagination as a mere mode or direct extension of the more fundamental act of perception. Images are nothing more than a repetition and recombination of what we have already perceived. Hume's is a reductionist attempt to explain the genesis of images through reference to antecedent factors - perception and sense. As a result, imagination becomes at best a particular and separate faculty of the human mind. However it is precisely in this capacity - at its putative best - that imagination is often labeled as the worst faculty in that it misleads and deceives both our senses and intellect. Pascal has

7

encapsulated this view by calling imagination "the mistress of falsehood and error.[13]

The other group of philosophers (Plato, Plotinus, Bruno, Ficino, Vico, Fichte, Schelling, Coleridge, Breton, Bachelard) envisages imagination as inherently discontinuous with perception. Instead of being a transitional operation leading to a supposedly superior state of mentation (sheer intellection, pure reason) imagination is seen here as an original noetic faculty essentially independent from perception and sensation.

Now one would expect that imagination as an autonomous activity of the psyche is relatively easy to delimit from other acts of mentation. We find however that this is impossible, for, in spite of its autonomy, imagination ramains an extremely ambiguous and ephemeral affair, difficult to describe in its own terms or in terms of its relationship with other mental acts. A clear indication of such difficulty is the temptation among the theorists of imagination to indulge in tautological statements. For example, psychologists, in their effort to contrast "true" image with "eidetic images," hallucinations, etc., use such pleonastic terms as "imagination image" "imaginary image," "imaginative image."[14]

The ambiguity and elusiveness of imagination is principally due to the fact that it never acts on its own, but always through or in tandem with other faculties (willing, feeling, sensation, thinking, believing). In Jung's words, "fantasy is just as much feeling as thinking, as much intuition as sensation. There is no psychic function that, through fantasy, is not inextricably bound up with the other psychic functions."[15] Hillman suggests that imagination is "prepositional" in that it enables us to see things in their mutual interpenetration and transparency; it is a "subtle sensing of the prepositional relations among events." In

8

this capacity imagination acts as "a permeating ether that dissolves the very possibility of separate faculties, functions and realms."[16] Paradoxically however, it is by placing itself at the service of all the other faculties, by becoming, as it were, invisible, that imagination emerges, in Baudelaire's words, as "the queen of the faculties": "All the faculties of the human soul must be subordinated to imagination, which puts them all into its service."[17] Somewhat in the manner of an ideal Roman Catholic Pope, imagination is the servus servorum.

*

The classical definition of hallucination is "perception without an object." Edward Casey, the foremost American phenomenologist of imagination, elaborates by saying that hallucination has to do with mistaken belief in "the perceived presence of something that is not given in perceptual experience at all."[18] In view of this definition our task is to contrast hallucinations with imaginative presentations in which the perceptual component is nonessential or has only an adventitious character.

One of the basic features of hallucinations is their "paranormal" character in that they occur alongside ordinary perceptions or tend to replace such perceptions for an indefinite period of time. We are using the adjective "paranormal" rather than "pathological" or "psychotic" in order to avoid lumping together all hallucinatory phenomena under the heading of "aberrational." For clearly, such experiences as eidetic images, "visions" induced by drugs or under hypnosis, synaesthetic sensations, misreadings of written texts, etc., are not symptoms of sickness of any kind. However, they may be considered as hallucinations insofar as they compete with or replace ordinary perceptions. Hallucinations always appear in a specific sensory form and their contents are experienced as projected entities existing externally to the perceiving subject.

In contrast to the paranormal character of hallucinations, imagined objects or events never interfere with or replace actually perceived items in this world. There is no competition between imagination and perception; we can imagine and perceive concurrently. According to Jung, the image or fantasy idea "never takes place of reality and can always be distinguished from sensuous reality by the fact that it is an 'inner' image."[19] The reason for this is that the sensory quality of images - their form, color, texture - are not derived from external objects. As the archetypalist Patricia Berry says, "with imagination any question of objective referent is irrelevant. The imaginal is quite real in its own way, but never because it corresponds to something outer."[20]

The phenomenon of halluciantion has been widely used to discredit imagination. Empirical psychiatrists like to stress that the so called visionaries are often hysterical and schizophrenic types or that religious visionary experiences may be generated by extreme asceticism or systematic practice of meditation leading to abnormal concentration and tension. This may or may not be so. Suffice it to say that the identification of visions with hallucinations ignores the fact that religious visions usually lead to a re-organization and strengthening of an individual's total personality whereas the common hallucinations leave no such trace in the make-up of the human subject. I therefore tend to agree with Mary Watkins, the author of the classic Waking Dreams, that "in regard to awareness of the imaginal the hallucinator is asleep."[21] I might add that from the imaginer's point of view not only the hallucinator but the ordinary perceiver as well is a somnambulist to the extent that his senses are not fully awake to the potential richness of what's "out there." It is also for this reason that, for example, the Eastern meditators do not hesitate to equate the so called normal perception of the world with hallucination calling both of them maya - an illusive projection of the cosmos as a separate entity from the projector.[22] But this is also the point of view of what in archetypal psychology is called the soul. From the soul's perspective, a world without imagination is a world of abstractions, occupied by ghostly creatures that are more fictitious than the "ghosts" of our fantasy life. The real ghosts are our literalisms, not the ones we bump into at night.

Imagination and Fancy

The distinction between imagination and fancy, even though generally accepted in literary circles, is more of a desideratum than an actuality. There is an almost universal condemnation of fancy or day-dreaming as being not only useless, but positively harmful, especially when it pretends to be innocently playing with images. To the medieval alchemist Paracelsus (Theophrastus Bombastus of Hohenheim), fancy is "the madman's cornerstone;" to others, the aimless imagery of daydreaming is the first step to iniquity and perdition. The paltry delectations of reverie are said to glue us to the external world, and at the same time make us insensitive, complacent, self-conscious; in short, fancy leads to spiritual death. When Milton shows Satan seducing Eve, he makes day-dreaming the prelude to the Fall (P.L. IV 800):

> Squat like a Toad, close at the eare of Eve
> Assaying by his Devlish art to reach
> The Organs of her Fancie, and with them to forge
> Illusions as he list, Phantasms and Dreams.

Clement of Alexandria, an early Church Father (Stromata IV, XVIII), comments on Christ's warning - that he who looks on a woman with lust, has already committed adultery - saying: "he who looks so as to lust is day-dreaming." And then he adds: "whosoever looks instead on a beautiful body marvelling at the grace from above bestowed on it by the Supreme Artist, does not fall prey to fancy, but makes a spiritual use of imagination."

S.T. Coleridge dissociated creative or primary imagination from reproductive imagination which he also calls "visual Imagination or Fancy." "Fancy," he says, "arises wholly out of That Slavery of the Mind to the Eye and the visual Imagination or Fancy under the influence of which the Reasoner must have a picture."[23] To free the mind from the despotism of the eye is the first step toward its emancipation from the influences of the senses, sensations and passions. In the 13th Chapter of Biographia Literaria, fancy, a mere handmaid of perception, is said to be "no other than a mode of Memory emancipated from the order of time and space;" it is mechanical and passive; a "mirrorment... repeating simply, or by transposition," and "the aggregate and associative power" acting only "by a sort of juxtaposition." Essentially, fancy is associative imagination depending on sensuous perception and as such has nothing truly creative about it.

By contrast, imagination "recreates" its elements; it is "synthetic," a "permeative" and a "blending, fusing power." At other times Coleridge describes true or poetic imagination as a "coadunating faculty" which dissolves, diffuses in order to unify. Creative imagination is "essentially vital" in that it "generates and produces a form of its own" and its rules are "the very powers of growth and production."

Possibly a better term for "imagination" is "fantasy" whose Indo-European root is bha, meaning "light," "vision," and also "sound" and "magic utterance" and which in Greek gives rise to the words "phantom" and "phenomenon." Like fantasy, imagination has to do with magic creation, skill, trickery and the general idea of phenomenal reality as such. Its Hindu correlative is maya, the form-creating, bewitching and subtly alluring power of Brahman.

Taking the Hindu notion of maya as a clue, we may suggest that the distinction between true imagination (the vera imaginatio

12

of Paracelsus) and fancy depends upon the way in which images are responded to and worked. Our criteria refer to _response_. In terms of Hinduism, _maya_ is an illusion - something fanciful - only when we become entangled in the welter of forms and images displayed by its creative power and proceed to hypostatize them into literal and material entities. But as soon as these contraptions are no longer taken as being literally true, the phenomenal world of _maya_ is transformed into the real world, which is no other than the world of imagination.

Thus: whether images are real or fanciful depends on our attitude, our response to them. In themselves (in their hypothetical whatness) they are neither true nor false, neither good nor bad, neither demonic nor angelic. According to a basic maxim of archetypal psychology, images are not what we see but the way in which we see (Edward Casey). If this sounds tautological, it also points to the soul's delectation to move in circles - a theme to be discussed in Chapter IV.

Image and Psyche

Among a plethora of philosophically and psychologically oriented attempts to overcome the dualism between inner and outer (spiritual and material, subjective and objective) Jung's position is unique in that it avoids surreptitiously falling into one or the other of these extremes. Jung achieved this balanced view not by intellectual acrobatics, but as a practicing healer who was not afraid to relate his clinical experience to ancient wisdom and the spiritual disciplines of the East as well as to the mythical thought of prehistoric societies. What came out of this synthesis was the startling insight that the psyche is image and imagining.

According to Jung, the best way to understand experiences in which inner images cannot be distinguished from outer reality is by studying all phenomena as psychic happenings that, in the form of images, may derive either from external or internal

13

sources. In the following passages Jung attempts to capture his central insight.

"Everything of which we are conscious is an image" and "image is psyche."[24] Or again: "Every psychic process is an image and an imagining."[25] Our experience of reality, all that we think, feel or perceive, is psychic: "the world exists only so far as we are able to produce an image of it."[26] What we call consciousness never relates itself directly to any material objects; even if images are answers to external facts, they are nevertheless answers of the psyche. What appears to us as immediate, tangible reality is a world of carefully processed, meaningfully structured images.

Contrary to the tenets of both materialism and spiritualism, the world we inhabit is a psychic world. The Jungian psyche is no longer based on matter (the brain) or on mind (intellect or metaphysics), but on esse in anima conceived as a third reality between mind and matter. In the image-making activity of the soul, idea and thing, inner and outer, come together and are held in balance.[27]

We are steeped in a world that is a creation of our psyche: "We are so enveloped in a cloud of changing and endlessly shifting images that one might well exclaim with a well-known sceptic: "Nothing is absolutely true - not even that it is not quite true!"[28] What Jung is saying in these series of statements is that the world of common experience or the phenomenal physical world which is "rationally" apprehended by sight, touch, etc. and can be measured or mapped out in standard units of time and space is, in its most simple and basic form, an exceedingly complicated structure of psychic images.

Jung admits that there are unprofitable, futile, false or morbid fantasies and imaginings whose sterile nature is easily recognizable. A faulty performance, however, proves nothing against the normal performance. One would be hard-pressed to

14

deny that all the works of man - his culture - have their origin in creative imagination. "What right, then, have we to disparage fantasy?" asks Jung. "In the normal course of things, fantasy does not easily go astray; it is too deep for that, and too closely bound up with the tap-root of human and animal instinct... The creative activity of imagination ... raises man to the status of one who plays. As Schiller said, 'man is completely human only when he plays'."[29]

To envisage images as psychic events means that in every sensation there is a "subjective factor," a subjective, unconscious disposition which "alters perception at its source, thus depriving it of the character of purely objective influence."[30] The "subjective factor" constitutes a "psychic mirror world" reflecting a reality which is covered with "the patina of age-old subjective experience and the shimmer of events still unborn."[31] Jung's mirror-analogy suggests that the images of the psychic world are, in a sense, our fate. Contrary to Locke and sensationalist philsophies, we do not start our life as tabula rasa (clean slate), but are always and at every moment burdened with the experiences of our remotest ancestors which, like riverbeds, channel the flow of our individual lives. There are things we are fated to repeat as the celestial bodies repeat their orbital revolutions.

To Jung the word "image" does not denote the psychic reflection of an external object but is derived from poetic usage and stands for a fantasy-image which is related only indirectly to the perception of external reality. Images are distinguishied from sensation and perception or from the quasi-real character of hallucinations by the fact that they are "inner" images. The inner image is a homogeneous product with a meaning of its own, "a condensed expression of the psychic situation as a whole," i.e., of the unconscious as well as the conscious situation of the moment.[32]

Archetypal psychology, elaborating on Jung, regards the image as "an irreducible and complete union of form and content. Image is both the content of a structure and the structure of a content."[33] Jung himself expresses the inseparability of the image and its content in these words: "Image and meaning are identical; and as the first takes shape, so the latter becomes clear. Actually, the pattern needs no interpretation: it portrays its own meaning."[34] According to Hillman, "an image is complete just as it presents itself."[35] We must stick to the images (Lopez-Pedraza) in their presentation because their meaning is not separate from their being. Images mean what they are and are what they mean.

By saying that images need no interpretation Jung is hinting at the ingrained habit of the rational mind to inquire behind images as if they were spooks, hallucinations or symptoms of psychic disorder. This habit is due to our literal-mindedness: something must be literally so-and-so or it "ain't" real. There is no medium, no grey areas, no penumbra except for poets, artists and the insane. We have even coined the respectable hybrid "psychosomatic" to dismiss an illness that cannot be treated with the ordinary tools of the trade. It's a grim world, divided between good and evil forces that do not mix and whose perpetuation in the after-life has been canonized in the conceptions of eternal heaven and hell. What place can imagination possibly have in this universe of orderly, rational discourse and neatly apportioned zones of reality?

Evangelos Christou, one of the pioneers of archetypal psychology, maintains that imagination has a logos (logic) of its own differentiating it from such mental or quasi-mental processes as thinking, willing, wishing, perceiving. His word for the specific character of imaginative activity is (psychological) "experience."

> In the sense of psychological factualness or reality, spirits may or may not be imaginary, a sensation may or may not correspond to a physical object, but all are real in the sense that they can be experienced and this experience constitutes a world in its own right.[36]

Imagination is a psychological experience endowing events (inner as well as outer) with meaning. According to Hillman, "between us and events, between the doer and the deed, there is a reflective moment..."[37] It is this moment - this unknown component - which, turning events into experiences, makes meaning possible. Note, however, that "meaning" is not something added, as it were, from outside or fabricated through the intervention of reason. Meaning is experienced together with the event, i.e., it is imagined.

Thus when Jung states that images in the strict sense (as distinguished from after-images) are always "inner," he is not implying that they are literally "inside" us. For the outer world also has an inner dimension and things "out there" have their own interiority. The "inner" means "subjectivity," the "reflective moment" which "constitutes a world in its own right."

In trying to assign a locus to imagination as a sui generis activity, the best strategy, in my opinion, is to follow the French Islamic scholar and mystic Henry Corbin (died in 1978) who has coined the adjective "imaginal" in order to distinguish it from the derogatory connotation of "imaginary." Corbin proposed this term, as well as the Latin locution mundus imaginalis (in French monde imaginal), as pointing to an order of reality that is ontologically no less real than what we call the physical reality on the one hand, and the spiritual or intellectual reality, on the other. The characteristic faculty of perception within the mundus imaginalis is imaginative power which noetically or cognitively is on a par with the power of the senses or the intellect. According to Corbin, the imaginal world functions as an intermediary between the sensible world and the intelligible world.

17

In this there is an agreement between Corbin and the great theoretician of the Romantic movement, Coleridge, who saw creative imagination as the threshold between self and not-self, between mind and matter, between conscious and unconscious. To Coleridge creative imagination is not only the source of art but also the living power and prime agent of all human perception. It is a way of discovering a deeper truth about the world - a meaning that is intensely subjective and at the same time belongs to the interior constitution of all things.

PART ONE

I: THE GHOST OF IMAGINATION

NOTES

The Collected Works of C. G. Jung, trans. by R.F.C. Hull, have been published in the United States by the Bollingen Foundation (Bollingen Series XX). Since 1967, the American publisher has been the Princeton University Press. The volumes are referred to herein as CW.

¹Jean-Paul Sartre, L'Imaginaire (Paris, 1940), p. 26. Tr. by Bernard Frechtman as The Psychology of Imagination (London and New York, 1949).

²Joseph Campbell, The Masks of God: Primitive Mythology (New York: Penguin Books, 1959), p. 25; cf. p. 83. For experiments showing the difficulty of maintaining the distinction between inner and outer reality, see S. Segal, "The Perky Effect: Changes in Reality Judgments With Changing Methods of Inquiry," Psychon. Sci., 12:393-394, 1968; E.H. Gombrich, Art and Illusion: A Study in the Psychology of Pictorial Representation. The A.W. Mellon Lectures in Fine Arts, 1976. Bollingen Series XXXV. 5. (Princeton University Press, 1960), p. 5, 205.

³Mircea Eliade, The Quest; History and Meaning in Religion (Chicago: The University of Chicago Press, 1969), p. 86. A contemporary psychologist, contrasting intense visualization with the usual perceptual experience, writes: "The fullest perception of the object ... is characterized by an inexhaustible and ineffable quality, by the profoundest interest in the object, and by the enriching, refreshing vitalizing effect which the act of perception has upon the perceiver" (E. Schachtel. Metamorphosis. New York, Basic Books, Inc., 1959, p. 177).

⁴Gaston Bachelard, On Poetic Imagination and Reverie. Tr. with an Introduction by Colette Gaudin (Indianapolis: The Bobbs-Merrill Co., Inc., 1971), p. 16.

⁵Krasinsky, Tibetische Medizin-Philosophie, quoted by Titus Burckhard in "Cosmology and Modern Science," The Sword of Gnosis, ed. Jacob Needelman (Baltimore, Md.: Penguin Books, Inc., 1974), p. 148.

⁶David Hume, Treatise of Human Nature, I. I. ii.

⁷Ibid., I. IV. vii.

[8] Aristotle, De Anima 427 b, 18-22 (Hett's trans.).

[9] Ibid., 428a. 11.

[10] Immanuel Kant, Critique of Pure Reason, A 124; Kemp-Smith (New York: St. Martin's Press, 1929).

[11] Ibid., A 78 - B.

[12] See Martin Heidegger, Kant and the Problem of Metaphysics. Tr. by James S. Churchill (Bloomington: Indiana University Press, 1962), pp. 172-175.

[13] Blaise Pascal, Pensées, ed. L. Lafuma (Paris: Seuil, 1962), p. 54.

[14] See M.J. Horowitz, Image Formation and Cognition (New York: Appleton-Century-Crofts, 1970), p. 23; A. Richardson, Mental Imagery (London: Routledge & Kegan Paul, 1979), p. 94.

[15] CW 6, par. 78; cf. 7, par. 490.

[16] James Hillman, "Image-Sense," Spring 1979, p. 134, 136.

[17] Charles Baudelaire, Curiosities esthetiques et L'Art romantique, p. 329.

[18] Edward S. Casey, "Toward Archetypal Imagination," Spring 1974, p. 7; cf. his pioneering work Imagining: a Phenomenological Study (Bloomington: Indiana University Press, 1976). I am also indebted to his essays: "Comparative Phenomenology of Mental Activity: Memory, Hallucination and Fantasy Contrasted with Imagination"; "Imagining, Perceiving, and Thinking." Private copies.

[19] CW 6, par. 743.

[20] Patricia Berry, "An Approach to the Dream," Spring 1974, p. 61.

[21] Mary M. Watkins, Waking Dreams (New York: Harper Colophon Books, 1976), p. 19.

[22] See W.Y. Evans-Wenz, Tibetan Yoga and Its Secret Doctrines (London: Oxford University Press, 1935), pp. 161-66.

[23] From a note written on a flyleaf of Coleridge's copy of the De Divisione Naturae of John Scotus Erigena. Quoted by Owen Barfield in What Coleridge Thought (Middletown, Conn.: Wesleyan University Press, 1971), p. 20.

[24] CW 13, par. 75.

[25] CW 11, par. 889.

[26] CW 11, par. 766.

[27] See CW 6, par. 78 ff.

[28] CW 8, par. 623.

[29] CW 16, par. 98.

[30] CW 6, par. 647. William James has observed that apperception is the "sum-total of effects [of the perceiver's] entire psychostatistical conditions, his nature and stock of ideas ... character, habits, memory, education, previous experience, and momentary mood" (Principles of Psychology. Dover Publ., 1950, II, p. 107).

[31] CW 6, par. 649.

[32] CW 6, par. 745; cf. par. 748.

[33] Berry, "An Approach to the Dream," p. 67.

[34] CW 8, par. 402; cf. 12, par. 329; 17, par. 162.

[35] James Hillman, "An Inquiry into Image," Spring 1977, p. 68.

[36] Evangelos Christou, The Logos of the Soul (1963) (Zürich: Spring Publications, 1976), p. 36.

[37] James Hillman, Re-Visioning Psychology (New York: Harper & Row, 1975), p. x.

[38] See Henry Corbin, "Mundus Imaginalis or The Imaginary and the Imaginal," Spring 1972, p. 15; cf. p. 7.

II: MIND AND MATTER

Production and Transmission

To appreciate fully the uniqueness of the Jungian hypothesis of the psyche as a third reality between mind and matter, we must contrast it with two ideologies that have dominated the history of Western philosophy and pscyhology - materialism and spiritualism. Such an excursion is necessary if only because these Weltanschauungen represent the basic framework for most of the significant writing in the area of humanities, particularily in parapsychology - the only "science" which has deliberately set out to achieve a "reconciliation" between the supposedly antagonistic realms of matter and spirit. In my opinion, much of the confusion and deceptive rigorousness prevailing among the proponents of this "reconciliation" could be eliminated by taking seriously the Jungian view that what is called matter and spirit are nothing more than abstractions and that a truly rigorous thought has no choice but to move on the borderline between all artificially erected contrarieties.

Materialism, in its crudest form, is based on the evolutionary hypothesis that the "spirit" (which usually is never distinguished from "pysche" or "soul") arises from a physical substratum, be it the brain, hormones, "instincts," "drives" or what not. The brain, that gray stuff of cerebral convolutions, engenders thought and consciousness in its interior, much as it engenders cholesterin, creatin and carbonic acid. In a word, thought is the secretion of the brain.

This theory, which was explicitly formulated in the eighteenth and nineteenth centuries, sounds plausible enough if one adverts to the fact that arrests of brain development occasion imbecility; that blows on the head abolish memory or consciousness; that brain stimulants and poisons change the quality of our thinking. It has also been claimed that various special forms of thinking are functions of special portions of the brain. For example, when we are thinking of things seen, it is our occipital convolutions that are active; when we are conscious of things heard, it is a certain portion of our temporal lobes; when of things to be spoken, it is one of our frontal convolutions. If the objection is raised that the organic movements by which the brain exercises the function of receiving impressions are unknown, the standard reply is that the operations of the stomach and intestines, designed to effect digestion and so on, are equally hidden from our scrutiny. The conclusion seems to be inevitable that the brain, just like the stomach, digests impressions and emits them metamorphosed into ideas, to which the language of physiognomy or gesture, or the signs of speech and writing give an outward expression.

Among those who have most compellingly argued against the materialistic hypothesis I would like to single out William James and F.C.S. Schiller of Oxford, late of Cornell University. In James' view, the productive function of the brain is not the only kind of function with which we are familiar. There is also the permissive or transmissive function which is ordinarily left out of consideration. For example, colored glass, a prism or a reflecting lens have the function of sifting and limiting the energy of light in color or determining it to a certain path and shape. Likewise the keys of an organ open various pipes and let the wind in the air-chest escape in various ways. The voices of the pipes are determined by the columns of air trembling as they emerge. But the air is not engendered in the organ. The organ only transmits portions of air "to whom it may concern."

Let us now imagine, says James, the whole universe of material things as a mere veil hiding and keeping back another world, or with the poet, "Like a dome of many-coloured glass" staining "the white radiance of Eternity" (Shelley). Imagine further that "the dome, opaque enough at all times to the full

24

super-solar blaze, could at certain times and places grow less so, and let certain beams pierce through into this sublunary world. These beams would be so many finite rays...of consciousness, and they would vary in quantity and quality as the opacity varied in degree."

On James' hypothesis, these beams would come from "the absolute life of the universe" or the "absolute world soul" to which the various brains give a finite and special form. "Glows of feeling, glimpses of insight, and streams of knowledge and perception float into our finite world" and our brains which represent thin and half-transparent places in the veil. - The amount of "the absolute life," transmitted to the brain, would depend on the "barrier of its obstructiveness." When the barrier is low, a greater amount of universal life pours over than, let's say, during a heavy sleep. When the brain stops acting, or decays, the energy flow will vanish altogether. Nevertheless the reservoir of energy in the world soul would remain intact, and consciousness ("as such") would continue.

James admits, however, that from a strictly scientific point of view, both hypotheses - the materialistic and idealistic or spiritualistic - are metaphysical in nature and as such equally fantastic. In strict science, it is immaterial whether we talk about production or transmission; in either case we mean nothing more than the bare fact of concomitance; when the brain-activity changes in one way, consciousness changes in another; when the currents pour through the occipital lobes, consciounsess sees things; when through the lower frontal region, consciousness says things to itself, etc. Thus it appears that all our talk either about transmission or production must be reduced to imaginative hypothesizing. For when science is asked to explain the exact process by which the brain produces consciounesss, it confesses her total ignorance. Ignoramus et ignorabimus. In James' words: "The production of such a thing as consciousness

in the brain is the absolute world-enigma - something so paradoxical and abnormal as to be a stumbling block to nature, almost a
self-contradiction."[1]

The advocates of transmission theory do not deny the close
connection of thought and mind with the physiological structure
of the brain, with glands and the body in general. According
to Schiller, whose views largely coincide with those of Henri
Bergson, the role of matter is to regulate, limit and restrain
consciousness which it encloses. Thus in lower animals where
the material encasement is coarse and simple, only a minimum of
intelligence is transmitted through the matter. Animals are in
the stage of brute lethargy whereas men have passed into the
higher phase of somnambulism allowing glimpses into the reality
of a transcendent world.

Schiller regards materialism as a hysteron proteron, a
putting the cart before the horse. The connection between
matter and consciousness must be inverted so as to say that
matter, instead of producing consciousness, contracts it and
confines its intensity and its manifestation within certain limits.
Furthermore, if it is assumed that the body is a mechanism for
inhibiting consciousness, it will be necessary to invert also our
ordinary ideas on the subject of memory. Rather than trying to
account for memory, we shall have to account for forgetfulness;
"it will be during life that we drink the bitter cup of Lethe, it
will be with our brain that we are enabled to forget."[2]

The apparent advantage of the transmission theory - at
least to those who abhor materialism - is that it explains or, at
any rate attempts to account for the lower in terms of the higher.
One is seduced into believing that the superior status of man
within nature, his spiritual essence, his God-likeness is salvaged
from debasement and all is well in the best possible of the worlds.
In my opinion, however, to treat matter as a kind of afterthought
of spirit is no less debilitating than to treat spirit as an appendix

26

of matter. Both theories, the productive and the transmissive, are still wedded to the Cartesian dualism; it is only that in the transmission theory the two terms of the dichotomy are reversed so as to subordinate the body to the mind. In either case man is de-humanized. For it hardly matters whether we reduce him to the animal or to the angelic level: something gets substracted from his median status with the aim of concocting an artificial thing - a spirit-being or a beast-like creature. What is forgotten in this operation is that both matter and spirit are metaphysical constructs (images) and that the reality from which they spring is the psyche. In Jung's words: "The psyche is the starting point of all human experience, and all the knowledge we have gained eventually leads back to it. The psyche is the beginning and end of cognition."[3]

Psyche and Consciousness

Materialism (including the proponents of production theory), while denying any kind of autonomy to psyche and psychical processes, generally admits that the physical substrate of our mind has the quality of consciousness even though the latter is said to be unexplainable in strictly scientific terms. Most modern psychologies, in the wake of this truncated theologizing, have chosen to deal primarily with the conscious mind of man. In these psychologies without psyche the total being of man is presumptively identified with consciousness and its concept-based, abstract frame of reference. It is seldom realized however that this simplistic view is of a relatively recent origin. If we omit for the moment the ancient religions and mythologies, we find that up to the time of scientific revolution and prior to Descartes (1596-1650) many religious and speculative thinkers took for granted factors lying outside and yet influencing the conscious mind. As L.L. Whyte[4] has shown, the knowledge of unconscious mentation had always been there, beginning with St. Augustine

27

through men as diverse in their outlook as Thomas Aquinas, Jacob Boehme, St. John of the Cross, Paracelsus, Kepler, Dante, Cervantes, Shakespeare, Montaigne. It is only in the modern era, starting with the Newtonian revolution in science and the "Cartesian catastrophe" in philosophy, that conscious awareness was singled out as the defining characteristic of an independent mode of being called mind.

Opposition to Cartesianism, whether in the form of materialism or in the various forms of subjective idealism, invariably issued in the sacrifice of one of the dual terms to the other. It was always the case of either matter tending to absorb spirit or spirit swallowing up matter. Generally speaking, within the mainstream of Western thought it is the spirit that, in the shrunken form of conscious subject, has usurped the first place. But this is far from saying that the West has thereby undergone a process of "spiritualization." On the contrary, having asserted himself as the central certainty, the conscious Ego (ego cogitans) extended this initial certainty over the object, proceeding to reduce it to mere extended stuff in space. The object is divested of all qualities except those which are measurable, numerable, and calculable. "The subject separates itself from the object in order to ensure its own mastery over it. Dualism is man's self-assertion in the face of nature ... nature sinks to the level of material for exploitation, and man towers as the master over it."[5]

The Cartesian identification of man with conscious thinking and ultimately with an imperial ego has led to the refusal on the part of most contemporary psychologists to deal with their own subject matter, the psyche. The soul has been successfully exorcised from the only field that is traditionally devoted to its study and replaced by such euphemisms as "personality dimensions," "mind," etc. It took the behavioral sciences to extinguish this faint echo from the lost territory of the soul - a territory

28

which according to Jung "reaches so far beyond the boundaries of consciousness that the latter could easily be compared to an island in the ocean. Whereas the island is small and narrow, the ocean is immensely wide and deep and contains a life infinitely surpassing in kind and degree, anything known on the island."[6]

Reductionist Enterprise

Behaviorism (founded by John Broadus Watson in 1913) has banished such metaphysical terms as "consciousness," "emotion," "purpose," from psychological vocabulary. Half a century later, B.F. Skinner, in his standard work Science and Human Behavior, issued the edict that mind and ideas are non-existent entities, invented for the sole purpose of spurious explanations. The British philosopher and parapsychologist Cyril Burt has summed up this purge in the following words: "Psychology, having first bargained away its soul and then gone out of mind, seems now, as it faces an untimely end, to have lost all consciousness."

Behaviorism, which started as a revolt against the excessive use of introspection (Würzburg school), is modeled on the mechanistic physics of the nineteenth century. The behaviorists's guiding ambition is measurement of human behavior by quantifiable methods and the subsequent control of behavior by manipulation of stimuli (stimulus-response theory). In experimenting with what is called "operant condition," animals are preferred to human beings and rats and pigeons to monkeys or chimpanzees. At the heart of this procedure is the attempt to reduce the complex activities of man to the hypothetical atoms of behavior found in lower animals. It is (humbly!) claimed that bar-pressing experiments with rats and the training of pigeons provide all necessary elements to describe, predict and control human behavior, not excluding the language of art and science. One is of course not bothered in the least that, by the logic of this kind of reasoning, the behaviorist's own scientific endeavor is reduced to the level of conditioned reflex and thus hardly to be taken seriously as an advance in human knowledge.

It is true that present day behavioral scientists have convinced themselves that they have outgrown the sterile orthodoxy of their elders. New hypothetical mechanisms, intervening variables, auxiliary hypotheses have been added to the old fabric. Nevertheless the basic concepts and the general outlook of behaviorism have not changed. More ominously, the terminology and jargon of this ideology, parading as science, has become part of much of the contemporary mentality. It is the prevailing wisdom of our age that human life is shaped by a series of responses to external conditions - beginning in early childhood with toilet training, continuing with education according to the Skinnerian principles of reinforcement of correct responses and ending with the affluent society of adults, conditioned by mass media into perfect consumers. Such is the infallible recipe for the progressive stultification of mankind!

Behaviorism is based on the philosophical belief commonly known as reductionism. In the most general sense, reductionism is an attempt to explain the higher in terms of the lower or the whole in terms of its parts. The reductionist fallacy lies not in trying to understand one type of reality in terms of another - virtually all explanation in science proceeds in this fashion - but in the spirit of "nothing-but-ism," i.e., in the belief that life is merely an extension of matter at a certain level of organization and that mind is merely an extension of life at a certain level of complexity. Man is a complex biochemical mechanism whose activities consist of "nothing but" a chain of conditioned responses which can be explained, predicted and controlled by methods exemplified in the conditioning of rats and pigeons. It is at this point that science is deserted in favor of metaphysics, a belief system assuming that there are no truths save those of science. To what extremes the zoomorphic approach of materialistic reductionism may lead is illustrated by the following passage from Desmond Morris' The Naked Ape:

> The insides of houses or flats can be decorated and filled with ornaments, bric-a-brac and personal belongings in profusion. This is usually explained as being done to make the place 'look nice.' In fact, it is the exact equivalent to another territorial species depositing its personal scent on a landmark near its den. When you put a name on a door, or hang a painting on a wall, you are, in dog or wolf terms, for example, simply cocking your leg on them and leaving your personal mark there.[7]

Reductionism is also wedded to the evolutionistic hypothesis which characteristically expresses itself as the search for origins. Evolutionism believes that there must be a literal, objective and historical beginning to everything. We want to know whence came mindedness, what is the provenance of the universe, matter, life, man and we are not at rest until we have produced a simple, single and all-embracing answer. I am of course not denying that this search may furnish useful and even exciting pieces of information about homo sapiens, his modes of adaptation to the environment, his brain, his sexual proclivities, etc. All that and much more is within the province of legitimate scientific endeavor. But it is crucial to distinguish science as an empirical pursuit from the scientific pursuit as a psychic and emotive activity. In the latter role science is one of the manifestations of the psyche, a fantasy which is conditioned by the "subjective factor" as much as any other "non-scientific" approach. In Jung's words, the scientific thinking

> is also a psychic function, thanks to which matter can be organized in such a way as to burst asunder the mighty forces that bind atoms together ... The psyche is a disturber of the natural laws of the cosmos, and should we ever succeed in doing something to Mars with the aid of atomic fission,[8] this too will have been brought to pass by the psyche.

II: MIND AND MATTER

NOTES

[1] William James, *William James on Psychical Research*, compiled and ed. by Gardner Murphy and Robert O. Ballou (Clifton: Augustus M. Kelley, 1973), pp. 291-94.

[2] F.C.S. Schiller, *Riddles of the Sphinx* (London: Swan Sonnenschein, 1891), p. 393.

[3] *CW* 8, par. 261.

[4] See L.L. Whyte, *The Unconscious Before Freud* (New York: St. Martin's Press, 1978), pp. 25-28.

[5] William Barrett, *The Illusion of Technique* (Garden City, N.Y.: Anchor Press, 1978), pp. 191-92.

[6] *CW* 11, par. 141.

[7] D. Morris, *The Naked Ape* (London, 1967). Quoted by Arthur Koestler, *Janus; a Summing Up* (New York: Random House, 1978), p. 14; cf. pp. 19-20; 23-26; 223-24.

[8] *CW* 8, par. 422.

III: REALITY OF THE PSYCHE

Imaginal Reduction

We have already observed that, according to Jung, the only medium through which the psyche can be known is the psyche itself; it can only perceive itself in and through itself: "... no explanation of the psychic can be anything other than the living process of the psyche itself." Psychology can never be a science in the generally accepted sense of the word; it has no Archimedean point from which to observe and judge itself, for its "object is the inside subject of all science."[1] Jung and archetypal psychology will therefore follow the circular model extolled by men like Heraclitus, Parmenides, Empedocles, Plato, Plotinus, Nicholas of Cusa and William Blake. Psychological reasoning merges its subject with its object and ties up its beginning with its end. Expressed differently: for the psyche, subject and object, inner and outer are reciprocal realities.

From this it follows that the only kind of reduction we may practice is the reduction to the psyche. Moreover, since, as Jung has shown, psyche is identical with its images, the reduction to the psychic becomes, in archetypal psychology, "imaginal reduction." According to Hillman, imaginal reduction aims at demonstrating, by means of symbol and metaphor, that behind all "isms" (including scientific empiricism) lies a world of separate primordial reality - the imaginal world. From the perspective of the soul, images are the basic given of all psychic life and the only reality we apprehend directly: everything we know is transmitted to us through psychic images. Hillman dramatizes Jung's position by stating that images are the fundamental facts of human existence and that it is from the stuff of these images that we create our world, our reality.

> To live psychologically means to imagine things ... To be in soul is to experience the fantasy in all realities and the basic reality of fantasy ... In the beginning

33

> is the image: first imagination then perception; first
> fantasy then reality ... Man is primarily an imagemaker
> and our psychic substance consists of images: our
> existence is imagination. We are indeed such stuff as
> dreams are made on.[2]

So it should not come as a surprise that "imaginal reduction"
shuns elegant solutions. Instead of trying to explain and expli-
cate, the psychological standpoint prefers to complicate by
concentrating on the enigma and the penumbral regions of human
existence. It follows the method of "infinite regress" seeking to
account "for the unknown in the still more unknown, ignotum
per ignotius."[3] It is also because of this preference for the
hidden and the mysterious that we must regard all the reductionist attempts (in the spiritualistic as well as in the materialistic
mode) as equally fallacious. They are all fantasies of the soul
pursuing her own circumambulatory course and using every
opportunity to make it more devious.

I should like to quote at this juncture a passage from Jung
describing as clearly and schematically as possible the status
which he assigns to psychic reality.

> It is characteristic of Western man that he has split
> apart the physical and the spiritual for epistemological
> purposes. But these opposites exist together in the
> psyche ... 'psychic' means physical and spiritual ...
> this 'intermediate' world seems unclear and confused
> because the concept of psychic reality is not yet
> current among us, although it expresses life as it
> actually is. Without soul, spirit is as dead as matter,
> because both are artificial abstractions; whereas man
> originally regarded spirit as a volatile body [emphasis
> mine], and matter as not lacking in soul.[4]

The key sentence in this declaration is: "Without soul, spirit is
as dead as matter." Most of the official philosophy in the West,
having forgotten the 'psychic factor," has condemned itself to
generating imposing monisms of various shades and predilections.
But all mono-vision (a German writer calls it Monotonotheismus) -
materialistic, capitalistic, scientistic, idealistic, and spiritualistic -

leads to the death of both matter and spirit since, as Jung points out, only a matter that is "not lacking in soul" and only a spirit that is "a volatile body" can be fully alive.

Following Jung and the Platonic tradition, we shall replace the dualistic division of man with a tripartite anthropology: instead of two - mind and matter - our "game-plan" envisions three parts, placing the soul as the third (tertium quid) between the perspectives of mind (spirit, logic, idea) and of body (matter, nature, empirics). It is to this realm of psychic reality that we shall refer such vital experiences as dreams, imagination, fantasy, occasional ghosts and other "paranormal" manifestations (telepathy, precognition, etc.). I realize that this is a large order. What I intend, however, is no more than to provide a guiding principle allowing to view all these phenomena as quite normal once it is understood that the activities of the soul cannot be limited to what our day-light consciousness purports to be possible or decent.

The Substantialist View of the Soul

For the purpose of a more adequate grasp of the Jungian position I would like to interrupt these cogitations in order to take a glance at the concept of soul as it was formulated in Greek philosophy and further elaborated in the Middle Ages. Without going into all the niceties of scholastic distinctions, it can be stated that traditionally the soul is understood as a substance, a fixed unchanging something behind our thoughts, intuitions, emotions, perceptions, actions and imaginings. The soul is a mysterious, concrete agent existing on a non-phenomenal plane and yet somehow involved in everything we experience. It is as if we need something more than the phenomena, something which goes beyond or stands behind the phenomenal world of our experience, and to that "more" we give the name of soul-substance. We seldom realize, however, that this "more" is

35

merely a verbal explanation which follows the strategy expressed in the maxim "whatever you are totally ignorant of, assert to be the explanation of everything else." Nothing in the way of real comprehension is added by claiming that the soul, being a simple and active substance, is incorruptible and naturally immortal or that this invisible vapor, locked up in the body and released at death, can only be annihilated by a direct action of God.[5]

In the medieval Aristotelian and Thomistic theology, the soul is the principle of life, the one primary source or subject of all vital activities; as such it is the "form" or the entelechy of a physical organic body. Soul and body constitute one substance and this composite substance is endowed with life whose principle is soul. "Soul and body make a living creature" (Aristotle, De Anima, II, i, 413a)

It is important to emphasize that the Aristotelian view is based on common experience which ascribes psyche to the living as distinct from the dead. A live body or a living being is distinguished from "dead" body or a non-living being by the spontaneous, immanent, self-produced movement; it moves and changes not only when acted upon by other agents and forces, but by its own initiative (entelechy). The soul as the life principle is common to all forms of life, including the animal and plant kingdoms.

On the Aristotelian premise, the soul cannot subsist without a body and their separation means that both suffer death. Aristotle's soul is a mortal soul. Paradoxically it became even more so when it was identified by Christian Aristotelians with mind or spirit, which they conceived as a power enabling man to transcend his own mechanically conditioned organism altogether. For by superimposing upon the naturalistic psyche of Aristotle the notion of an other-worldly and spiritual soul, the medieval theologians succeeded only in preparing the way for the Cartesian worldless consciousness (res cogitans). An other-worldly soul is a soul without a world, a lonely soul adrift in a cosmos that knows it not. What I am saying is that a purely spiritual soul, even though it may have all the appurtenances of an abstractly conceived immortality, according to Jung, would have to be "as dead as matter." It is mortal from a surfeit of spirituality, as it were, from lack of breath.

In contrast to this spurious immortality Jung is pointing to the existence of a subtle matter distinct from gross matter as well as to the existence of a subtle spirit distinct from gross spirit. Gross spirit is "pure spirit" just as gross matter is "pure matter": both of them are abstractions and as such dead or rather still-born. Death is an affliction peculiar to both spirit and matter insofar as they are unrelated to the soul.

Aristotle was certainly right in pronouncing the soul mortal. John Dewey, discussing the Aristotelian concept of soul, writes: "The soul does apparently die in the body. It hides itself so effectively that the materialist says there is no soul; but it has died as dies the seed, to quicken and transform the body."[6] It is this kind of transformation and the "immortality" resulting from it that I should like to fantasize about (Part II).

Much more far-reaching in its implications was the distinction made by Aristotle between passive intellect (intellectus possibilis) or simply mind (the reasoning power of man) and an active or poetic intellect (nous poiētikos). The latter is an agency that permeates the potential phantasms of the soul with its spiritual light and awakens their sleeping, secretly tense and vigilant intelligibility. According to the Schoolmen anterior to Aquinas, the active intellect constitutes what is highest, most powerful and most worthy in the essence of man (Nic. Ethics, II7a 14-20). The Jungian Marie-Louise von Franz has suggested that the active or agent intellect has an important place in the philosophy of the Arab Platonist Avicenna where it functions (like Tao in Chinese philosophy and the "universal harmony" in Leibniz) as a

37

quasi-cosmic reality present in both man and nature. According to von Franz, it is also the equivalent of Jung's psychological conception of the luminosity (twilight consciousness) of unconscious archetypal contents.[7]

I do not feel it necessary to discuss the various opinions surrounding the Jungian hypothesis of the "collective unconscious." Suffice it to say that the expression "unconscious archetypal contents" in the present context is not meant to suggest that the psyche contains a special kind of material which is forever inaccessible to consciousness. The deeper psyche is not a noumenon in the Kantian fashion, unknowable and hermetically sealed off from the world of phenomena. Archetypal psychology does not deny the existence of certain unconscious processes occurring in human experience, as illustrated by Freud and Jung in such phenomena as forgetting, slips of tongue, dreaming, habit, neurotic symptoms, etc.[8] All these "factors" are real enough so long as they are treated as such in the consulting room of the psychoanalyst or in our own bedrooms. But it is precisely by treating them as literal entities that we obscure their imaginal background which possesses its own reality and shines in its own light - the glowing light of the Jungian "luminosities." We are "unconscious" of this peculiar kind of light only because we cannot find anything that stands in opposition to it: the "luminosities" are not opposed either to the day-light of consciousness or to the "dark night of the soul." Their only enemy is literalism.

Multiplicity and Luminosity of Archetypes

The concept of archetypes, like that of the unconscious, is controversial among the critics of Jung both outside and inside the Jungian school of thought. There is however a substantial agreement among the Hillmanians that the archetype is the most ontologically fundamental of all Jung's psychological concepts.

In Hillman's thought, archetypes are not unknown and unknowable noumenal entities but wholly immanent in images. They are not nouns denoting transcendental contents behind the images, but adjectives pointing to the value, richness, import and effect of images.[9] In other words, images are themselves archetypal, fully meaningful in their own right and on their own terms. Psyche does not consist of images but is image and imagining.

Archetypal images (unlike symbols) do not represent any-thing other than themselves. In cosmological terms, they are not representations but presences of the macrocosm within micro-cosm. According to Jung, the whole psychic human being is "nothing less than a world, a microcosm," i.e., "something boundless: infinite or infinitesimal."[10] Humans are worlds present to themselves, i.e., wholly and unabashedly narcissistic worlds. By the same token, the archetypal images which consti-tute these "worlds," are themselves image-worlds, infinite in number and unpredictable, mercurial in their behavior. The ontological structure of the psyche is radically imaginal: it is not single, unitary or monotheistic, but multiple, polycentric and polytheistic.

By saying that images are mercurial, I am referring to their ambiguous character, their duplicity. In the language of alchemy, images are utriusque capax, capable of being both spiritual and material, good and evil, light and dark, conscious and unconscious. For the same reason what is called matter and spirit are not two substantial "somethings," irremediably opposed to each other, but perspectives which the psyche may adopt towards any reality "out there": anything can be envisioned as either material or spiritual; a plant or a stone may be more "spiritual" than a human being just as a human being may be more "materialistic" than the groceries which he consumes.

We are now in the position to state that what Jung calls the "luminosity" of archetypes refers to the imaginal realm of the soul which is neither fully conscious nor fully unconscious. In his important essay "On the Nature of the Psyche" Jung avers that the contents of the unconscious are not plunged in complete darkness, but are only relatively unconscious, just as the contents of consciousness are hardly ever perceived in all their aspects, but are also partially unconscious. The light of consciousness has many degrees of brightness and is therefore relative. Consciousness

> embraces not only consciousness as such, but a whole scale of intensities of consciousness. Between 'I do this' and 'I am conscious of doing this' there is a world of difference, amounting sometimes to outright contradiction. Consequently there is a consciousness in which unconsciousness predominates, as well as a consciousness in which self-consciousness predominates.

For example, on the primitive level, ego-consciousness is far from being stable: there is a mere "luminosity." For here - as on the infantile level - consciousness is not a unity, not yet centered by a firmly-knit ego complex. It is

> just flickering into life here and there ... At this stage it is like a chain of islands on an archipelago. Nor is it a fully integrated whole even at the higher and highest stages; rather it is capable of indefinite expansion.[11]

The Jungian psyche is a field of multiple and luminous particles which are like sparks or scintilla, and which correspond to tiny conscious phenomena. One of Jung's clearest formulations of his concept of "multiple luminosities" occurs in Mysterium Conjunctionis. The doctrine of scintillae, he says,

> testifies to the personality- or ego-character of psychic complexes: just as the distinguishing mark of the ego-complex is consciousness so it is possible that other, 'unconscious' complexes may possess, as splinter psyches, a certain luminosity of their own.[12]

These autonomous or relatively autonomous entities would be like "vibrations" present in the atmosphere or "pieces" of the Polynesian mana, largely unattached to a particular individual, free-floating.

It is conceivable that what we call thoughts and ideas represent another form of such free-floating phenomena. In his autobiography, Jung says that Philemon, a figure of his fantasy, helped him realize the autonomy of thought and ideas. It was a "crucial insight":

> ... there are things in the psyche which I do not produce, but which produce themselves and have their own life. Philemon represented a force which was not myself ... He said I treated thoughts as if I generated them myself, but in his view thoughts were like animals in the forest, or people in a room, or birds in the air, and added: 'If you should see people in a room, you would not think that you had made those people or that you were responsible for them.' It was he who taught me psychic objectivity, the reality of the psyche.[13]

From what we have said it seems obvious that the Jungian unconscious should not be understood topographically, i.e., as a literal place inside the organism or as a separate system containing innate unconscious ideas inherently distinct from the total world process. Rather than positing, in a dualistic fashion, two discrete compartments - conscious and unconscious - we must imagine psychic life in terms of degrees of intensity, alternation and interfusion. Quite simply, we are always both conscious and unconscious. It is like in the famous dream of Chuang Tsu who dreamed that he was a butterfly. When the sage suddenly awoke he did not know whether he was Chuang Tsu who had dreamed that he was a butterfly, or whether he was a butterfly dreaming that he was Chuang Tsu. There is a fascintaing echo of the ancient Chinese sage in the following words of Hillman:

> We are dreaming all the time ... Part of the soul is continually remembering in mythopoetic speech, continually seeing, feeling, and hearing sub specie aeternitatis ... Our lives seem at one and the same moment to be uniquely our own and altogether new, yet to carry an ancestral aura, a quality of déjà vu.[14]

Anima Mundi and the Subtle Embodiment

In the tradition of sophia perennis (Plato and Neoplatonism) the individual soul is continuous with anima mundi, a world soul that animates the universe and flows into the human subject. For example, among the Gnostics, the world soul is conceived as that part of God which is imprisoned in nature and constitutes the quintessence of physis. Man is a partial phenomenon possessing an "accrescent soul," prospsyches psyche, a soul that has "grown into" him. According to Jung, the "accrescent soul was a second soul that grew through the mineral, vegetable, and animal kingdoms up to man, pervading the whole nature ..."[15]

The concept of anima mundi goes back to Plato's doctrine that a soul had been diffused through the body of the world by the Demiurge, "wherefore, using the language of probabilities [i.e., the language of myth] we may say that the world became a living creature" (Timaeus, 30). From Plato on, the concept recurs, with many variations, in the Stoic philosophers, in Plotinus, Nicolas of Cusa, as well as among the Cambridge Platonists (More, Cudworth) and in the nature philosophy of the German Romantics. Foremost among the latter was F.W.J. Schelling (1775-1854) who set out to demonstrate that nature was "visible spirit" and that spirit was "invisible nature." Spirit and matter, acting simultaneously in dynamic duality and organic unity, constitute the world soul - an organizing principle which holds everything together in a living whole. In Schelling's system matter and spirit exist only in their reciprocal relationship. Others have conceived the soul as a sphere whose center is everywhere and whose circumference is nowhere - an idea which has been ascribed to the legendary Egyptian sage Hermes Trismegistus. The image of an infinite sphere was originally applied to God, but Nicolas of Cusa (1401-1464) used it also for the universe, God's creation, and the Renaissance philosophers (Bruno, Ficino, Vico) considered it equally suitable for the individual human mind.[16]

It is only by the end of the seventeenth century that Western science "discovered" a world of dead matter, permeated by movement due to uniform, quantitative forces and devoid of anything remotely "spiritual." In Jung's words, "man himself has ceased to be a microcosm and eidolon of the Cosmos, and his 'anima' is no longer the consubstantial scintilla, or spark of the Anima Mundi, the World Soul."[17]

Another important tradition in which the soul is conceived in wider terms than man, is alchemy. In Western alchemy (as in the East), the individual soul is only partly identical with our conscious being. The soul functions in the body, but "the greater part" of its operatio takes place outside the body. This "greater part" is said to imagine "many things of the utmost profundity." According to the alchemist Ruland, the soul as the vice-regent of God "has absolute and independent power to do other things than those the body can grasp."[18] If we were to ask, what is the place or the medium of realization of these "other things," the answer must be that it is neither mind nor matter, but an intermediate realm of subtle reality which can be expressed only by an image. The alchemical opus is directed toward the actualization of the psychic reality of the imaginal and away from the perceptual and the natural reality of the physical.[19]

One of the most emphatic statements concerning the realm of subtle reality is found in Ruland's Lexicon alchemicae: "Imagination is the star in man, the celestial or supercelestial body" (Astrum in homine, coeleste sive supracoeleste corpus).[20] What the alchemist is in effect saying is that imagination creates not immaterial vaporous phantoms but a subtle or imaginal body. G.R.S. Mead, one of the few serious writers on the subject, observes that the notion of "subtle embodiment" may prove to be that mediating ground in concrete reality which is so badly needed to provide a basis of reconciliation between the two dominant modes of opposed and contradictory abstractionizing that characterize the spiritualistic and materialistic philosophy of the present day ...[21]

Reconciliation or not - it seems evident that to a literalistic mentality, based as it is on either/or style of ratiocination, the subtle body can be no more than a half spiritual, half material hybrid, a benign monster created by wayward and overheated imagination. There are signs, however, that scientists themselves are beginning to reconsider their assumptions about the basic constitution of things. I shall go into this question of assumptions and paradigms in the Second Part. As of now it is only fair to warn the reader that, for reasons to be explained later, I am not interested in the widespread attempt on the part of "spiritual" writers and some Jungians to validate the psyche and psychic phenomena by recourse to the recent developments in microphysics and astronomy. It is true that Jung, being anxious to gain scientific respectability for his revolutionary insights, at times did slide into the empiricist temptation. Yet, as the following quotation shows, even in drawing parallels between discoveries in modern physics and depth psychology, he never lost sight of the psyche as a "subtle embodiment."

> The moment when physics touches on the 'untrodden, untreadable regions,' and when psychology has at the same time to admit that there are other forms of psychic life besides the acquisitions of personal consciousness - in other words, when psychology too touches on an impenetrable darkness - then the intermediate realm of subtle bodies comes to light again ... We have come very close to this turning-point today."[22]

Soul and Spirit

Plotinus has said that the ultimate One cannot be named: "we can but circle, as it were, about its circumference"

44

(Enneads, 6.9. 3-4). In recent times a similar thought has been expressed by the 14th Dalai Lama of Tibet: "The creative soul craves spirit ... People need to climb the mountain not simply because it is there but because the soulful divinity needs to be mated with the spirit."[23] I do not intend to find out whether the Plotinian "One" is "more or less" the same as the highest peaks of the Himalayas. For the present purposes it is enough to say that, if the soul needs spirit, the reverse is also true: the spirit must use soul as its medium.

In the Jungian vocabulary "psyche" is a comprehensive term denoting the totality of psychic processes, conscious as well as unconscious. The word "soul"[24] refers to a "functional complex" or partial personality; it is also often applied to anima which stands for a deeper generic force behind our conscious functions. Essentially anima is the archetypal structure of consciousness or "the archetype of life," i.e., the actual life of the psyche, its spontaneous involvement in the endless labyrinthine problems of human existence.[25]

Jungians, including Hillman, use the words "soul" and "psyche" for the most part interchangeably. The reason for this is that they are not meant to be scientific concepts but symbols. As a symbolic term, "soul" (or psyche), according to Hillman, is a deliberately ambiguous concept resisting all definition.[26] One may just as well use such words as "heart," "life," "warmth," "humanness," "emotion," etc. A soul may be said to be "troubled," "dismembered," "immortal," "spiritual," "lost," "innocent," "inspired." The psyche, which, as Jung said, can never become an object of observation without at the same time being its subject, is more like a hall of mirrors where one mirror reflects one's reflection in another mirror and so on ad infinitum.

The Jungian conception of the psyche is more akin to pre-civilized view of the soul as the source of life, the prime mover, a ghostlike presence which has objective reality. To

Jung, soul is not at all a subjective presence or subject to the will, but a self-subsistent agency, something independent, capricious, unfathomable and ungraspable. So it is safe in this, as in many other instances, to side with the brilliantly obscure Heraclitus who said that "you could not discover the limits of the psychē even by traveling every path: so deep a logos does it have."[27]

Jung also accepts the possibility of a plurality of souls (complexes, partial personalities) in one and the same individual. For the possibility of a dissociation of personality exists not only in pathology but also within the range of the so called normal behavior. The soul, far from being a homogeneous unit, is "a boiling cauldron of contradictory impulses, inhibitions, and affects ... The unity of consciousness or of the so called personality is not a reality at all but a desideratum."[28]

Our emphasis on psyche as a polycentric field of powers is necessary in order to offset the widespread tendency among the Jungians to glorify the Self as the unifying center of personality. This strategy has de facto resulted in reducing Jung's psychology to a psychological version of Christianity and/or Hebrewism with Christ and/or Yahweh worshipped under a scientifically more respectable guise of the Self. We must resist all reductionist attempts, including the reduction of the soul to something vaguely "spiritual" and monotheistic.

A polycentric view of the psyche has a long and venerable history. James Frazer, among many other anthropologists, has shown that primitive man regarded the soul as an impersonal presence with which he could converse; he also associated himself with a plurality of souls, at least four and sometimes as many as thirty. In Frazer's words,

> the divisibility of life, or ... the plurality of souls, is an idea suggested by many familiar facts, and has commended itself to philosophers like Plato as well as to savages. It is only when the notion of a soul becomes a theological dogma that its unity and indivisi-

bility are insisted upon as essential. The savage, unshackled by dogma, is free to explain the facts of life by the assumption of as many souls as he thinks necessary.[29]

The overriding concern of archetypal psychology is to avoid substantializing the soul. Thus Hillman: "By soul I mean ... a perspective rather than a substance, a viewpoint towards things rather than a thing itself." To this he adds two more qualifications: first, "soul" refers to the deepening of events into experiences; second, "soul" means "the imaginative possibility in our natures, the experiencing through reflective speculation, dream, image, and fantasy -- that mode which recognizes all realities as primarily symbolic or metaphorical."[30] What Hillman is suggesting is that the soul, rather than being an immaterial "something" behind our thoughts, emotions, etc., an agent behind our actions, is an all-pervading presence which cannot be localized. As a perspective, rather than a substance, the soul is free of any literal location. It is not in the body, or in the brain or in other physical place. The place of the soul is precisely "where the action is," that is to say, the soul is wherever our "love," our inclinations, emotions and moods are. And, of course, if these "loves" are somehow experienced "in" the body or the brain or outside the body (in "things" like trees, rocks, animals), then that is precisely where the soul has found a temporary abode. The soul may assume many shapes because it is essentially an "animal" which in the Greek sense means not "beast" but any "animated being," including ghosts, demons, gods, the ensouled stars - even the ensouled universe as a whole.

I must digress at this point in order to dispel a potential distortion that would equate our view with the philosophical-psychological theory known as panpsychism. Panpsychism is a sub-species of monism holding that all things in the universe

47

have an "inner" or psychological being. According to the proponents of this school of thought, which includes such illustrious names as G.T. Fechner, Josiah Royce, Hermann Lotze, S. Alexander, G.W. Leibniz, F.C.S. Schiller, etc., the whole world of sense is but a veil of an infinite realm of mental life. What is commonly called "mind" (mindedness) was _always_ there; even the material substance of a single-celled animal such as protozoa already has a kind of embryonic mindedness. Thus when matter had reached a certain level of organization, as for example in the case of man, nothing new was introduced. The consciousness which emerged out of living matter must also have been latent in all living as well as non-living matter.

Panpsychism is rooted in the desire to avoid any kind of discontinuity between inorganic matter on the one hand and the more organized level which matter has reached in animals and men, on the other. Among recent writers who have attributed some kind of protomindedness, _i.e._, a rudimentary form of life, sensation and even volition, to entities such as molecules, atoms, and subatomic particles, may be listed A.N. Whitehead, C. Hartshorne, Bernard Rensch and L.C. Birch. According to E.W. Sinnott (a colleague of the famous biologist Dobzhansky),

> biological organization [concerned with organic development and physiological activity] and psychical activity [concerned with behavior and leading to mind] are fundamentally the same thing. To talk about 'mind' in a bean plant ... is more defensible than trying to place an arbitrary point on the evolutionary scale where mind[31] in some mysterious manner, made its appearance.

Panpsychism (quite apart from its scientific credibility) suffers from the literalistic fallacy. It assumes that "mind" is an objective datum, a something or other which is "always there" and whose existence is amenable to impartial observation and scientific detection. The basic flaw in this assumption is that it claims to account for the nature of reality in terms of a single principle.

In our view things may or may not be ensouled; sometimes they are, sometimes they are not; now they are alive, now dead and then again alive, but never always there as alive or dead. There is never an either/or, but always "now this," "now that." The soul's perspective is that of radical relativism implying that reality is primarily imaginal and that all our perceptual and cognitive processes are rooted in imagination. It is out of this "groundless ground" that we create our world, indeed, many worlds whose ontological status is synchronous with the status of the kind of imagination that creates them. Archetypal psychology is more comfortable with the naive "panpsychism" of primitive peoples and children - individuals who have not yet succumbed to the temptation of the moderns to confuse the map with the territory. It is a "pan-psychism" from which we must first amputate "pan" and then "ism."

Turning to "spirit" we note that the Latin words spiritus (from spirare, "to breath") and animus are the same as the Greek anemos ("wind"). The older Greek term for "wind" is pneuma which also means "spirit." In Arabic "wind" is rih, and ruh is "soul, spirit." The word "spirit" in its early usage refers to a dynamic principle whose hallmarks are spontaneity of movement, spontaneous capacity to produce images independently of sense perception and the autonomous and sovereign manipulation of these images. As an agency which stimulates, incites and inspires, spirit is hardly distinguishable from psyche.

Curiously, however, it is precisely as a spontaneous force that spirit has become the classical antithesis of matter. According to Jung,[32] this artificial oppositon is largely due to the Christian prejudice that spirit is so vastly superior to the life of nature that the latter must be regarded as no better than dead. In the Western tradition the concept of spirit has been restricted to the supernatural or anti-natural and has lost its essential connection with pyche and life. When finally, with the rise of scientific materialism, spirit was degraded to a servile attribute of matter, its original spontaneity and emotionality withdrew into psyche; to some extent it was also preserved in esoteric and transmundane circles as the enemy of matter. As a result of these developments, the primal identity between psyche and spirit was lost. Spirit has come to mean in most cases something that is either antithetical to matter (supernaturalism, Cartesian dualism) or - an appendix to matter (materialistic monism).

Jung's position in this regard is much less simplistic. As we already indicated, the psyche, far from being a homogeneous structure, is an interplay of many forces which are only loosely bound together; there is a marked tendency within the psyche to split into parts. These parts, called complexes, may "detach themselves from consciousness to such an extent that they not only appear foreign but lead an autonomous life of their own."[33] Complexes are psychic fragments which appear and disappear according to their own laws. They often behave like independent beings endowed with personality, especially in the voices heard by the insane, in automatic writing and as spirits or ghosts among primitives. According to Jung, the psychological basis for the belief in spirits and in plurality of souls is the fact that "psyche is not an indivisible unity but a divisible and more or less divided whole."[34]

Jung is convinced that the tendency of the psyche to split into parts is a normal phenomenon and need not be reduced to the condition of hysterical multiple personality or schizophrenic alterations of personality. The difference between normal archetypal images and the dissociated products of schizophrenia is that "the former are entities endowed with personality and charged with meaning, whereas the latter are only fragments with vestiges of meaning - in reality they are products of disintegration."[35]

If we now substitute "image" for the word "complex," we may suggest that "spirits" are archetypal images universally present in the pre-conscious make-up of the psyche. They are "luminosities" that arise and can be "seen" in states of reduced intensity of consciousness (in dreams, reveries, visions). We call them compulsions, phobias, neurotic symptoms only because, as Jung points out, we live in an utterly godless and profane time and because we ignore psyche and pursue a cult of consciousness to the exclusion of all else. "Our true religion is a monotheism of consciousness, a possession by it, coupled with a fanatical denial that there are parts of the psyche which are autonomous."[36]

The soul is a Protean-like being. The image of Proteus was employed by the Neo-Platonists of the Renaissance in order to show that the psyche is ever in flux, never fixed into one stance or image. Man is not one but many, flowing everywhere as the anima mundi and potentially all things.

I referred earlier to a passage from the Dalai Lama of Tibet in which he stated that the "creative soul craves spirit." In the same passage the soul is said to be "at home in the deep, shaded valleys." John Keats, writing to his brother, says that the world is "the vale of soul-making." Then he continues: "How then are souls to be made: ... How but by the medium of a world like this? This point I sincerely wish to consider because I think it a grander system of salvation than the Christian religion."[37]

We need not compare the effectiveness of Christianity as a salvific message to the soteriological value of soul-making. Suffice it to say that the main reason for the tepidity and shallowness surrounding much of the present-day Christian existence may well lie in the circumstance that, having exchanged soul for (disembodied) spirit, it has lost connection with life and the world, with "the deep, shaded valleys" of the world. It is

51

certainly significant that already in St. Paul's letters, pneuma or spirit had begun to replace psyche or soul. According to D.L. Miller, in the New Testament psyche is used only fifty-seven times to pneuma's 274 occurrences. So much is this the pattern that Paul comes to call psychikoi bad and pneumatikoi good (I Cor. 2:13-15; cf. I Cor. 15:44-46).[38]

Traditionally the soul belongs to the valleys or, as Jung puts it, "she tends to favour the body and everything bodily, sensuous, and emotional. She lies caught 'in chains' of Physis" but she also "desires beyond physical necessity."[39] In Greek mythology psyche, besides being soul, denoted a nightmoth or butterfly. According to Hillman, the place of the soul is "a world of imagination, passion, fantasy, reflection, that is neither physical and material on the one hand, nor spiritual and abstract on the other, yet bound to them both."

In contrast to soul's intimate relationship with imagination and fantasy, i.e., with the concrete, multiple and immanent, the images of the spirit, says Hillman, "blaze with light, there is fire, wind, sperm. Spirit is fast, and it quickens what it touches. Its direction is vertical and ascending; it is arrow-straight, knife-sharp, ... and phallic. It is masculine, the active principle, making forms, order, and clear distinctions."[40] Other words may be used to denote the outstanding characteristics of spirit: it is abstract, unified, prophetic in style, humorless, impersonal, timeless.[41] But note that in all these descriptions of spirit Hillman uses the expression "the images of spirit" (emphasis mine) in order to indicate that what we call spirit or spirits cannot be divorced from the soul. Spiritual flights, spirit's search for ultimates, for oneness of all things, etc. is essentially a psychic adventure. For, according to one of the central maxims of archetypal psychology, "all things are determined by psychic images, including our formulations of the spirit."[42] Unfortunately in our culture spirit has been uprooted and subsequently identified with immaterial essence, "pure thought" and similar miscreations.

Nevertheless the soul craves spirit. Icarus on the way to the sun, Bellerophon, ascending on his white winged horse, Phaethon, driving the sun's chariot - all these are mythological figures of the spirit. Even if they were forced to fall onto the valleys of the soul, they could fly only because they were able to "use their imagination." It is the function of the spirit, then, to convey to the soul, in Jung's words, "a certain 'divine influx' and the knowledge of higher things, wherein consists precisely its supposed animation of the soul."[44]

We must reiterate, however, that in all this the soul or psyche is the ontologically prior reality; it is the soul which journeys towards the peaks (A. Maslow's peak-experiences) or degrades itself into gross matter. As in the Plotinian system, the soul has affinities with every grade in the hierarchy. The human soul is a wanderer among the worlds: it may unite itself to the sphere above, and become spirit (a spiritual soul) or it may remain entangled in an environment which is beneath its true dignity. But then perhaps it is the case that the soul has no special dignity of its own. Psyche, as Keats said in his "Ode to Psyche," had no temple dedicated to her. Heraclitus calls psyche "the vaporization out of which everything else is derived." (fr. 43, Wheelwright). If so, the special dignity of the soul may very well consist in her refusal to become disengaged from transience, mortality, lunacy and all the other infirmities that are an indelible part of the human condition.

NOTES

[1] CW 8, par. 429.

[2] Hillman, Re-Visioning Psychology, p. 23.

[3] Ibid., p. 152.

[4] CW 13, p. 51, note 2.

[5] The substantialist view of the soul was canonized for the Catholics at the Councils of Vienne (1311-1312) and the Lateran (1513). See Denzinger-Banwart Enchiridion Symbolorum, 481, 738.

[6] John Dewey, "Soul and Body," in The Philosophy of the Body, ed. Stuart F. Spicker (Chicago: Quadrangle Books, 1970), p. 119.

[7] See Marie-Louise von Franz, ed., Aurora Consurgens. Bollingen Series LXXVII (Pantheon Books, 1966), p. 166 ff.

[8] See James Hillman, The Myth of Analysis: Three Essays in Archetypal Psychology (New York: Harper Colophon Books, 1972), p. 173 ff; Roberts Avens, Imagination is Reality; Western Nirvana in Jung, Hillman, Barfield & Cassirer (Spring Publications, 1980), pp. 73-84.

[9] See James Hillman, "On the Necessity of Abnormal Psychology," Eranos 43-1974 (Leiden, E.J. Brill), pp. 103-104.

[10] CW 16, par. 206.

[11] CW 8, pars. 385, 387; cf. pars. 365-370 on "The Dissociability of the Psyche."

[12] CW 14, par. 47; cf. 8, par. 396.

[13] C.G. Jung, Memories, Dreams, Reflections, recorded and ed. by Aniela Jaffé. Tr. from the German by Richard and Clara Winston (New York: Vintage Books, 1963), p. 183; cf. CW 8, par. 388 ff.

[14] Hillman, The Myth of Analysis, p. 177.

[15] CW 14, par. 374.

[16] The infinite sphere of the Middle Ages whose center is nowhere and everywhere, has found an application in Fred Hoyle's idea of the expanding universe which he illustrates by the analogy of a balloon with a large number of dots on its surface and blown up gradually to infinite size. In The Nature of the Universe (1950) Hoyle writes: "The balloon analogy brings out a very important point. It shows we must not imagine that we are situated at the center of the universe, just because we see all the galaxies to be moving away from us. For, whichever dot you care to choose on the surface of the balloon, you will find that the other dots all move away from it. In other words, whichever galaxy you happen to be in, the other galaxies will appear to be receding from you." Quoted in Rudolf Arnheim, Visual Thinking (University of California Press, 1969), p. 290.

[17] CW II, par. 759.

[18] CW 12, par. 396.

[19] See Berry, "An Approach to the Dream," p. 63.

[20] Quoted by Jung in CW 12, par. 394.

[21] G.R.S. Mead, The Subtle Body in Western Tradition (London: Stuart & Watkins, 1967), p. 2.

[22] CW 12, par. 394.

[23] Quoted by Hillman in "Peaks and Vales; the Soul/ Spirit Distinction as Basis for the Differences Between Psychotherapy and Spiritual Discipline," Puer Papers (Spring Publications, 1979), p. 59.

[24] The word "soul" is from the Old Germ. saivala, Germ. Seele and may cognate with the Greek aiolos, meaning "quick-moving, changeful of hue, shifting." The Greek word for psychē is related to psuchein, "to breathe"; psychos means "cool" and psychosis, "animation." The German Geist goes back to the Indo-Iranian gheizd whose root means "to move powerfully"; it is also akin to the Old Norse geisa, "to rage," and the Anglo-Saxon gaestan, "terror." The Hebrew ruah is a synonym for anger and "is used to cover such emotions as sadness, trouble, bitterness, and longing, which are regarded as 'located in the ruah'." See James Hillman, Emotion (London: Routledge & Kegan Paul, 1960), p. 232.

[25] See CW 13, par. 62; 7, par. 339, 521; 6, pars. 797-99. For a full exploration of anima and the relevant literature see Hillman's two essays on "Anima" in Spring 1973, pp. 97-132 and Spring 1974, pp. 113-46.

[26] See James Hillman, Suicide and the Soul (Zürich: Spring Publications, 1976), p. 46.

[27] Diels-Kranz, fr. 45; English tr. by K. Freeman in Ancilla to the Pre-Socratic Philosophers (Oxford: B.H. Blackwell, 1948).

[28] CW 9i, par. 190.

[29] James Frazer, The Golden Bough. One Vol. abridged ed. (New York: Macmillan Co., 1934), p. 690; cf. p. 178. The idea of multiple souls is central in the Greek shamanistic tradition and survived in varying forms into the Classical Age. See E.R. Dodds, The Greeks and the Irrational (University of California Press, 1951), Chapter 5.

[30] Hillman, Re-Visioning Psychology, p. x.

[31] E.W. Sinnott, Cell and Psyche: the Biology of Purpose (Chapel Hill: University of North Carolina Press, 1950), pp. 48-50.

[32] See CW 9i, pars. 389, 391, 393.

[33] CW 8, pars. 252-253.

[34] CW 8, par. 582.

[35] CW 8, par. 254.

[36] C.G. Jung, "Commentary on the Secret of the Golden Flower," in Psyche & Symbol, a Selection from the Writings of C. G. Jung, ed. Violet S. de Laszlo (Garden City, N.Y.: Doubleday Anchor books, 1958), p. 313.

[37] H.B. Forman, ed., The Letters of John Keats (London: Reeves & Turner, 1895), letter dating from April 1819, p. 326.

[38] See David L. Miller, "Archelous and the Butterfly: Toward an Archetypal Psychology of Humor," Spring 1973, p. 15.

[39] CW 15, par. 673.

[40]Hillman, _Re-Visioning Psychology_, pp. 68, 69.

[41]See Hillman, "Peaks and Vales," pp. 59-69.

[42]_Ibid._, p. 64.

[43]_CW_ 14, par. 673.

IV: THE UROBORIC PATH

The Saint and the Poet

Jungian pyschology starts from the premise that the psyche is an original structure, which cannot be reduced to an appendage either of the material or the spiritual world. It is a self-regulating and self-sustaining system composed of parts which are in a state of constant strife and perpetual flux. This process of inner polarity is indispensable for the very life and aliveness of the psyche. What Jung calls the Self or "wholeness" is ordinarily never reached (except in the case of a Buddha or a Christ). The wholeness of personality is a spirit fantasy - something one has to learn to enjoy for its own sake and not for the results it may bring. For it is the fantasy itself that is fulfilling, not the goal. Wholeness is in the images themselves, not in a Beyond that is empty of all images.

We may translate this into Buddhist language by a detour of William Blake's classical formula: "If the doors of perception were cleansed everything would appear to man as it is, infinite." Significantly, Blake is not telling us that a cleansed perception discloses an imageless and wholly transcendent Infinite. When our senses are fully awakened, the Infinite, like the Buddhist nirvana, is found in samsara, i.e., in the Heraclitean world of flux where, in Jung's words, "thesis is followed by antithesis, and between the two is generated a third factor, a lysis which was not perceptible before."[1] The "third factor" is the soul, the anima mundi, the kind of Infinite which presences itself in the things at hand or rather in their imaginal, soulful appearances. It is like in those Buddhist stories which tell that the most sacred scriptures are its unwritten pages - an old pine tree gnarled by wind and weather or a skein of geese flying across the autumn sky.

59

Evidently, to an exclusively rational approach which thinks of opposites as total and absolute, the "third factor" must remain inaccessible - tertium non datur. Opposites never unite on their own level, of their own accord or by a divine fiat. A supraordinate "third," existing at a different level from the opposites themselves, is always required. Nature (and psyche is nature in her animated form) thrives on paradox and is not bound by the rules of rational logic. She uses opposites to create a new thing - the soul, a miracle in the center of existence. - I now invite the reader to pay attention to the following passages of Jung expounding the centrality of the psyche.

> Living reality is the product neither of the actual, objective behavior of things nor of the formulated idea exclusively, but rather of the combination of both in the living psychological process, through esse in anima.

> Idea and thing come together ... in the human psyche, which holds the balance between them.[2]

Or again:

> I do not contest the relative validity either of the realistic standpoint, the esse in re, or of the idealistic standpoint, the esse in intellectu solo; I would only like to unite these extreme opposites by an esse in anima, which is the psychological standpoint. We live immediately only in the world of images.[3]

In one of his letters Jung writes:

> I am indeed convinced that creative imagination is the only primordial phenomenon accessible to us, the real Ground of the psyche, the only immediate reality. Therefore I speak of esse in anima, the only form of being we can experience directly.[4]

Among the "occult" thinkers of the past, the equivalent of the esse in anima is coincidentia or conjunctio oppositorum - a traditional formula expressing the ineffable nature of God. For example, Nicolas of Cusa speaks of the dwelling place of the divine reality as being "gird round with the coincidence of contradictories, and this is the wall of Paradise wherein Thou dost abide."[5] Jung, however, ordinarily assignes this divine place to the soul:

> The confrontation of the two positions generates a tension, charged with energy and creates a living, third thing - not a logical stillbirth in accordance with the principle tertium non datur but a movement out of the suspension between opposites, a living birth that leads to a new level of being, a new situation.[6]

W.B. Yeats, a kindred soul, also turns his gaze away from Cusanus' "wall of Paradise" and back to a world of flux and sheer enantiodromia: "If it be true that God is a circle whose centre is everywhere, the saint goes to the centre, the poet and artist to the ring where everything comes round again."[7]

By saying that the "saint goes to the centre" whereas "the poet and the artist, to the ring where everything comes round again," Yeats expresses a basic difference between the mystical and imaginal approaches. Western mystics and mystical writers have for the most part tended to subordinate imagination to a pure intellectual vision of God. The reason for this unfavorable view of the imaginal lies primarily in fear - fear of the essential freedom and power of imagination, especially in the moral realm. To the mystic, fantasy is connected with the lower parts of the soul, with passion and appetite; hence it could not be used as an instrument of moral improvement. For example, Hugo of St. Victor, while making imagination a necessary link in the communion between spirit and body, cautions that reason must never fall in love with this linking faculty. To Richard of St. Victor and Bonaventure, imagination is a kind of handmaid to reason, a comparatively low kind of contemplation by which one ascends to the imageless vision of the Perfrect Form of Beauty. Throughout the Middle Ages imagination is at best an instrument of the intellect and is defined in the light of a predominantly rationalistic ideal. It is a dangerous power that interferes with a rationally guided will - a magician whose trickery and false coinage, called phantasma proterva, is synonymous with demonic apparition.[8]

We cannot share the passion of the mystic who "goes to the centre." Rather, we align ourselves with the artist who returns to the "ring where everything comes round again." This is not to say that archetypal psychology is indifferent to the idea of a center. On the contrary, it is so fond of it that it multiplies centers ad infinitum. We may also put it in Oriental terms by suggesting that our center is in mandala, which means the "centerless center."

Curiously, Jung seemed to be unable adequately to understand the subtlety of mandala symbolism, which he interpreted as the "premonition of a center of personality, a kind of central point within the psyche to which everything is related."[9] In common with the mainstream of Western psychology, he insisted upon an ego-centered consciousness and, at least temperamentally preferred to see mandala as pointing from this ego to a larger Self which he, in turn, tended to identify with the religious archetype of Christ or God "within us." But it is also Jung who never tires of repeating that the psyche is not only the object of psychology, but - "fatally enough" - also its subject. According to Jung, the psyche cannot be transcended, which is the same as saying that it is multi-centered and revolving in circles. The Self is not the Center or an ideal to be reached, but a signpost on the circuitous journey of the soul - a journey whose center is everywhere and the circumference nowhere.

Rainbow and the Dream-Rose

Jung's psychology is a song of praise, a hymn to the circular character of the psyche which can never get out of itself to become conscious of its own structure. The psyche never talks of anything but itself and its complementary twin, the natural universe. What it says are such things as, "I am a woman" or "I am a serpent," "I am a hero (climbing the peaks)," "I am sun rising in the morning and setting in the evening," "I am oceans and rivers," "a boy and a girl," "a bush and a bird and a dumb fish of the sea." Psyche and the world reflect each other and together create a mirror-world whose governing law is that of imagination. Imagination is a non-derivative, self-propelling power, for its energy, unlike that of a dynamo or a robot, is supplied by the imagination itself. Imagination can be known only through imagination. In saying this I am following the ancient Greek and the alchemical maxim that the like is known only by like, i.e., every mode of understanding corresponds to the mode of being of the interpreter. Put in philosophical terms, being and thought - these two perpetual antagonists of the rationalistic inquiry - belong togehter. If I may add an observation from another "field," it is also conceivable that the Gospel parable of the Feast (Matt. 22:2-10; Lk. 14:16-29) means exactly what it says, namely, that it is hopeless to convey the meaning of symbolic images to people who are blind to them.

Owen Barfield, 'the British literary critic and one of the most subtle of contemporary thinkers, has suggested that it is inadequate to picture our cognitive processes as a commercium, a relationship between subject and object in the course of which the impressions received from the outer world are miraculously transformed into ideas. Knowledge in the sense of insight into the nature of things, occurs within the space of the soul, spanning, like a rainbow, the opposite poles of inner and outer worlds.

According to Barfield, the most obvious bridge between the "subjective" experience (emotion) of the psyche and the "objective" qualities in nature, is color. The two poles, subjective and objective, light up between the extremes of light and darkness or, more precisely, in their reciprocal interplay.

"Thus, outwardly the rainbow - or, if you prefer it, the spectrum - is the bridge between dark and light, but inwardly the rainbow is what the soul itself is, the bridge between body and spirit."[10]

Soul or imagination is not concerned either with mere matter or with pure spirit; to use a portmanteau term, it is a psychosomatic activity which, like a rainbow, links these two extremes harmoniously together and produces a "new level of being," a "third," which is none other than the soul itself. The soul creates itself by imagining itself and it exists only while it imagines. The truth and reality of the soul is created and exists in the created. Imagination is a self-originating, autonomous occurrence, sheer presencing, a "something" which, as a Buddhist would say, is "just so." In the strict sense of the word, it is a colorful experience.

There is an old tradition in the Iranian Sufism (Najm Kobrā, Semnanī) which holds that the mystic really and actually sees light and darkness by a kind of vision that is developed in conjunction with a growing interiorization. This visionary apperception is due to the development of subtle organs or suprasensory senses. According to Henry Corbin, "the colored photisms, the suprasensory perceptions of colors in the pure state, result from an inner activity of the subject and are not merely the result of passively received impressions of a material object."[11] - The Sūfi doctrine of colors is based on the alchemical method, which teaches that the like aspires to its like, that the like can be seen and known only by its like. This method is also related to the old correspondence idea, that there is homology between the events taking place in the outer world and the inner events of the soul.[12]

In the Western tradition it was Goethe who, by sheer coincidence, has mapped out a path that corresponds in all essentials to the Sūfi theory of colors. In his Farbenlehre Goethe writes:

The eye owes its existence to light. From auxiliary, sensory apparatus, animal and neutral, light has called forth, produced for itself, an organ like onto itself; thus the eye was formed by light, of light and for light, so that the inner light might come in contact with the outer light. At this very point we are reminded of the ancient Ionian school, which never ceased to repeat ... that like is known only by like. And thus we shall remember also the words of an ancient mystic that I would paraphrase as follows: If the eye were not by nature solar, how would we be able to look at the light? If God's own power did not live in us, how would the divine be able to carry us off in ecstasy? [13]

In Goethe's theory, "physiological colors" are not at all physiological in the sense of a material organism, but pertain to the subject, to the "eye which is itself light." The act of seeing is not a unilateral, subjective affair, but an interaction, a reciprocal action. In Corbin's words: "The perception of color is an action and reaction of the soul itself which is communicated to the whole of being; an energy is then emitted through the eye, a spiritual energy that cannot be weighed or measured quantitatively."[14]

*

The philosopher A.N. Whitehead has said that the poets are entirely mistaken when they credit "the rose for its scent, the nightingale for its song, and sun for its radiance" and that "they should address their lyrics to themselves and should turn them into odes of self-congratulations on the excellence of the human mind. Nature is a dull affair, soundless, scentless, colorless, merely the hurrying of material, endlessly, meaninglessly."[15] There is also the well-known T.S. Eliot's line "We are the music while the music lasts."

Whitehead may well have, in the above passage, parodied the way in which nature is viewed by mechanistic science. If, however, his statement is construed so as to imply that all meaning must be located in the individual's consciousness, then we must issue an emphatic non licet. Poets are (partly) right when they credit the rose for its scent, for the scent, like color and sound, is the result of an interaction between the poet and the rose; roses too imagine. The poet's rose is neither out there in the fields nor in his consciousness but precisely between the two. The real rose lights up in the void between the poet and the thing called "rose," i.e., within the imaginal space of the soul. Real roses are the imaginal or the dream-roses. In the same spirit I should like to "correct" Eliot by saying not that "we are the music while the music lasts," but rather that "we last while the music is." The music is not in us; rather, we are "in" the music. If you will, call it the Pyhtagorean harmony of spheres or Leibniz's harmonia praestablita, but then you must add the proviso that there seems to be no one to have done the pre-establishing. Perhaps the secret lies in being so attentive to the music that the question "Who is playing?" becomes completely irrelevant. For if there is a Player, He, of all the others, must be so absorbed in the play, so unreservedly giving of Himself that to introduce a distinction between the player and the play would be equivalent to destroying both.

When St. Augustine was asked, "What did God do before the world was made?", his rejoinder was that He created a hell for the inquisitive. Augustine's remark must be understood in the context of his belief that creation is a continuous activity - a belief that was also held by Origen, Scotus Erigena and Thomas Aquinas. Thus when the Book says "In the beginning God created the heaven and the earth," the words "In the beginning" have the same import as the phrase "once upon a time," which means that what happened once is always happening. The creation is now. Perhaps the most lucid explanation of this matter was given by Rabbi Bunan: "The Lord created the world in a state of beginning. The universe is always in an uncompleted state, in the form of its beginning. It is not like a vessel at which the master works and he finishes it; it requires continuous labor and unceasing renewal by creative forces. Were there a second's pause by these forces, the world would return to primeval chaos."[16]

That there is not "a second's pause" means that the Creator is in a continuous, reciprocal relation with the created. Hence it is not only the Creator who creates - He is himself in an equal measure created by what he creates. "In the beginning" is neither the Creator nor the created (i.e., the world or a work of art) but the relation between the two. And the beginning is always beginning anew. In the context of our discussion, we may therefore just as well say: in the beginning is Imagination.

In seventeenth century Europe, people followed Bishop Usher's calculation of the date of the creation of the universe - as October 6, 4004 B.C. I submit that we are not much wiser in claiming to know who is man by connecting him to his simian ancestors or treating him as a Giant Rat or by placing the appearance of Genus Homo some 3,750,000 years ago. What is at work in all such attempts is the inveterate tendency to solve the riddle of existence by reducing it to historically or scientifically ascertainable origins. As a result man qua man - the pre-eminent enigma, the creature of the Between - tends to evaporate. And a part of this enigma is that both ascent and descent, Heaven and Earth, spirit and matter, are, to use a Buddhist expression, "mutually arising." Or, as Heraclitus, the first depth psychologist of the Western tradition (Hillman), stated: "The way up and the way down are one and the same."[17] In the words of another fragment: "This universe, which is the same for all, has not been made by any god or man, but it always has been, is, and will be - an everlasting fire, kindling itself by regular measures and going out by regular measures."[18]

Soul and the World of Myth

Almost a century ago the great anthropologist James C. Frazer, the author of the <u>Golden Bough</u> (first ed. 1890), advanced the theory that mankind everywhere passes through three stages of intellectual development, from magic to religion, and from religion to science (similar to Auguste Comte's theological, metaphysical and positive phases). He saw the basis of myth in magic - the tendency to control nature by rites and spells. Only when the more intelligent among the early men discovered the limitations of their magic might, did they appeal, in supplication and propitiation, to demons, ancestor-spirits or the gods of religion. In the course of time the shrewder intellects saw that the spirits and other higher beings were impotent in certain matters and so science was born. Frazer assumed that with the progress and development of science and technology the crass superstitions of magic would ultimately fade away.[19]

Frazer's thought as well as that of a whole generation of the nineteenth century anthropologists (Spencer, Tylor, Lang) was governed by the evolutionary prejudice that the latest in time is the best and the highest. For these men intelligence had begun with the Greeks and culminated in Western Europe. Other types of wisdom, different life goals from those of the Western man, were regarded as rudimentary forms of modern culture and their worth had to depend on their degree of approximation to modernity. To this cultural ethnocentrism, allied with the Western belief in the superiority of the scientific point of view, is due another supererogatory assumption, <u>i.e.</u>, that myths are accounts of physical history corresponding to the world of gross facts. Mythology, in this view, is a naive fumbling effort to explain the world of nature - a false etiology, and the rituals of the early man - only a misguided technology.

In contrast to anthropological evolutionism, the function of myth, in our view, has been best expressed by Plato: "We have

need of myths for the enchantment of the soul" (Laws, 903 B).
In Jungian thought, myths are dramatic, personified descriptions
of a non-human or quasi-human realm of tragical, monstrous,
fantastic figures which are beyond the grasp of the conscious
mind. These figures constitute the very basis, the delight and
the archetypal ground of psychic life. Myths are not invented
by a primitive untutored mentality but experienced. They are
"original revelations of the preconscious psyche, involuntary
statements about unconscious psychic ... processes."[20]

According to the tenets of archetypal psychology, the world
of the psyche is coextensive with the world of myth, for the
latter, far from being part of a dead past, is superbly alive in
our symptoms, fantasies and last but not least, in our sumptuous
rational ideas and constructs. For Hillman "mythology" and
"psychology" are interchangeable notions: "Mythology is a
psychology of antiquity. Psychology is a mythology of
modernity."[21]

Foremost among the contemporary philosophers who have
taken myth seriously is Ernst Cassirer, a critical idealist of
neo-Kantian persuasion. According to Cassirer, the primitive
thought has an independent logic which must be understood in
terms of its own premises. Instead of treating myth merely as a
prelude to the emergence of reason (as among the nineteenth
century anthropologists) or a stage in man's intellectual development, he sees the mythical world of the primitive as embodying a
unitary spiritual energy which manifests itself in creation of
images. These images confront man in the shapes of elemental
spirits, in the rustling of leaves, the murmuring and roaring of
the wind, in the voices of the forest. The world of the primitive
is fully alive because it is neither purely subjective nor purely
objective, neither spiritual nor material, but ensouled.

The mythical image is a cocrescence of name and thing: it
does not re-present the thing but is experienced as a genuine

69

presence containing the power, the significance and efficacy of the thing itself; it is the thing and the thing is alive. In myth the phenomenal (appearance) and the real are fused into one or, to put it differently, every phenomenon is always and necessarily an incarnation, a pure expression rather than representation. The meaning of images dwells in the images themselves as life dwells in the body. For the primitive, therefore, our contrast between representation and reality or between reality and appearance is meaningless: the world is fully present in the mode of its appearance. Whatever affects the mind, feeling or will has the lineaments of a fully objective, living and undoubted reality. There is no discrepancy between wish and fulfillment.

Thus when we see the archaic man filling the world with sacred trees, rocks, ghosts or with anthropomorphic gods and goddesses, we should not glibly assume that he is trying to twist reality into the categories of his own ego. Contrary to the nineteenth century evolutionists, the early man is not projecting into nature his owns ideas of souls, ghosts and ancestral spirits which he had fashioned out of his private dreams, hallucinations or cataleptic states (animism). In Cassirer's view, the idea of projection or animation of a dead matter (Cartesian res extensa) is based on the theological prejudice that "person" is the only carrier of soul and that what we call subjectivity, interiority or inner life is exclusively and literally possessed by our ego-personality. The spirits and demons of the myth are not projections or personifications, but objectifications of instantaneous, fleeting, intense impressions which occupy and possess the primitive mind.[22]

Henry Frankfort corroborates Cassirer's point of view by stressing that the ancient man experienced the world emotionally "in a dynamic reciprocal relationship." He simply does not know an inanimate world. For this very reason "he does not 'personify' inanimate phenomena nor does he fill an empty world with the ghosts of the dead, as 'animism' would have us believe."[23]

Now "projection" is at best a tricky word. Already Ludwig Feuerbach (1804-1871), the German philosopher of the nineteenth century and predecessor of Marx, Freud and Nietzsche, proclaimed, in the wake of Kant's destruction of natural theology, that religion is to be understood as a gigantic projection of the noblest attributes of man onto the cosmos. What religion is "really all about" is human reality, human fears and hopes. God for Feuerbach is nothing other than a compendious summary devised for the benefit of the limited individual - "the commonplace book where he registers his highest feelings and thoughts, the genealogical album into which he enters the names of the things most dear and sacred to him."[24] In a word, religion and theology must be reduced to anthropology.

Jung's use of the word "projection" is more ambiguous than that of Feuerbach. To begin, he defines projection as resulting from "the archaic identity of subject and object."[25] In this he is indebted to the French sociologist L. Lévy-Bruhl (d. 1939) who had coined the expression "mystic participation" to characterize the "supernatural" orientation of the so called primitive mentality. The primitive lives in a magical world, involving objects and beings in a network of mystical participations and exclusions. According to Jung, this magic, endowing nature with qualities of feeling and emotion, comes from a projection of collective unconscious. In the world of the primitive "everywhere his unconscious jumps out at him, alive and real."[26]

Reading these lines one is tempted to lump together Jung and the animists who imagined that the archaic man was surrounded by a pre-existent dead nature about which he then formed neurotic theories or onto which he unconsciously projected his neurotic fantasies. (If we accept this view, we are, in effect, paying the pre-historic man the dubious compliment of being at the same time post-scientific man). That Jung at times

71

seems to be playing into the hands of his opponents is due to his adoption of a spatial metaphor suggesting that the psyche (in this case the collective unconscious) is literally inside the organism or at any rate distinct from all that is adjacent and external to it.

There is enough evidence, however, in Jung's writings that what he calls "our comfortable theory of psychic projection" is not tenable in the light of a more sympathetic understanding of the early man's experience. In effect, the process of psychic projection must be reversed: "Instead of deriving the mythical figures from our psychic conditions, we must derive our psychic conditions from these figures."[27] As we shall shortly see, in the last resort it will be necessary to think in terms of a yet more original occurrence, an act or a state of affairs - a common presence - that "projects" both the "I" and the "not-I." And we shall refrain from asking "whence" or "onto what."

Consider for a moment the Polynesian idea of mana. According to Codrington, Lévy-Bruhl, Jung and others, mana is an image of psychic energy, a life force (Seelenstoff, Potenz) which every sentient creature feels as the driving power within it. To the mind of the primitive there is existent and permeating, on earth, in the air and in the water, in all the divers forms assumed by persons and objects, one and the same essential reality, both one and multiple, both material and spiritual. Mana is present everywhere at once like an impersonal force, and yet it is individual in certain persons.

Evidently the primitive is not engaged in any kind of anthropomorphizing; he is not making personalities out of inanimate objects. When he speaks to objects (iron, axe, tree), flattering or trying to deceive them, it is because, in Lévy-Bruhl's words, "he feels in them the presence of a force which is neither exactly personal nor impersonal and which he does not differentiate from them."[28]

72

Like the Jungian anima, mana is the soul of things enabling everything to exist. It is the source of life, the prime mover, a ghostlike (neither material nor spiritual) presence which has objective reality. As Jung puts it: "To the primitive man the psyche is not, as it is to us, the epitome of all that is subjective and subject to the will; on the contrary, it is something objective, self-subsistent, and living its own life."[29] Jung also observes that to some extent this is true of the civilized man as well. For example, we are unable to suppress many of our emotions; we cannot change a bad mood into a good one; we cannot command our dremas to come and go. We only flatter ourselves by believing that we are masters in our own house. Like the primitive, we are more often than not dependent on the processes of a quasi-conscious psyche which has purposes and intuitions of its own. "... life and psyche existed for me before I could say, 'I,' and when this 'I' disappears, as in sleep or unconsciousness, life and psyche still go on ..."[30]

According to Hillman, personifying, which we tend to associate with myth, has nothing to do with the projection of human feelings and emotions onto a detached and pre-existing nature. Rather, it is a spontaneous activity of the soul, a way of experiencing the world as a "psychological field."

> We do not ... personify at all ... where imagination reigns, personifying happens. We experience it nightly, spontaneously, in dream. Just as we do not create our dreams, but they happen to us, so we do not invent the persons of myth and religion; they, too, happen to us. The persons present themselves as existing prior to any effort of ours to personify. To mythic consciousness the persons of the imagination are real.[31]

In view of these considerations, we may now ask with Jung a question that many people, including the parapsychologists, find "tantalizing":

> does the psyche in general - that is, the spirit, or the unconscious - arise in us; or is the psyche, in the

73

early stages of consciousness, actually outside us in the form of arbitrary powers with intentions of their own, and does it gradually come to take its place within us in the course of psychic development? Were the dissociated psychic contents [complexes] ever parts of the psyches of individuals, or were they rather from the beginning psychic entities existing in themselves according to the primitive view as ghosts, ancestral spirits and the like?[32]

Jung the scientist is reluctant to commit himself to the belief in the "existence of real spirits." He is convinced that these phenomena are "exteriorized effects of unconscious complexes," but he wants to avoid the "question of whether spirits exist in themselves" until such time as sufficient proof of their existence is adduced.[33]

But then there is also Jung the Platonist, boldly speculating on a dream of his (after his illness in 1944) in which he saw in the front of an altar, a yogi in deep meditation. "When I looked at him more closely, I realized that he had my face. I started in profound fright, and awoke with the thought: 'Aha, so he is the one who is meditating me. He has a dream, and I am in it.' I knew that when he awakened, I would no longer be." To Jung the dream points to the Eastern and the Platonic idea that this world of maya is a projection, "a dream which seems a reality as long as we are in it."[34]

It would take us too far afield to engage in a discussion of the Eastern views. As I already indicated earlier, maya, far from being "illusion," is the Hindu and Buddhist equivalent of the psychic realm or the anima mundi. For example, in Hindu mythology maya is represented as Maya-Shakti, the creative energy of Brahman, the divine play (lila) of universe with all its innumerable gods, goddesses and demons. Brahman is not at all a "pure act" or "unmoved mover" transcending this world of transiency, but, in Heinrich Zimmer's words "that through which we live and act, the fundamental spontaneity of our nature;

Proteus-like, capable of assuming the form of any specific emotion, vision, impulse or thought."[35]

There is a beautiful passage in Jung where he describes anima ("the archetype of life") in words that could be just as well applied to Maya-Shakti:

> With her cunning play of illusions the soul lures into life the inertness of matter that does not want to live. She makes us believe incredible things, that life may be lived. She is full of snares and traps, in order that man should fall, should reach the earth, entangle himself there, and stay caught, so that life should be lived; as Eve in the Garden of Eden could not rest content until she had convinced Adam of the goodness of the forbidden apple.[36]

To say with the Hindus that we are "projected" by the creative energy of Brahman is the same as saying that we, as individual souls, are real imaginal manifestations of this energy. If you will, Brahman is the anima mundi, engaged in a continuous process of making or poiēsis. It is a "making" that occurs on the level of soul or imagination where the outer (the Maker or the Artificer) and the inner (the product or the artifact) coincide. On this plane it is impossible to say whether it is the artist who produces the artwork or the artwork - the artist. As Jung has remarked, "it is not Goethe who creates Faust, but Faust which creates Goethe." In the same context he compares a great work of art to a dream: they are never univocal but plurisignative. A dream "presents an image in much the same way as nature allows a plant to grow ..."[37]

Projections are like dreams: we do not make them nor do we know who makes them; they just happen. To use Gabriel Marcel's metaphor, projections, in the sense of "making" or poiēsis, are "absolute improvisation(s)"[38] in which spirit and matter, Brahman and maya, the creator and the created coincide. And the "where" of this coincidence or the "locus" of projection is neither the "I" nor the "not-I," but a common presence - the psyche. The psyche is the projector and the projected in one.

On the whole, we would agree with Socrates when he expresses uncertainty concerning the precise character and the provenance of demons and spirits. In Apology (31 D) he says of the demonic: "You do not know whence it comes and whither it goes." He also indicates that this force is not within and at the disposal of a person, but is received from a larger sphere and acknowledged with reverence and awe.

Returning to Cassirer's theory of mythical thought, we find the same essentially Platonic and Jungian version of the genesis of myth. Like Jung, Cassirer reverses the usual anthropomorphic nature of the mythical process. The primitive, instead of transfering his own finished personality (ego) to the god, first discovers himself as active spiritual principle through the figures of his gods; the human "I" finds itself only through a detour of the divine "I."[39]

Owen Barfield, independently of Jung and Cassirer, has reached a similar conclusion. He too is convinced that the picture of the primitive as "always projecting his insides onto something or other," i.e., as animating a dead world with arbitrarily concocted shapes of monstrous or benevolent beings, must be reversed to say that "it was not man who made the myths but myths or the archetypal substance they reveal, which made man."[40] For quite possibly, the primitive had no "insides" to begin with: instead of being a camera obscura (something like a box with one single, very small aperture), he was more like an Aeolian harp or wind harp on whose strings wind could be made to produce harmonious sounds. In a like manner it is the anima mundi (call it the Collective Unconscious or the Freudian Id) which breathes through the strings of individual brains and nerves and fluids, producing the ever-present and luxuriant imagery of myth.

According to Barfield, man - "in the beginning" - is not an

76

independent subject confronting an objective, alien world; rather the so called subjectivity, ego, personality and so on, emerges from a common ground or presence, embracing both man and nature. Our subjectivity is a "form of consciousness that has contracted from the periphery into individual centers." It is conceivable, says Barfield, that

> the task of Homo Sapiens, when he first appeared as a physical form on earth, was not to evolve a faculty of thought somehow out of nothing, but to transform the unfree wisdom, which he experienced through his organism as a given meaning (emphasis mine), into the free subjectivity.[41]

What Jung, Cassirer and Barfield have accomplished is to turn upside down the still widespread nineteenth century evolutionary notion of myth. We can see now that man started his career on earth not as an unconcerned onlooker facing a separate, unintelligible and dumb world about which he subsequently invented all manner of myth, but that he had to extricate his self-consciousness and his "freedom" out of a larger realm of reality - mana, soul or anima mundi. He found himself through the intercourse with the not-self - the mundus imaginalis of archetypal imaginal beings.

So one should not find it absurd to imagine that this "secular world" of ours is an imitative projection of another, "more subtly" embodied realm of reality. But we may just as well reverse this proposition and suggest that beings in that "other world" imitate us. In the primitive societies there is a widespread idea that the "other world" is a mirror image of this one - what is up here is down there, right is left, black is white. For example, the Ainus of Japan even say that the dead think of themselves as living and see the living as ghosts: "they think of us just as we think of them."[42] We must, therefore, resisit the temptation to decide once and for all who is "right" - "we" or "they." From the psyche's perspective it all depends on "who they think they are" as well as on "who we think we are." Furthermore, images are never contrary or contradictory but complementary. So it is "imaginable" that spirits, ghosts, etc. on the one hand and men on the other, are related not in terms of "real" versus "unreal" but in terms of complementarity. In the most fundamental sense we are all indispensable to one another.

The basic assumption behind the Copernican revolution, effected by Cassirer et al. is that the so called external world has a dimension of interiority which is not radically distinct from our own. Put in philosophical language, our ideas and thoughts cannot be sharply separated from being (reality). Just as the primitive does not invent myths, but experiences them, just as dreams and "inspirations" come to us, so our allegedly objective ideas and thoughts are archetypally determined; they too carry a hidden numinous power which is beyond our conscious control.

Martin Heidegger has attempted to express this by saying that man (Dasein) has a "pre-conceptual understanding of Being" through which he comprehends himself as fundamentally related to the world.[43] The primary datum of human life is not the Cartesian cogito ("I think") but the sum ("I am") or the act of existing with the world and having a world. We encounter the world on a level that precedes the split between subject and object, thought and being. In the final analysis, man is not the author of his thoughts but a kind of missionary who carries out the words of Being in his thought-responses. Psychologically, this means that our conscious and personal life is grounded in what Jung calls "collective unconscious" which in the present context we have identified with the world of myth and imagination. Our psyche, on its level of depth, is inhabited by a multitude of mythical persons and we can never be certain whether we imagine them or they imagine us. It is only that, in our eagerness for scientific respectability, we no longer call these numinous powers "gods", but phobias, obsessions, etc. The gods, as Jung said, have become diseases. But ideas too carry diseases. The psychic epidemics we call wars are let loose upon the world in the name of noble, "spiritual," "transcendent" ideas and ideologies.

It is not usually realized that the word "idea" comes from eidos, and among the Pre-Socratics as well as in Plato, combines the act of seeing and the visible object, subject and object. Ideas are not only what we see (as when we say "I see" meaning " I understand") but also modes of being. For as Plato said, idea is "the eye of the soul."[44] Hillman, commenting on the Platonic view, has observed that "the soul reveals itself in its ideas." We are always in the embrace of an idea and "we see what our ideas, governed by archetypes, allow us to see."[45] In a deep sense, we see with the eyes of the soul and they are the same eyes with which the world sees us. Alchemists compared this kind of seeing to shining fish eyes or to the eyes of the Lord that range over the whole earth (Zachariah 3: 9). Jacob Boehme says that "the soul is an Eye of the Eternal Abyss, a similitude of the Eternity," or , that "the Soul is like a ball of fire or a fiery Eye."[46]

Closer to our time, Goethe, unlike his friend Schiller who was steeped in Kantianism, could see ideas with his own eyes. But what he saw was not so much a Kantian Idea, divorced from the Ding an sich (the noumenon), but a Platonic Idea in its original meaning - the plant archetype (Urpflanze). He saw with the eyes of the soul an Urphänomen, i.e., an archetypal image in the Botanical Garden of Padua.[47] In Goethe's view, all phenomena of nature variously reveal and express the perduring archetypes. It is up to us to stretch the mind and to see the universal in the concrete and the particular, the spiritual in the material and the material in the spiritual. But again, the only organ, equipped with this kind of vision, is the psyche - the mediatrix between all pairs of opposites.

Psyche, said Jung, is image. Reduced to our frame of reference, this means that we perceive reality with or via imagination. Our perception of the world is not a process we passively undergo, but an active intervention and shaping. Simultaneously, however, we are perceived and shaped by the world. "I" and "the world" is an interaction, a reciprocal relation. And the soul, which is never identical either with the "I" or the world, "happens" (as dreams happen) in this relationship; indeed it is this relation itself, the rainbow spanning the two extremities of ego-consciousness (light) and the unconscious (darkness). What is in the middle, is neither light nor darkness but the penumbral region of the soul, the place of subtle embodiment. To travel in this region is to renounce all Cartesian certainities, including the certainity of immortality. For here we are in the sphere of making, not in that of being or becoming. To make something in the sense of poiēsis one must trust imagination even if it occasionally leads us astray. As we shall learn from Plato, error and errancy is no less an integral part of soul-making than truth, veracity and moral rectitude.

Jung and Plato

As I have repeatedly stressed, the age-old conflict between nature and spirit, matter and mind, subjective and objective reality is primarily due to the oblivion of the soul. The whole endeavor of Jungian psychology consists in an attempt to resuscitate this forgotten organon by replacing the crude and banal duality of body and mind with a tripartite division of man or a threefold understanding of human nature: body, soul and spirit. In so doing Jung alines himself with Plato, the Neoplatonic thinkers of the Renaissance (Ficino, Bruno, Vico), the poets and philosophers of the Romantic Movement of the eighteenth and nineteenth century (Schelling, Fichte, von Schlegel, Goethe,

Coleridge, Blake) and the alchemist thought of the Middle Ages. From this large company of kindred souls I shall single out Plato as the true ancestor of Jung at his best and most original.

Notoriously Jung's psychology is such a medley of themes and intellectual disciplines - philosophy intermingled with mysticism, rigorous thinking with the loftiest flights of fantasy, clinical observations with forays into occultism and magic - that it is all but impossible to extract from it a consistent view of man or the world. Not surprisingly, we find the same kind of ambiance and lack of systematic arrangement also in Plato and among the Neo-Platonists - perhaps an indication that it is the very subject matter, the psyche, which forbids neat and comprehensive presentation. Apart from the tendency to pose as a jack-of-all-trades, what makes Jung's thought essentially Platonic - in spite of the fact that he tried to imitate Aristotle and the scientific method by collecting empirical evidence from his patients and exotic cultures - is the triadic view of man.

The Jungian concept of the psyche as the third thing is not the result of logic; it is a creative solution which owes its appearance to the flowing of opposites into one another. The emergence of a "third" is a "miracle", i.e., a potentiality of which logic and reasoning is thoroughly unaware.

In Timaeus (31 B and C) Plato declares: "That two things of themselves form a good union is impossible." "For, he continues, there must be a bond (desmos) between them, holding them together. The best bond is one that makes itself and the elements it connects into a complete unity." Plato's problem was one of unusual difficulty. Having constructed the cosmos on the pattern of eternally unchanging Ideas (forms) - the highest and most completely perfect of the intelligible things - he realized that there is a gap between the transcendent world of Ideas, a world without body or color or motion, and the variegated garments of the physcial world.

Plato's creative solution to this problem is Eros, a great daimon (daimon megas) who is midway between mortals and immortals, "for everything daimonic is midway between divine and mortal" (Symposium 202c). As Diotima explains to Socrates, the daimon mediates between gods and men, closing the gap between them and filling mortal men with a desire for that which is immortal. Eros in Plato is a metaxy - a principle of relationship or betweeness holding together heaven and earth and making them participate in each other.

The Platonic Eros has nothing to do with vapid "Platonic love;" rather he is a god to be dreaded for the havoc he makes of human life. In Plato's words, "he is anything but tender and beautiful, as many imagine him," but "rough, unkempt, unshod, and without a house, and he lies on the bare earth, sleeps at the doorsteps, and in the streets under the open sky" (Symposium 203 CD). He is also portrayed as a mighty huntsman, bold, impulsive, intense, always pursuing the beautiful and the good. According to Paul Friedländer, one of the great exegetes of Plato, Eros is "active not only in men's souls, but in the bodies of all living beings and in vegetation... in all forms of existence, as the power reconciling hostile opposites such as cold and warm, bitter and sweet, dry and wet, ruling in harmony and reaching into the cosmic order."[48] Eros is not merely a human attitude but a metaphysical factor in all nature. He is the miracle in the center of being, a hierophanic, archetypal agency preserving the universe from dissolution into chaos.

As I mentioned a while ago, Plato's insistence on the mighty character of Eros was necessary in order to forge a unity between the world of eternal ideas and the world of sheer becoming and passing away. The more sharply Plato has separated the intelligible and the corporeal worlds, the changeless and the changing, the stronger a bond had to be created between the two. The superhuman strength of the bond is a guarantee that it will be more "real" than the terms which it unites. For the metaxy of the soul, unlike the realms of pure ideas and pure change, is a new creation, a creative act that supercedes the old creation. By the expression "the old creation" I am referring to the Parmenidian monistic universe where eternity and time, being and becoming do not mix (according to the maxim "what is, is, and what is not, is not"). As James Olney in his recent book on Jung and Yeats perceptibly observes, this universe is "shorn of fiction and poetry, it is divested of its bright garments of mythology and of all the stories that begin 'Once upon a time'." Plato's great achievement is that in Timaeus he "restores 'likeness' as a valid tool for the epistemologist and ontologist; it reestablishes time and process as realities of a kind rather than mere illusions; it returns correspondence, simile, and analogy to the universe; and it opens the way to myth and to the 'likely story', to Yeats' symbols and to Jung's archetypes."[49]

We must hasten to add, however, that Jung and Hillman have introduced an important correction to the usual interpretation of Plato's view of time and the changing cosmos as a likeness (icon) of Being (Ideas). The correction, simply stated, consists in dropping the "of." Instead of asserting with Plato that the world is an image of Being (Ideas), we may now propose that image is Being or Reality. This new a priori (we may call it an imaginal a priori or "imaginal reduction") will lead us to suggest that what is called eternity must be somehow located in time provided that time is envisioned as a dimension of the soul, i.e., as the time of the soul which "is" between "pure" eternity on the one hand and "pure" process, on the other. For the present, we must pay attention to Plato's account of creation.

In the myth of the Timaeus, the Demiourgos, having created the universe and the lesser gods, turns over to the latter the task of creating mankind. Demiourgos explains to the gods that they are, by his will, immortal but that the universe, in order to be complete (not perfect) must contain not only immortal creatures but mortal as well. And yet those mortal creatures are to have a soul - an immortal principle. So the daimones who, as we remember, are mid-world spirits, set about their task of "weaving mortal to immortal" (41d). Note well that the completeness of the universe requires a kind of intermingling of the mortal and the immortal. To us, Westerners, imbued as we are with "monotonotheistic" mentality, this is a strange notion. We are Parmenidians at heart, dedicated to the principle "what is, is; what is not, is not." It's either mortality and decay or everlasting life. The proposition that we could be, let's say, more or less "immortal" or "mortal" is a sign of confused thinking which we condescendingly leave to the poets and psychopaths. To a Plato, however, completeness seems to lie not in perfection (be it the perfection of a god or that of a thing) but rather in perfectibility, in a kind of motion and striving that is its own goal.

According to Timaeus, heaven has given to each of us a daimon who represents the highest part of us and raises us toward our kinship in heaven. For we are indeed "a plant whose roots are not in earth, but in the heavens" (90a). And it is the daimon who, if properly cultivated, makes us immortal and divine and will establish for us a blessed relationship with eternity. The man who neglects his daimon will become as mortal as it is possible for him to be. But he who loves wisdom and pursues it all his life will become as immortal as is possible for human nature. - "Because he is forever caring for (therapeuonta) the divine element (to theon) in himself and maintaining in best order the daimon that dwells along with him, he will be supremely blessed (eudaimona)" (90 C). The verb therapeuein means both "to care for, to heal" and "to do service to the gods, to worship." Thus it is only through daimon-therapy, i.e., through concern and reverence for the divine, the daimonic or - in

84

Jungian terms - the psychic element within us, that we realize and strengthen our immortality. According to Plato, the only way to accomplish this is by imitating the ordered (cosmic) course of the universe of the lesser gods, those heavenly bodies whose circling provides the model for our circulation.

In a similar way, Jung, when he begun drawing mandalas, realized that "there is no linear development; there is only circumambulation of the Self. Uniform development exists, at most, only at the beginning; late, everything points to the center."[50] But, even though Jung, because of his monistic temperament, was unable to appreciate the idea of a "centerless center," he does insist that the Self is not a goal to be reached but only circumambulated. In one of his letters he suggests that the existence outside time, as we know it, is characterized by "relative eternity."[51] I take it to mean that human "immortality" depends on how well we circulate, that is, how intensely we care for the imaginal ground of our personal souls. It seems that, besides Jung and Hillman, it was Yeats who has given one of the best formulations to this insight:

> Our imaginations are but fragments of the universal imagination, portions of the universal body of God, and as we enlarge our imagination by imaginative sympathy, and transform with the beauty and peace of art, the sorrows and joys of the world, we put off limited man more and more and put on the unlimited 'immortal man'.[52]

The notion of circular movement would also imply that, in Jung's words, "existence outside time ... runs parallel with existence inside time. Yes, we ourselves may simultaneously exist in both worlds (emphasis mine), and occasionally we do have intimations of a twofold existence." What Jung seems to be saying here is that we are both mortal and immortal or, as Plato would have it, capable of immortality as well as mortality; to that extent we already, i.e., here and now participate in both worlds. We are,

85

in a real sense, in them because they are in us as ever present real images.

Now because "immortality" is a highly ambiguous notion, it is fitting that Plato introduces the story (myth) of Eros and the creation of the soul by Demiourgos only when he sees that Socrates' dialectical arguments in favor of immortality of the soul have by no means convinced his interlocutors. This is as much as saying that psyche needs mythos (literally "a likely tale" - eikotas mythous, Tim. 59 c-d), i.e., creative and imaginative speech, not logic, to express its paradoxical and contradictory nature. In Laws (903 B) Plato says: "We need myths for enchantment of the soul." Jung, when he was about to articulate his thought about life after death, preferred to "tell stories - mythologize."[53] The advantage of the mythological mode is that it can express the ideal and the universal in a sensible concrete image and thus, unlike the logical mode, is not compelled to separate thought from being, essence from existence and reality from appearance. Like Eros which Diotima explains to Socrates, myth is a great daimon mediating between man and the idea of man, between the mortal and the immortal.

In Jung's opinion, it was a deadly mistake when Christianity transformed the Greek daimones and the daimonion into "demons" -purely malicious beings - and set about exorcising them. For by getting rid of the daimonic, Christianity also exorcised the soul, converting it into an immaterial substance that, after the demise of the body, goes to its everlasting reward either in the vapid realms of heavenly jubilation or is relegated to the gruesome chambers of hell. Plato and Jung remind us that the soul can be lost not only in hell but also in the exceedingly healthy and rarefied atmospherics of heaven.

To repeat, what Plato and Jung are saying is that the soul necessarily partakes of both the realms of being and becoming, immortality and mortality and is confined to neither. The Platonic myth expresses soul's double citizenship in terms of a circular path, conveying the idea that there is a kinship between the human soul and the cosmos, between the movement of the souls and that of heavenly bodies. Man is a small cosmos (microcosm) included in the large cosmos (macrocosm) and both of these are living, self-moving souls. In this way the fate of the soul is built into the universe. Plato first envisions the great cosmic order and only then determines human existence within this order. Like the Pre-Socratics (Alkmaion, Empedocles, Heraclitus), he intends to deduce immortality of the human soul, its aliveness from the eternal movement of the cosmos. The self-moving character of the soul is analogous to the sideral movement, which means that the individual psyche and the world-soul are in a necessary mutual relation: the "perfect" human soul reflects the order and the movement of the universal soul.

But we must insist with Jung and archetypal psychology that perfection is an unattainable ideal, a fantasy which is certainly healthy (and thus "holy") as long as it is not hypostatized into a literal state or place. The fantasy of spiritual perfection or spiritual ascent is an essential part of the soul's peregrination among the worlds: when the soul imagines that it is "in heaven," that is precisely where it is so long as the imagination lasts. Our point is only that even "in heaven" the soul does not cease to be soul. From this it must be concluded that even "in heaven" there is no perfection, which is the same as saying that there is no heaven without soul and no soul without heaven.

The only perfection we can imagine is that of a circular movement which must needs include not only peaks but also vales. So Plato adds that the soul, while revolving upon itself, is composed of rings of the Same and Different (Tim. 36 c - 38 c). These rings or circles are represented in the sideral sky by the fixed stars and by the planets; in the human soul - by truth and knowledge on the one hand, and opinion and belief, on the other. Opinion, however, is never exclusive of error, distortion, paranoia and perversion. The soul is the Knight Errant whose home is the ceaselessly blowing spirit and it follows, in Hillman's words, the errant path of fantasy and "listens to the deviant discourse of the imagination."[54] It is a central tenet of archetypal psychology that "the psyche does not exist without pathologizing" and that our infirmities and afflictions too connect us with gods. The gods of the myth are not only perfect but quarreling, cheating, sexually obsessed, revenging, vulnerable, torn apart. Their immortality (athenos) means that the "infirmitas they present is also eternal."[55]

This is a mysterious, awesome thought - a thought that attests its own impotence. Where do we go from here? There is no answer. For it is only in abstracto that we can dissociate the movement from the goal. In reality or, if you wish, in life as it is concretely lived, the movement, the mover and the goal are indistinguishable. We must imagine the movement itself as being the goal. "How can we know the dancer from the dance?" asked Yeats ("Among Schoolchildren"). Well, we don't for, if we knew, we could no longer dance.

In archetypal psychology, the soul is by definition polymorphous, a protean figure with many centers, malleable, openended. We circle around a center that is never reached because it is ubiquitous. In Waldo Emerson's words, "The eye is the first circle; the horizon which it forms is the second; and throughout nature this primary figure is reflected without end. It is the highest emblem in the cipher of the world."

The ancient symbol for soul's circulation is uroboros, the coiled serpent representing time and the eternal return of the same. Heidegger, in a discussion of Nietzsche's metaphor that man must bite off the head of the serpent which has crawled into his mouth, suggests that the image of uroboros points to the necessity of facing and positively affirming the transience of time.[56] What Heidegger presumably means is that the uroboric course is not so much an eternal circling in the literal sense of the word as following the Greek god Hermes. Hermes is the psychopomp, the guide of souls, the conductor of the dead to the underworld. So the underworld - Hades - is not excluded from the soul's journey; that too is part of its "eternity" and of its "heaven." Hermes, according to Karl Kerenyi, is the primordial mediator and messenger who always stands in "a middle between being and non-being," who is "at home while wandering, at home on the road itself." Hermes is hodios ("belonging to the road"), constantly in motion. But even more significantly, the roads which he travels are genuine roads of the earth, running "snakelike, shaped like irrationally waved lines ... winding, yet leading everywhere."[57]

That is precisely the great mystery of "immortality": the "genuine roads of the earth ... leading everywhere." It is also the mystery of the Hermetic circle whose center is everywhere and circumference nowhere. For the snakelike roads of the earth are the same roads which the soul is destined to travel. They lead "everywhere" because there are no limits to the soul's circulation, no sudden metamorphosis of darkness into light, of error into a healing truth (as, for example, in Hegel). There is no finality of any kind except the finality of infinitude which must not be confused with eternity or ever-lastingness. According to Heraclitus, the road (hodon) which the soul travels, is an up-and-down way where up and down, like the beginning (archē) and end (pera) are the same (DK, fr. 60 & 107). The Heraclitean "end" is not a simple return to the same, a vicious, sterile and dull round ("one damned thing after another") in which the contraries are fragmented into opposites. David Miller, the author of The New Polytheism, has adequately described it as "a depth, a peri-meter broken through like a horizon exploded. The deep 'end' is ultimately soul which is without end."[58]

The Hermetic circle conveys the sense of endless possibilities which can never become fully actualized or exhausted. Provisionally I should like to suggest that the symbol of "endless possibility" is the very opposite of immortality in the conventional sense of consummation of all things in a hypothetical after-life or a nunc stans. "Endless possibility" means neither immortality (timelessness) nor mortality (time) but perseverance in the middle between the two; a cosmic balancing act, an acting out, not of a prepared script, but creating the script by acting it out.

IV: THE UROBORIC PATH

NOTES

[1]C.G. Jung, Memories, Dreams, Reflections, p. 35.

[2]CW 6, par. 77.

[3]CW 8, par. 624.

[4]C. G. Jung Letters, I: 1906-1950, ed. Gerhard Adler in collaboration with Aniela Jaffé. Tr. from the German by R.F.C. Hull. Bollingen Series XCV:1 (Princeton University Press, 1973), letter dated 10 January 1929.

[5]Nicholas Cusanus, Vision of God, tr. by Emma Gurney Salter (London: J.M. Dent and Sons, 1928), pp. 43-44.

[6]CW 8, par. 189.

[7]W.B. Yeats, Essays & Introductions (London and New York: Macmillan, 1961), p. 287.

[8]M.W. Bundy, "The Theory of Imagination in Classical and Medieval Thought," University of Illinois Studies in Language and Literature XII (Urbana, 1927), p. 267; cf. pp. 274-75.

[9]CW 9i, par. 634; cf. II, pars. 80-82; 13, par. 56.

[10]Owen Barfield, Worlds Apart (Middletwon, Conn.: Wesleyan University Press, 1963), p. 197.

[11]Henry Corbin, The Man of Light in Iranian Sufism. Tr. from the French by Nancy Pearson (Boulder and London: Shambala, 1978), p. 139.

[12]See Proclus, The Elements of Theology. A Revised Text with Translation, Introduction and Commentary by E.R. Dodds (Oxford: Clarendon Press, 1963), p. 1963, Proposition 29. According to the Neoplatonic principle of epistrophe or reversion, all phenomena can be led back to the inner states corresponding to them. Epistrophe is a recall of all things and events, given in the empirical space-time, to their imaginal background, i.e., to their subtle essences.

[13]J.W. Goethe, Farbenlehre. Kröners Taschenausgabe, Vol. 63 (Stuttgart, 1949). Einleitung, p. 176. Quoted in Corbin, The Man of Light in Iranian Sufism, p. 139.

[14]Corbin, The Man of Light in Iranian Sufism, p. 141.

[15]Quoted in J.De Marquette, Introduction to Comparative Mysticism (New York: Philosophical Library, 1949), p. 15.

[16]Quoted in Francis Huxley, The Way of The Sacred (Garden City, N.Y.: Doubleday and Co., Inc., 1974), pp. 73-74.

[17]Philip Wheelwright, Heraclitus (New York: Atheneum, 1964), fr. 108.

[18]Ibid., fr. 37.

[19]See E.E. Evans-Pritchard, Theories of Primitive Religion (Oxford University Press, 1965), pp. 27-28; B. Malinowski, Magic, Science and Religion (New York: Doubleday and Co., 1948), pp. 18-19.

[20]CW 9i, par. 261; cf. pars. 262-263; 267; 8, par. 33 ff; 13, par. 299.

[21]James Hillman, The Dream and the Underworld (New York: Harper & Row, 1979), p. 21.

[22]See Ernst Cassirer, The Philosophy of Symbolic Forms, Vol. 2 (New Haven: Yale University Press, 1944), p. 200, 235; An Essay on Man (New Haven: Yale University Press, 1962), pp. 82-83, 86, 94.

[23]Henry Frankfort et al., Before Philosophy; the Intellectual Adventure of Ancient Man (Baltimore: Penguin Books, 1967), p. 14; cf. pp. 35-36.

[24]Ludwig Feuerbach, The Essence of Christianity (New York: Harper & Row, 1957), p. 132.

[25]CW 6, par. 783; cf. pars. 741-743.

[26]CW 10, par. 44; cf. par. 43.

[27]CW 13, par. 299; cf. 9ii, par. 4.

[28]Lucien Lévy-Bruhl, The 'Soul' of the Primitive (London: George Allen & Unwin, 1965), p. 26.

[29]CW 8, par. 666.

[30]CW 8, par. 671; cf. par. 673 on the consciousness of being "practically immortal."

[31]Hillman, Re-Visioning Psychology, p. 17; cf. pp. 12-15.

[32]C.G. Jung, Modern Man in Search of a Soul (New York: Harcourt, Brace and Co., 1933), pp. 147-48; cf. CW 8, par. 599, 600; E.H. Gombrich, Art and Illusion, A Study in Psychology of Pictorial Representation. Bollingen Series XXXV. 5 (Princeton University Press, 1969), pp. 107-109.

[33]CW 8, pars. 599-600.

[34]Jung, Memories, Dreams, Reflections, pp. 323, 324.

[35]Heinrich Zimmer, Philosophies of India (New York: Meridian Books, 1957), p. 79.

[36]CW 9i, par. 56; cf. 13, par. 126; James Hilmann, "Anima," Spring 1973, pp. 119-20.

[37]Jung, Modern Man in Search of a Soul, pp. 170-71.

[38]Gabriel Marcel, Être et Avoir (Editions Montaigne, n.d.), p. 21.

[39]See Cassirer, The Philosophy of Symbolic Forms, 2: 211-218.

[40]Owen Barfield, The Rediscovery of Meaning and Other Essays (Middletown: Wesleyan University Press, 1977), p. 75.

[41]Owen Barfield, Speaker's Meaning (Middletown: Wesleyan University Press, 1967), pp. 113-14; cf. Rediscovery of Meaning, p. 17; 148-49; Saving the Appearances, A Study in Idolatry (New York: Harcourt, Brace & World, 1965), Chapters I-X.

[42]Francis Huxley, The Way of the Sacred, p. 44.

[43]Martin Heidegger, Being and Time. Tr. by John Macquarrie and Edward Robinson (New York: Harper & Row, 1962), p. 25.

[44]See Paul Friedländer, Plato I. Bollingen Series LIX. (Princeton University Press, 1969), pp. 14-18.

[45]Hillman, Re-Visioning Psychology, p. 221.

[46]See CW 9i, par. 704.

[47] Friedländer, _Plato_ I, p. 21.

[48] _Ibid._, p. 55.

[49] James Olney, _The Rhizome and the Flower; The Perennial Philosophy_ - _Yeats and Jung_ (Berkeley: University of California Press, 1980), 136.

[50] Jung, _Memories_, _Dreams_, _Reflections_, p. 196.

[51] _C. G. Jung Letters_ 2, p. 561.

[52] W.B. Yeats, _Essays & Introductions_, pp. 138-39.

[53] Jung, _Memories_, _Dreams_, _Reflections_, p. 299. The Neo-Platonic scholar W.R. Inge has observed that it is only in myth that thought and form come into being together in contrast to allegory where thought is grasped first and then arranged in a particular dress. In myth "the thought is the vital principle which shapes the form; the form is the sensible image which displays the thought" (_Mysticism in Religion_), Chicago University Press, 1948, p. 100).

[54] Hillman, _Re-Visioning Psychology_, p. 161.

[55] Hillman, "On the Necessity of Abnormal Psychology," p. 96; cf. _Re-Visioning Psychology_, pp. 88-104.

[56] See Martin Heidegger, _Nietzsche_ I, pp. 289-97.

[57] Karl Kerenyi, _Hermes, Guide of Souls_ (Zurich: Spring Publications, 1976), p. 77; cf. pp. 14-15.

[58] See David L. Miller, "Images of Happy Ending," _Eranos_ 44-1975 (Leiden, Brill), p. 87.

V: BACK TO IMAGES

Just-So-Isness of Images

Having surveyed the Jungian notion of the psyche, we seem to be as perplexed as ever about the exact nature of images: what are these elusive and illusory shapes and figures, these "airy nothings" that the soul is said to be continuously, compulsively producing? If we attend to this question more closely, we find that we are asking about the meaning of images. The assumption behind the question - an assumption which has become an almost ineradicable habit - is that images always mean something besides what they are or how they appear. It is as if images had fronts and backs and our sacred task were to find out how it looks behind the façade.

We may begin to dismantle this dualistic assumption by stating that it is impossible to ask what images are for the simple reason that there are no images in general. A general or universal image is a contradiction in terms or, at best a symbol or, when divested of all concreteness, a concept. Images are by definition particular, unrepeatable, unique. What follows from this is that images cannot be known if by "knowing" we mean separating the whatness (essence) of an image from its concrete manifestation, its "just-so-isness" or thusness (existence).

As I have stressed on several occasions, images are accessible only to imagination (on the principle that only the like knows the like). For example, if we wish to know what a bird is or what it signifies - whether this warm-blooded vertebrate is seen in dreams or in waking states - it would be useless to begin our inquiry by consulting a dictionary of symbols. By finding out that birds stand for "spirits of the dead," for "ascent to heaven" or for "Holy Ghost," we only would have found that the "real bird" has escaped our grasp. For all birds are rather like the blue bird of Maeterlinck - they lose their colors when put into a cage. It would seem then that the only way of getting to know the bird must come from the bird itself. All that I, as a subject, have to "do" is to undo myself, i.e., to adopt an attitude of letting be, a posture of total attention to this particular bird-event, to this image as it moves and changes according to its own desires. I must let the bird invent itself in the mirror of my imagination. Then it may also happen that, in Blake's words, "ev'ry Bird that cuts the airy way,/ Is an intense world of delight" (K 160).

The upshot of such an attitude is the realization that the only real birds are imaginal birds. Put differently, the essence of birds and, by the same token of any other "thing" ("dead" or "alive"), shows itself when the thing is approached, not as an object of scientific curiosity or in terms of its practical usefulness, but as an image that exists in its own right and for its own delight. In contrast to symbols which always point beyond themselves, images mean what they are and are what they mean. In the words of Mary Watkins, "the imaginal resists being known except in its own terms. Image requires image. Image evokes image."[1]

Thus there is a necessary reciprocity, a correlation between what I see and the way I see; as stated earlier, an image is not what I see but the way in which I see. In this view the ability to perceive the imaginal realities must be attributed to a special kind of awareness (intuition?) - an awareness that is no longer a tool of the ego, but of what Jung calls the Self, to which we prefer to give back the religious and poetical name of "the soul." Charles Tart, a transpersonal psychologist, uses the term "basic awareness" to denote something that seems to be qualitatively different from the physical structure of the brain and spatial constraints limiting the body. "Basic awareness" transcends space and time and "may have the capacity to function in some wider universe that we do not comprehend or may at least have the potential for such capacity."[2]

The "wider universe," postulated by Tart, in our opinion, is none other than the space of the soul and the peculiar spatiality of images. Images are neither inside nor outside of man, but have their own spatial and temporal features that are essentially different from the "profane" or the ordinary perceptual space and time. The soul *is* at any time wherever it *imagines* to be. This is as much as saying that the soul is not a substance, but a perspective or, in Hillman's words, "the imaginal possibility in our natures."[3] The locus of the soul is identical with the way in which the soul sees. And, as we must have realized by now, the soul's way of seeing consists in a movement from the literal surface of things to their metaphorical, subtle essences. It is a vertical motion from what is merely visible (with the "naked eye") or from the province of the "despotism of the eye" to the less visible and hidden.

In archetypal psychology, the vertical direction refers not to literal or spatial depth but to a process of interiorizing. Depth is not physically located beneath the surface of things. Quite on the contrary, from the standpoint of ordinary perception, imaginal space lacks depth in the sense of gradual recession of planes. Imaginal objects (images) present themselves *frontally*; we cannot get back of, or around them: we have to take them as they present themselves.[4] Consequently, the kind of depth we have in mind can be perceived anywhere and at any level of being so long as our perception is guided by imagination. Paradoxically, depth is on the surface of things, in their aspectivity or physiognomy which is the very opposite of a superficial or literalistic view. We are confronted here with a peculiar *transparency* which is also a luminous darkness (the "luminosities" of Jung) where the enveloping "stuff" is not separate from the enveloped substrate, where the inside is fully present in the outside and the real in the apparent.

The world of images is indeed "another world" but only in the sense that its "otherness" reveals not a numinous "wholly Other" (R. Otto), but the depth and the interiority of its own structures. Images are visible, but only to what is invisible in us, i.e., to imagination. In the last analysis, images are the psyche itself in its "imaginative visibility" (Hillman).

The expression "imaginative visibility" points to the sensate character of images. Images are sensate but not perceptual, i.e., they may or may not be visually seen. Visibility "does not have to have hallucinatory properties which confuses the act of perceiving images with imagining them. Nor do images have to be heard as in a poetic passage."[5] All such notions of "visibility" tend to literalize images as distinct events presented to the senses. The sensate character of images must not be, therefore, confused with their sensual or secondary qualities which are physically, spatio-temporally real. These qualities represent, so to speak, the public character of images. What we ordinarily perceive is the surface of the canvas and paint in the case of a painter, the printed or the spoken word in the case of the poet. However, artists and poets typically direct our attention to something beyond the range of the physically perceptible, to what Shakespeare called "the forms of things unknown" and it is the poet's task to give to this "airy nothing/ A local habitation and a name" (A Midsummer-night's Dream, V., i, 12-17).

What this means is that the sensual qualities of an image are not derived from external, perceivable objects. As Patricia Berry points out, "with imagination any question of objective referent is irrelevant. The imaginal is quite real in its own way, but never because it corresponds to something outer."[6] We are dealing here with a radically different gnoseological category, the category of the imaginal or imagination, which has no place in the traditional Weltanschauungen of spiritualism and materialism. One can never overemphasize that images are neither spiritual nor material, but belong to the Platonic realm of metaxy where, as Henry Corbin will later propound, the spiritual assumes body and the body is spiritualized.

Images are easily confused with after-images of sense perception because, like the latter, they have a body of sorts. But just as images, instead of being derived from perceptual, material objects, are products of pure psyche, so this "body of sorts" is not a perceptual, material body, but a psychic or subtle body. In Berry's words, it is a body "in which the secondary combinations and all the sense qualities of the image that would for perception be outlandish, incomplete, overwhelming or distorted in some respect or another, here make sense."[7]

Distorted Image

Distorted, incomplete, outlandish images make sense. How is this possible? Historians of art (E.H. Gombrich, Rudolf Arnheim) have pointed out that diagrammatic completeness or life-likeness of images is the outstanding characteristic of primitive art. Australian aborigines who were shown pictures of birds with one foot missing, are reported to have expressed dismay at the absence of a fully represented bird. The sculptor in ancient Egypt was known as "one who keeps alive." The most famous of the myths that crystallize belief in the power of art not only to portray or imitate, but to make, is that of Pygmalion. In Ovid, Pygmalion is a sculptor who wants to fashion a woman after his own heart and falls in love with the statue he makes. He prays to Venus for a bride modeled after that image, and the goddess turns the cold marble into a living body.

According to Gombrich, we owe it to the Greeks to have broken the spell which resides in a complete, potent image, rivaling creation, for the sake of illusion, surrounding the incomplete figure.[8] From now on the incompleteness of artistic images is perceived not simply as a matter of fragmentation or insufficient apprehension, but as a positive quality appealing to imagination. The creation of an imaginal realm of art led to the replacement of making by the matching of reality through the new skill of mimesis. We would be mistaken, however, says Gombrich, if we regarded this skill as an attempt to imitate nature. For "nature cannot be imitated or 'transcribed' without first being taken apart and put together again."[9]

Precisely. Art as a special activity is born only when nature is no longer experienced "artistically," i.e., when it has been "taken apart" and made into an object of observation and experimentation instead of being a realm in which we participate. I am referring to what Cassirer called the stage of mythical thought when the boundary between things (objects of nature) and their appearances was fluid and images were not detached from their originals. According to Cassirer, art represents a later stage (beyond the original image) in which "the image world acquires purely immanent validity and truth. It does not aim at something else or refer to something else; it simply 'is' and consists in itself ... Thus for the first time the world of the image becomes a self-contained cosmos with its own center of gravity."[10]

The point I want to make is that at the mythical "stage" there is no need for an "image world" with a "purely immanent validity and truth," because at this stage art and life are not two separate realms to begin with. Art is as "natural" as life itself and imagination is present not only in man (as a separate faculty) but in the nature as well. Nature as a whole is permeated with "immanent" life akin to that of the primitive artist and it is enough for the latter to "imitate" nature since the life or the spirit or the soul in the "thing" lives on in his "imitation" so long as it is a life-like imitation.

Cassirer also acknowledges that the original potency of myth consisting in a cocrescence of the image and the thing continues to live in the present. For the human spirit "has no absolute past; it gathers up into itself what has passed and preserves it as present."[11] Thus it is conceivable that even a modern artist, unless he is devoted to the production of merely fanciful imagery, must be able to experience imagination as the common source of both art and nature. For the same reason he should not be surprised that the Australian aboriginee is displeased at the sight of a crippled bird. For the aboriginee, as it should be for the modern artist as well, the real bird is the imaginal bird and a crippled bird is a distortion not only of the natural but also of the artistically imitated birds. The point is that on this level - the level where imagination enlivens all things - it is immaterial whether anything is "distorted" or "whole": a bird may be perceived as the "real thing" or as an airplaine, as a flying crocodile or even as man with birdlike features. They all "make sense" because they are all equally imaginal. Art as a special and separate function enters the stage only when we begin to feel that we must distort reality in order to make it more real, i.e., when nature is no longer experienced as imaginative in her own right.

The British painter Lucien Freud has tried to express this state of affairs as follows.

> A moment of complete happiness never occurs in the creation of a work of art. The promise of it is felt in the act of creation, but disappears towards the completion of the work. For it is then that the painter realizes that it is only a picture he is painting. Until then he had almost dared to hope that the picture might spring to life.[12]

I submit that our painter, like Pygmalion, takes the word "life" too literally. Besides life that can be seen with the "naked eye," there is also an invisible life which may be seen in things that appear lifeless to the ordinary sight. In this sense a great painting is natural precisely because it is "unnatural." Lucien

Freud must know it. His complaint merely expresses nostalgia for a literal Paradise that never was. The real Paradise is the Paradise of art and imagination where things do "sping to life" even if the perception of this life requires the presence of a corresponding kind of life in the perceiver; what is more, it is a sort of life which is never experienced as merely human. That this is so is amply documented in the religious and primitive art.

There is a growing recognition among the serious students of anthropology, ethnology and depth psychology that, contrary to the anthropomorphic interpretation, the primitives seldom or never worshipped realistic likenesses of gods in human form.[13] The primitive art seems to be indifferent to things as they are seen or perceived and prefers to pay attention to things only as they live in imagination. In fact, the most holy images of gods are those which are the least appealing, the least human and the least beautiful. For example, the religious Greeks ranked the xoanon, an ancient image of the god made of wood, rough and scarcely human, above the works of a Phidias or a Praxiletes. At the Panathena it was the xoanon who was carried about in procession, not the glorious works of Phidias. It is the "black Madonnas" which for the Roman Catholics work miracles.

Clearly, what is imitated in all such cases is not the dead nature of scientific positivism, but nature as a storehouse of pictures which are actual revelations of the psychic essence of man. Thus the primitive art is life-like precisely insofar as life at this "stage" is free to assume any form it chooses. All that the "artist" is expected to do is to "imitate" the imagination which is at work in nature. His art is not a special activity designed to embellish life, but participation in the imaginal life of the cosmos as a whole - a life which is never "human" in a diluted humanistic sense. For the primitive mentality all "human-ization" of images means nothing less than desecration. As Nietzsche with his penetrating insight said, it is just the "monstruous, the sinister which is holy."[14] I can find no better way of describing the power of imagination and its essential independence from the natural reality than by quoting the following words of the poet and the Blakean scholar Kathleen Raine.

> From the earliest human records we see humankind creating abstract patterns and forms not found in nature; gods of strange unnatural aspect - the more unnatural and the more profoundly "human." Modern Amazonian savages asked Lévy-Strauss, that civilized Frenchman, why he and his kind did not paint their faces with abstract patterns in order (like the Amazonians) to affirm their humanity, their difference from animals around them. They knew what Western anthropologists would seem to have forgotten, that to be human is, precisely, to live our myths, to live according to an inner order which is not natural, which is, in terms of natural law, unnatural. The distortions and deformations of the human face and body, the paintings and tattooings practiced by primitives ... are supremely, specifically human, being expressions of a mental, an inner world, affirmed in opposition to, and in challenge of, in affirmation against, a natural order.[15]

In conclusion, it seems worth mentioning that, apart from the official condemnation of images by the Church Councils in the eight and ninth centuries, most types of religious mysticism have despised visual representations of the holy. From the German mystics of the Middle Ages and St. Theresa to the Quietists of the eighteenth century, images in concrete form as well as those that dwell in the soul, are systematically banned. The ostensible reason for this negative attitude toward images lies in the religious concern to preserve the transcendence of the divine: a human and material God is a scandal to the respectful unbeliever and the mystic alike. Man must not make any graven image because God confined in the image is capable of nothing. The mystic therefore must suppress sensory experience and seek to lose his self in an undifferentiated Absolute - the unnamable God of infinite negation.

In contrast to the mystic's way which strives to transcend

matter, we shall take the view, represented later in these pages by men like Blake, Swedenborg, Corbin and the Siberian shaman, that the material world offers no hinderance to the visionary eye. In our opinion, images of the holy, be they monstruous or beautiful, are not inferior replicas of the original but originals themselves. And precisely because they are original, i.e., new at every moment of their appearance, they must be incomplete and imperfect. Only the saint and the mystic strives for perfection whereas the artist, as Balzac has said, is continuously at work on the one masterpiece that is never created. If it should be accomplished, it could not be seen for in the perferct image there is nothing more to see.[16]

We are thus in favor of a radical immanence of all noumenal entities. Matter and sensory experience need not be transcended, but reorganized and transformed so as to become translucent to the holy. For, when the power of senses is increased, we find with Blake that "Each grain of Sand/ Every Stone on the Land/ Each rock and each hill/ Each fountain and rill/ Each herb and each tree/ Mountain hill Earth and Sea/ Cloud Meteor and Star/ Are Men Seen Afar" (K 709). Note that these human forms are not literally human and thus - not anthropomorphic. They are subtle, forever unfinished, moving bodies that are fated to "imitate" themselves and their own endless configurations.

The Dream and the Soul

Jung's identification of the psyche with the image and his understanding of the latter in the sense of a fantasy or poetic image has been unfolded in archetypal psychology to mean that the imaginative activity of the soul is most typically presented by the dream. In Hillman's work The Dream and the Underworld it is the dream rather than aesthetic experience that is taken as the paradigm of the psyche. The reason for this shift of emphasis is that dreams, even more than artistic experience, bespeak the image-making tendency of the soul by converting the dreamer himself into one image among others.

Furthermore, dreams, both private and public (in the mythologies of the world) are closely associated with death and are often seen as the psyche's preparation for death. The "dream-work" (Freud), assisted by conscious elaboration, builds an imaginal vessel or, in D.H. Lawrence's words, the Ship of Death. Probably the most provocative feature of dream-images is that they seem to be mainly concerned not with living but with imagining; what matters is not life, but soul and how life-experiences are used for the benefit of the soul. In our dreams there is a surprising disregard for the predilections of flesh and temporal existence, even for physical death itself.

Having indicated the main thrust of the Hillmanian approach to the dream, we must now place it in the larger setting of Greek mythology and the Freudian/Jungian theory of dreams. In addition, Hillman's views on dream and death should prepare the way for a more adequate grasp of the difficult Sūfi doctrine of mundus imaginalis ('alam al-mithâl) which provides a valuative and cosmic grounding for archtypes.

Men of all times and cultures have enjoyed the privilege of citizenship in two worlds corresponding to two modes of con- sciousness. The Greeks called them hypar (the waking world) and onar (the dream world), each having its own logic and its own limitations. Generally speaking, ancient peoples have accorded at least an equal significance and respect to both experiences. For example, Heraclitus is credited with the view that the soul has contact with the cosmic region (logos) only when free in sleep from the interruption of the senses.[17] In the earliest association of dreams with death, Homer tells us that dreams issue from the underworld of Hades and refers to sleep (hypnos) and death (thanatos) as "twin brothers" (The Iliad, XVI, 671 and 681). The Western tradition, however, has exhibited a predominantly negative attitude toward the dream, relegating it to the limbo of the "imaginary," which in turn is equated with the "unreal," hallucinatory, "fantastic," etc. About the only exception in this regard is the Romantic movement of the eighteenth and nineteenth centuries, which not unexpectedly swung to the opposite extreme of valuing the dream incomparably higher than waking reality. Thus a Hölderlin would declare that man is "a God when he dreams, but a beggar when he reflects."[18]

Hillman, in the wake of Jung's identification of the image with fantasy or poetic imagery, wants to understand dreams, not scientifically, but poetically. In the scientific approach, dream-worlds are regarded as concepts or symbols that acquire their significance from their objective correlatives. In contrast, a dream, understood poetically, far from being a message containing information about something other than the dream, is "like a poem or painting which is not about anything, not even about the poet or the painter." For as every artist would justifiably insist, painted lemons can and must be experienced without reference to "real" lemons. Art is not nature at secondhand, and one cannot paint lemons better than they "paint" themselves. If anything, a painted lemon or a flower is more real in that it is like the Goethean Urphänomen - a concrete universal, an archetypal image. In Hillman's opinion, it is the same with the lemon in a dream. "The poetic view does not posit an objective psyche to which the lemon refers and from which it is a message. Psyche is image, Jung said. We stick to the image because the psyche itself sticks there."[19]

Hillman is aware that his approach, which derives in part from Freud and Jung, is "shocking and difficult," "farfetched, impractical, and visionary"; yet he feels that it has to be radical in all these senses because it "bespeaks the territory of its origin, chthon [the Underworld as distinct from ge, the realm of nature, earth, fertility], the faraway pneumatic world that is a dimension not available in itself ..."[20]

Hillman credits Freud[21] with the Romantic idea that the dream contains a hidden and important personal message from another world. Unfortunately, this idea, which was nearest to Freud, disappeared among the post-Freudians. Freud himself, however, made a major concession to the prevailing rational empiricism of his day by viewing the residues of the day (Tagesreste) as the raw material of the dream. In this way he stays with the Lockean tabula rasa concept of the mind, holding that there is nothing in the mind that was not first in the senses. In the end, therefore, Freud returns the dream to the dayworld by translating or interpreting the realm of sleep into the language of waking life. Psychoanalysis becomes an instrument enabling the ego to rescue or "reclaim" the dream from its underworld madness and immersion in the pleasure principle - a progressive conquest of the id (das Es) by the principle of Apollonian rationality and mono-vision.

The over-all construct that Jung applies to dream is compensation. Jungians read dreams for their information regarding the process of individuation whose supposed aim is the creation of a more whole midway station embracing both the dream and the ego, the inner and the outer. The assumption here is that the dream is not complete in itself: it is always partial, one-sided, unbalanced. To understand it and to make it useful, the analyst must help the patient reestablish the "original harmony" between the opposites. Jung refers this principle to the Heraclitus' doctrine of enantiodromia, expressing the "regulative function of opposites." He adapts the Heraclitean saying, "The way up and the way down are one and the same," to mean les extrêmes se touchent.[22] From a purely philosophical standpoint, this ancient doctrine, opposed as it is to the either/or thinking of the Aristotelian tradition, is certainly important and probably even "true." But, says Hillman, in the consulting room of the

107

analyst things turn out rather differently. For the question now is: who is going to reestablish the lost harmony? The only "person" on the scene to do the work, is, of course, the old protagonist, the ego. In practice the compensation approach appeals to the dayworld perspective of ego and is guided by egocentric ideology, not by the dream. The principle of compensation, according to Hillman, is rooted in Western allopathic medicine, where healing means reversing the direction of a disease process by attacking it or by supplying the missing element. What has been overlooked in this procedure is that every dream (like every image) already contains its own opposite, that "every psychic event is an identity of at least two positions and is thus symbolic, metaphorical, and never one-sided." The Heraclitean "coincidence of opposites means that nothing has to be introduced by anyone from anywhere, because the opposite is already present ... Every dream has its own fulcrum and balance, compensates itself, is complete as it is."[23]

In sum, both Freud and Jung maintain that the dream must be translated into waking language. The difference betwen the two is that whereas Freud uses the dream in order to broaden the rational ego, Jung wants to extract from the dream what is absent in the daylight consciousness in order to achieve wholeness of personality (the Self). In sharp contrast to both of these positions, Hillman refuses to bring the dream into the dayworld "in any other form than its own"; the dream may not be envisioned either as a message to be deciphered for the dayworld (Freud) or as a compensation to it (Jung).[24]

Hillman prefers to follow the dream into a province where thinking moves in images, resemblances, correspondences; the dream will be met on its own ground which is that of unfathomable depth and polyvalence - in the underworld.[25] Just as images of the psyche are what they mean, just as the figures of myth and artistic creation possess their own consistency and message, so the dream imagery must be treated according to the Taoist principle of "letting be" and noninterference (wu-wei).

The underworld of the dream is a cosmos in its own right, distinct from but not unrelated to the dayworld. In Greek mythology this is indicated by the fact that Hades is the brother of Zeus. Their brotherhood means that the lower world is "contiguous with life, touching it in all parts ... its shadow brother, giving to life its depth and its psyche."[26] The underworld is a purely psychic world, a psychological cosmos whose mythological figures are metaphorical statements about the soul's comportment beyond life.

There is a useful analogy in Plato's Sophist (266c) where dream images are compared with shadows - "dark patches" interrupting the light and leading us to see a kind of "reflection," "the reverse of the ordinary direct view." In Hillman's interpretation, dreams are like dark spots, like absences of the dayworld. Nonetheless these images are visible, though "only to what is invisible in us. The invisible is perceived by means of the invisible, that is, psyche."[27] The shadow world in the depths replicates our daily consciousness, but it can be perceived only imaginatively; it is this world perceived and expereinced as a metaphor, i.e., in a state of interpenetration among all things, events and persons. From the perspective of underworld only shadow has substantial reality, "only what is in the shadow matters truly, eternatlly." For the shadow is not only repressed or evil reflection, which constantly accompanies us and which (according to Jung) must be integrated into a "better" whole, but the very essence of the soul. Sub specie aeternitatis, then, it is we, the "real people," who are the shadows of our souls. In the words of Heraclitus, "when we are alive our souls are dead and buried in us, but when we die, our souls come to life again and live" (DK, fr. 26). Hillman interprets the Heraclitean fragment as follows:

> To 'sleep' places us in touch with the 'dead,' the
> eidola, essences, images; to be 'awake' is to be in
> touch with the sleeper, the ego-conscious personality.
> In the Romantic sense;[28] during sleep we are awake
> and alive; in life asleep.

Hillman also distinguishes between the ego of daily life - the Herculean and controlling ego - and the ego of our dreams, the imaginal ego which is "at home in the dark, moving among images as one of them."[29] Since the dream does not belong to "me" but rather to the psyche, the dream ego merely plays one of the roles in the theatre. In fact, all persons we encounter in dreams, including myself, though they often present themselves in the guise of human beings with whom we are personally acquainted, belong neither to the external world nor to my psychic constitution, but to the shadowy "between" of the underworld - to the liminal, elusive and ambiguous twilight zone which alone is the home of the soul. In Hillman's words, "they are shadow images that fill archetypal roles; they are personae, masks, in the hollow of which is a numen." For example in the Egyptian cult of the dead, the shadow souls are at the same time images of gods. Our human person and all the other persons of the dream are "shadowed by an archetypal image in the likeness of a God, and the god appears as the shade of the human person."[30] Thus, says Hillman, we are made not only in the divine image but are constantly made and remade "by the divine image in the soul."[31]

Accordingly, Hillman's dream therapy consists not in translating the dream into ego-language but rather in translating the ego into dream-language. He wants to do the Freudian dreamwork on the ego, aiming at a transformation, a metanoia of the modern heroic ego that is caught in a whirlwind of activity for its own sake, into an imaginal ego, representing a more discontinuous circular pattern, an "uroboric course, which is a circulation of light and darkness."[32]

When we take the dream as a corrective to the "day-residues" (Freud) or as an instruction for tomorrow (Jung), we are using it for purposes that are alien to the dream-ego, i.e., for strengthening our heroic stance. Since, however, dream is not primarily a comment upon the world of our literalistic and rational consciousness but rather a digestive and assimilative process, we must imagine the dream-work as converting bits and pieces of the day, indeed all life events, "into psychic substance by means of imaginative modes - symbolization, condensation, archaization. This work takes matters out of life and makes them into soul."[33] Dream-work is essentially soul-making: "we work on dreams not to strengthen the ego but to make psychic reality, to make life matter through death, to make soul by coagulating and intensifying imagination."

In contradistinction to Freudian analysis, psychotherapy, or the Jungian process of individuation, Hillman would call his way "soul-making" or "initiation." Our nightly descent into dreaming is not a compensation but a mode of initiation which, instead of supplying missing parts to th ego-consciousness, voids it of attachments to and identification with the surface of things. Hillman's emphasis is on "psychology of craft" rather than on a "psychology of growth." Note however that the notions of growth, integration, etc., are rejected only to the extent that they are used to augment the hubris of the imperial ego. Soul-making encompasses organic growth and employs its images in the creation of psychic reality.

Soul-making is "making" in the original sense of poiēsis. The dream work, as I pointed out, consists in a shift of perspective from the heroic basis of consciousness to the poetic basis of consciousness, implying that "every reality of whatever sort is first of all a fantasy image of the psyche."[34] As a work of poiēsis (making of images in words) the dream work is made up not only of its material content but also of a form; dreams shape the given matter - the day residues - into a work of fantasy and imagination - a process during which the events of life and the life itself is transformed into a work of art. This, of course, is as much as saying that under ideal circumstances what we call "life" imitates dreams or that, on the level of depth, "nature" (the Greek gē) is mimetic to art. From the poetic perspective dreams and imagination are more real than what we mindlessly call "real life" and the "hard facts" of life.

Hillman's thought to some extent parallels the work of Gaston Bachelard who also emphasizes the necessarily polyvalent and ambiguous nature of imagination.[35] Just as dreams can never have only one interpretation, one meaning, in the realm of imagination, according to Bachelard, there is no value without polyvalence and duplicity. It is as Heraclitus observed: "The Lord whose oracle is in Delphi neither speaks out nor conceals, but gives a sign" (DK, fr. 93). Hillman follows Heraclitus in imagining the "dream work" to be an activity of a bricoleur (scrap dealer) rather than that of a censor. The task of a bricoleur is to take the leftovers from the day and to shape them into new figures within a new setting. The dream serves two principles, love and death. The bricoleur, who is in the service of the death instinct, "scavenges and forages for day residues, removing more and more empirical trash ... out of life"; the love instinct fuses and shapes the junk into a material for soul-making. "Imagination works by deforming and forming at one and the same moment." Bachelard, too, speaks of the deformative activities of imagination. Something in the psyche seems to want to be and yet to resist being twisted into unnatural monstrous shapes.

Hillman suggests that alchemy has resolved the dilemma by conceiving psyche's deforming tendencies as an opus contra naturam, a work against nature and yet for nature in its animated or ensouled form. For the psyche and her poetic genius the

112

merely natural states and circumstances are inadequate and "unnatural." Therefore, "the alchemical work had to deform nature in order to serve nature. It had to hurt (boil, sever, skin, dessicate, putrefy, suffocate, drown, etc.) natural nature in order to free animated nature."[36] The dream, like artistic imagination, is intent on saving nature - a far cry from subjecting it to man's control by means of technological machinery. Technology, in its present state, seems to be bent mainly on distorting and maiming nature. There is a war of cosmic proportions going on.

*

The closeness of soul to death is one of the most important themes in archetypal psychology. I would like to introduce this theme by first quoting R.M. Rilke, since few people have given such an accomplished expression to that strangest of all coincidences: the correlativity of life and death.

> Death is the side of life averted from us, unshone upon by us: we must achieve the greatest consciousness of our existence which is at home in both unbounded realms, inexhaustibly nourished from both ... The true figure of life extends through both spheres, the blood of the mightiest circulation flows through both: there is neither here nor beyond, but the great unity in which the beings that surpass us, the 'angels,' are at home ... We of the here and now are not for a moment hedged in the time-world, nor confined within it; we are incessantly flowing over and over to those who preceded us ... We are the bees of the invisible. Nous butinons eperdument le miel du visible, pour l'accumuler dans la grande ruche d'or de l'Invisible.[37]

In Suicide and the Soul, Hillman proposes that "the experience of death is requisite for psychic life."[38] Referring to a passage in Phaedo (64A) where Socrates speaks of philosophy as the practicing of death, Hillman interprets this dying to the

113

world of senses as the dying to the literal perspective that is necessary "to encounter the realm of the soul ..."[39] Experience of death acquaints us with "the very first metaphor of human existence: that we are not real."[40] We are not real to the precise extent that we deny our dependence on psychic reality. We are not real because we are reflections of the imaginal psyche; we are shadows of "shadows," that is, in our literalness - as concoctions of "spirit" and "matter" - we are shadows of our souls, for only the soul is not reducible to anything else and so constitutes our true, ontological reality. For the underworld of the psyche (the Jungian unconscious) is "a place where there are only psychic images. From the Hades perspective <u>we</u> <u>are</u> <u>our</u> <u>images</u>."[41]

These are extraordinary lines. Instead of viewing death as an exogenous event, befalling us from outside, Hillman has chosen to see it as something inherently, inalienably human, indeed, as "the <u>side</u> <u>of</u> <u>life</u> averted from us," as nourishing us <u>via</u> the imaginal soul: life would have literally no substance without the experience of death. In Hillman's view, therefore, death is the end of life only in a literal sense; imagistically or from the soul's perspective, death is the beginning of life as well. It is all radically relative: to the extent that we are afflicted with literalism, we are dead in life, in fact - more dead in life than in death. In the words of Heraclitus: "It is always one and the same thing that lives in us; living and dead, waking and sleeping, young and old. For the former turns into the latter, and the latter again becomes the former" (DK, 88).[42]

The discovery of the Hades - the archetypal background of life - "gives a sense of primordiality, of beginning at the beginning."[43] In Bachelard's words, it gives "a mad surge of life," for the "archetypes are reserves of enthusiasm which help us believe in the world, to love the world, to create the world."[44] Bachelard's observation should be understood in connection with

114

the highly unorthodox interpretation that Hillman gives to the Narcissus myth.

In the Freudian theory sleep is a return to primary narcissism and all dreams are narcissistic - disguised fulfillments of repressed sexual wishes. More specifically, the content of dreams represents the transfiguration of latent sexual urges into manifest imagery. In short, the dream work fulfills instinctual demands. The Jungian critique of Freud has pointed out that instinct has also a "spiritual" aspect called the archetype. Archetypes are the psychic instincts of the human species; in the form of images and symbols they complete instinct by guiding it toward the goal of wholeness or totality (the Self). Thus for both Freud and Jung the dream work fulfills an instinctual or archetypal need. Amazingly enough, however, this gratification, according to Hillman, is narcissistic precisely because it occurs within the dream itself: "the images made in dreams fulfill the desire of the instinct." It is "as if it were enough for the psyche to see its own reflection by means of images, as if it were enough to imagine in poetic form its physical body and needs, its love, and its own self." Nothing external is needed: the instinctual craving is stilled by the sheer presence of and participation in the image. The psyche sleeps in peace because Narcissus is contemplating not a mere reflection of his being but something more distant and reposeful - a work of art. We must imagine Narcissus imitating (as nature imitates art) his "own" soul-image, not the other way round. Or, as Hillman puts it, Narcissus "believes that he is looking at the beautiful form of another being. So it is not self-love of his 'own' image (narcissism) but the love for a vision that is at once body, image, and reflection."[46] Narcissus - "the patron saint of imagination" - is in fact a visionary and a poet whose perception and powers of imagination extend far beyond the compass of the "natural" nature. We must imagine Narcissus (rather than a Sisyphus) happy.

Thus Hillman would not interrupt Narcissus. He would not attempt to interpret the dream, because dreams can be killed by interpreters. Interpretation, even in the Jungian and Freudian psychotherapies, has become more and more linear and monistic in its concern with growth, self-realization, and life at the expense of depth and the inherent ambiguity of the imaginal soul. If, as Jung said, modern man is in search of a soul, this soul, adds Hillman, "is lost partly in life"[47]: it is lost through the attempts of modern psychotherapy to "explain" dreams by using the guidelines of the ego. The inevitable result of this rationalistic and subjectivistic bias is that the ego becomes strong at the cost of soul and imagination. Freud has said that the dream is the via regia (the royal road) to the unconscious. Unfortunately, psychology since Freud, by moving out of the unconscious toward the light of ego-consciousness too soon, too abruptly, has not only lost the soul, but - much more fatally - the memory of the loss itself. Gods have fled the soul. And yet, as Jung and Hillman remind us, gods are immortal - even in their infirmities.

"Gods are immortal - even in their infirmities." If it is asked how can gods be "infirm" and immortal at the same time, we may provisionally suggest, in accordance with our general standpoint, that "infirmity" in the sense of incompleteness is in no way exclusive of "wholeness" provided the latter is understood dynamically, i.e., as an interplay of forces whose outcome is strictly unpredictable. It is an un-ending "wholeness," a wholeing that, precisely because it has no end, must be finite, that is, contaminated with the ever-present possibility of distortion and even non-being.

It is with this idea of finite infinitude that we must work if we are to arrive at a conception of "immortality" that is based not on belief in a purely spiritual soul substance, but on the

Jungian hypothesis of psychic reality or the esse in anima. In our view, immortality on the one hand and mortality, on the other, are not mutually exclusive but complementary notions. Just like the psyche in the Jungian scheme is a middle term between the opposites of spirit and matter, so "immortality" must be envisioned as a "third" between the extremes of "ever-lasting life" and "mortality," between sheer evanescence and eternality (nunc stans). In other words, we must aim at the inclusion of time and finitude within the structures of timelessness and infinity.

To this end we must first explore with Casey some of the basic characteristics -such as autonomy, certainty, simultaneity - of what Jung called voluntary (conscious) and passive imagination which is dominated by the imaginer's ego, dwelling in the realm of "pure possibility" and enjoying shallow and temporary freedom.[48] In the course of this discussion I shall attempt to expand Casey's phenomenological description of imagining by connecting it at all crucial points with a different kind of imaginative experience leading, in Jung's words, through "a movement [born] out of the suspension between opposites" to "a new level of being, a new situation."[49] Ultimately this movement will culminate in Corbin's mundus imaginalis or achetypus whose instrument of cognition is archetypal or visionary imagination. At this point, imagination, according to Corbin, "posits real being."[50] In Casey's modified locution, such imagining "posits real imaginal being."[51] We shall also find that Haidegger's thought, especially his radical revision of the classical correspondence theory of knowledge, provides a helpful introduction not only to the highly esoteric speculations of Corbin and his spiritual company but to the entire question of subtle embodiment, to be discussed in the second part of this work.

117

Autonomy, Certainty and Simultaneity of Images

In trying to distinguish imagination from perception we already stated that, phenomenologically speaking, imagining is prior and therfore non-reducible to perception and such offshoot of perception as memory and hallucination. This means that imagining, as an experienced phenomenon, even in its ordinary and banal modes of activity, is autonomous and self-generating. Casey does not deny that epistemologically imagination pre-supposes perception for as humans (incarnated beings) we all have bodies and to be in body is to be a perceiver. However, the necessity to exercise perceptive faculty prior to imagining by no means pre-determines the latter's specific course. "Although it is epistemologically posterior to perception, imagining is not beholden to perceiving for its particular content on any given occasion."[52]

Besides autonomy, imagining possesses a kind of certainty not available in the world of perception and sense data. Imaginative experience, in contrast to perceptual experience, which is error-prone and always in need of correction, is non-corrigible. There is no possibility of being in error as to the character of what one imagines: "I cannot misimagine."[53] The reason for this freedom from error lies in the simultaneous nature of images. Imaginative presentations are monadic wholes containing no hidden corners in need of "further investigation" or additional "hard data." Whatever we imagine is given all at once (simul totum), presents all of itself; "only so much meets the eye as is there ... there is only what appears in each unrepeatable situation."[54]

According to Patricia Berry, simultaneity means that there is no priority in a image; all parts are co-relative and co-temporaneous. "Everything is occurring while everything else is occurring simultaneously." Berry also speaks of "full democracy of the image ... all parts have equal right to be heard, belong to the body politic ... and there are no privileged positions in the image.[55] Together with simultaneity goes the non-sequential and non-narrative character of images. For example, dreams are notoriously difficult if not impossible to write down because they do not seem to be amenable to a coherent story. There is no fixed order or sequence in dream images: the "image has no before and after."[56] Casey even doubts whether we can be said to imagine the _same_ object or event repeatedly since in the imaginative presentations there is no sense of a perduring spatio-temporal field in which narration could take place. As a result, "imaginings are inherently non-narrative in character; episodic at best (...) they disintegrate too quickly to possess a strictly narrative structure: 'one glimpse and vanished' (Samuel Beckett)."[57]

In my opinion, it would be entirely à propos to apply to the simultaneous character of images the Heideggerian category of truth understood in the Greek sense of _aletheia_, literally "un-hiddeness," "disclosure" or "unconcealment" (composed of two elements, alpha privative and the root _lethe_, "veil").[58] Images are unconcealed in that they are pure presences beyond the split of subject and object. This would imply that within the imaginal realm of the psyche, appearance (phenomenon) and reality (noumenon) are identical. Images mean nothing beyond themselves, point to no latent and unexplored areas of the psyche (the unconscious) but only to other images and their confirgurations _ad_ _infinitim_.

Consequently we may speak with Casey of "intrinsic completedness of imagination"[59] meaning that each imaginative act is strictly self-contained, complete in itself. In this respect images are like poems or paintings: they are not _about_ anything and least of all about "things" in the empirically verifiable reality. Like a painting, the image is mainly about itself or self-referential. This "plenary form" of images has been described by the philosopher R.G. Collingwood as follows:

> Everything which imagination presents to itself is a
> here, a now; something complete in itself, absolutely
> self-contained, unconnected with anything else by the
> relations between what is and what is not, what it is
> and that because of which it is what it is, what it is
> and what it might have been, what it is and what it
> ought to be.[60]

In the last resort what accounts for the certainty of imaginal
presentations is their ability to fuse, to synthesize the real and
the apparent, being and meaning. Western philosophy, however,
has never sought certainty - the indubitable, the ens
realissimum - in the realm of the imaginal. On the whole, philosophers have taken for granted Aristotle's remark that "imaginings
are for the most part false." As a result, Western thinking has
oscillated between two extremes, the spiritual and the material,
not realizing that "truth" (aletheia) may be right in the middle
between them.

But, as I have intimated, the kind of truth that belongs to
the middle realm of the soul offers no ready-made comfort:
paradoxically, it is uncertain and elusive in its very certainty.
As Heraclitus would have it, it is the kind of certainty that
"loves to hide" (Wheelwright, fr. 17). Put in terms of
Heidegger's characterization of aletheia, imaginative certainty is
revealing-concealing. Truth is a movement from concealment into
revelation and back into concealment, a movement that is
patterned upon the cosmic alternation of day and night, light
and darkness. Like the Platonic and the Neo-Platonic soul, it
moves on an uroboric course.

It is not surprising therefore that the official philosophy
has favored either the certainty of sensory experience (empiricism) or, having found it fallible, the eternal verities of reason -
whether the latter are presented in the form of compelling
syllogism or as a matter of faith handed down by a presiding

deity. In this existentially untenable situation we are goaded into choosing, in fear and trembling, between two mistresses, faith and reason. Philosophical and theological accommodations, such as they have been proferred (for example, in the form of Christian philosophy or in Teilhard de Chardin's evolutionism or under the sobriquet of dialectical materialism, to name but a few) have proved to be short-lived because they lack that life-giving spirit which is also the soul of a thing.

The latest fashion - if I may extend this digression - among these attempts to reach at all costs a unifying view of reality is the concerted exploitation on the part of trans-personal psychologists and religious writers, of the modern scientific discoveries purportedly containing explosive anti-materialistic implications. (I am referring mainly to such "epoch-making" findings in microphysics as the principle of complementarity, introduced in 1928 into quantum theory by Niels Bohr, the indeterminacy principle of Heisenberg and the Einsteinian $E = mc^2$.) The general point I want to make is that science is rhapsodized in these circles in the hope that it may corroborate the ancient claim of spiritualism, to wit, that spirit is superior or more primary than matter and that mankind is after all destined to evolve toward peaks of self-actualization and harmony. As I see it, the basic weakness in these and similar utopian fantasies lies in the tendency to stress the preposition "over": it's always either mind over matter or the other way round (as in materialism). It is as if the secret of life consisted in over-coming all obstacles, in triumphing over all shortcomings and iniquities. In other words, one is grimly determined to possess certainty of the Cartesian type - rational certainty bereft of ambivalence and insured against all perversion.

Now, as I stated a while ago, the kind of certainty available in the imaginative experience is characterized by the coalescence of appearance and reality, meaning and being. Enlarging upon this essential feature of imagination, we may also state with Casey that "imagining is all appearance and nothing but appearance."[61] Clearly the word "appearance," as used in the present context, is not equivalent to "illusion." In illusory situations, specifically in cases of perceptual illusion there is presumed to be a "true" state of affairs against which illusion can be measured and eventually corrected. An imaginative experience, by contrast, is non-corrigible because it cannot be legitimately compared to anything extraneous to it; it is self-sufficient and self-explanatory, i.e., wholly contained in the mode of its appearance. An image means exactly what it is.

Furthermore, imaginative presentations, according to Casey, are not only non-falsifiable, but also non-verifiable. This must be so because such presentations, being ineluctably first-hand in character, private and subjective in the fullest sense of these words, do not offer any possibility of inter-subjective confirmation. The imaginer may very well deceive others, for example, by not reporting his experience truthfully, but "he cannot deceive himself concerning his own imagining."[62] To suggest that the imaginer may deceive himself because he is in some respect "abnormal," "sick" or "out of touch with reality" would be equivalent to introducing criteria which are inapplicable to the case in question; in the last analysis, it would mean reducing imagination to faulty perception, hallucination and the like. The point is simply that causal thinking has no place in imagination if the latter is to be treated as an activity in its own right. The imaginal realm which is also the realm of the soul is not open for public inspection and hence it cannot be pinned down and dissected by means of the traditional logical and scientific categories. The logos of the soul is not the logos of the conventional logic.

"O My Things, How We Have Talked" (Bachelard)

The non-corrigible and self-explanatory nature of images

implies that their verification or falsification is beyond the province of the conventional reference or correspondence theory of truth. According to Casey, "the correspondence model of truth ... is not the only model at our disposal. In fact, the very specialness of imaginative exprience casts suspicion on the idea that the traditional correspondentional model adequately reflects the range of human experience of truth."[63]

Among the contemporary thinkers it is Martin Heidegger who has conducted the most devastating attack against the correspondence theory. We should not be surprised therefore to find that both Heidegger's philosophy and archetypal psychology, in spite of their widely differing styles of thinking and expression, are engaged in the same quest: the recovery of the imaginal ground not only of man, but of all being.

In Heidegger's view, the oblivion of this transpersonal ground (he calls it oblivion of Being) must be traced back to Plato and Aristotle, in particular to Plato's Allegory of the Cave (bk. VII of the Republic). For it is here that the world of things becomes a re-presentation, a standing in front of us (Gegen-stand, object) which we then confront in pursuit of "scientific objectivity" and the like. By encountering things as objects, we gradually convert them into tools for planetary manipulation. It is also at this juncture that truth, originally experienced as aletheia, simultaneous revelation and concealment, changes into idea, understood no longer as a mode of seeing (eyes of the soul) but as static presence separated from the beholder. In the process, ideas are hypostatized into things or literal entities "out there" so that, instead of seeing by means of ideas, we "see" ideas "objectively" as something to speculate about. Ideas have become objects for a subject.[64] As a result, truth is declared to consist in the correctness of judgment or in a correspondence of seeing with the object of vision.

This changed conception of truth developed through Aristotle into the Middle Ages where it was expressed in the classical formula: <u>veritas</u> <u>est</u> <u>adequatio</u> <u>intellectus</u> <u>et</u> <u>rei</u>. Truth is now located in the judgment and the judgment is true when it corresponds to the thing to which it refers. It is as if we carried images of things around in an inner psychic box to compare them occasionally with the things outside the box.

The seed, planted by Plato, developed into the Cartesian subject-object split and reached its culmination in Nietzsche's superman and the "will to power." From now on man's relationship with the world and all worldly entities (and, may I add, even to the "other-worldly" entities such as "ghosts" and astral bodies of the Psychical Research) is conceived in the confrontational terms of object-ness - objective control and domination which, as Heidegger sees it, is inseparable from the exaltation of the controlling subject. Objectivism and subjectivism (realism and idealism, materialism and spiritualism, etc.) belong to the same level of thinking: an object can only be an object for a subject and a subject stands always in opposition to objects.[65] Thus the more objective (scientific) we become, the more we are mired in a narrow subjectivism and the concommitant glorification of ego-consciousness and the Apollonian reason. In short, the representational theory of truth has led to the usurpation of all light and intelligibility, of all certainty by reason divorced from imagination. Certainty has been narrowed down to mean the Cartesian certainty of clear and distinct ideas.

To Heidegger, truth is an event of being (<u>Ereigniss</u>), a coming to pass from concealment to disclosure. This means that, contrary to the traditional metaphysics holding that Being is opposed to appearing, the <u>reality</u> (or being) of things is inseparable from the way in which they appear. Things - all things - <u>are</u> in their appearances as the stars are in their twinklings. Translated into the language of archetypal psychology, the world of things is essentially an imaginal, divine and personified cosmos, a presencing and a plenum in which, as the late Heidegger puts it, "the thing things."[65]

With this enigmatic expression Heidegger is voicing his opposition to the conventional view which conceives the thingness of a thing exclusively in relation to a subject. When things are considered as objects of representation or as needing to conform to the intellectual categories of a judging subject, they lose their soul. The scientific attitude or what Heidegger calls the calculating mood of science brings about the universal loss of things by dissolving their inner depth and self-sufficiency. Things become mere commodities when they are perceived in their complete unhiddeness and total objectification. The modern man cannot find his soul unless he finds the soul of things as well.

According to the late Heidegger, the thingness of a thing or the soul of things is prototypically disclosed in art and in poetic thought. For the poet the essences of things are not located beyond the visible world, but show themselves wholly in their modes of appearance. There is depth and fantasy in things when they are allowed to appear in their own being. Things, approached with a respectful attitude, an attitude of "letting be," "thing," i.e., they are enigmatic, alive, fantastic. The world of nature becomes a living organism once again, as it was to the early Greeks, teeming with divine, semi-divine and demonic beings engaged in a primordial strife (polemos) between light and darkness. But this conflict, contrary to the common sense view, is not destructive. Opposites in nature are not contradictory (as in logic) but polar; they live by virtue of each other and at each other's expense.

The world of nature is Dionysian, but Dionysos (the brother of Hades), as Hillman has observed, is not dumb. He is not only a blind force, the élan vital of vegetative life, but also "the soul of nature, its psychic interiority."[66] The Dionysian nature is physis and logos in one; it is physio-logical. Like imagination

125

and fantasy, Dionysos is never merely chaotic and dangerous, but also order-creating; even as a chthonian deity, he stands at the extreme limits of the Olympian light. He brings together the broad sky and the dark earth, the Olympyan gods and the chthonian powers. In this way, as the Heideggerian scholar Vincent Vycinas has it, "he announces something which is difficult to grasp, easy to lose, and which nevertheless is more real than anything real."[67]

Dionysos is the god of twilight - the elusive region between day and night, life and death, the spiritual and the earthly; he is at home in that transitional place of liminal and luminous realities where our perception is governed by imagination more than at other times. The liminal condition of twilight is also the threshold, a "no-place" and "no-time" which belongs to the circularity and wandering of the imaginal psyche. The logic of this psychic wandering is not the logic of contradiction or of the excluded middle, but a Dionysian one; it is the logic of the middle region, including the contraries and indeed thriving on their polemics. As Hillman says, the Dionysian logic is not "a progressive march whose retreats are only for a better leap forward (reculer pour mieux sauter)" but a discontinuous movement, which includes "the downward turns, the depressions, regressions, fallings away from awareness."[68] In a remarkable passage, explicitly naming the uroboric nature of the soul, Heidegger states that the soul's being is her wandering. This means, he says, that the soul is not first of all a soul, and then, accidentally as it were, also a stranger who does not belong to the earth. On the contrary, "the soul qua soul is fundamentally, by its nature something strange on earth."[69]

It is important to realize that the Heideggerian and the early Greek notion of physis is closer to the Jungian "psyche" than to nature in its present-day degraded "material" form. In Greek, as well as in primitive religions, physis was never perceived in our sense of "nature" or as motion of material things, of atoms and electrons. Rather it was a creative occurence in the sense of poēisis ("making"), the originating "bringing forth," "producing," "creating." As such physis is not separated from logos of the Apollonian mentality: the "making" of physis is a manifestation of its logos. To the Greeks logos is always the logos of physis. It is only later that logos, having been cut off from physis, becomes perverted logos, i.e., logic in the conventional sense. Conversely, physis, when thought of separately from logos, becomes perverted physis or what we today call "matter." The Pre-Socratic logic, reason, ideas are not opposed to nature; they are nature in her manifold manifestations. Logic and ideas belong to nature as images "belong" to the way in which they manifest themselves. To use Heidegger's language, Being, that notoriously abstract and empty non-thing is physis and physis is wholly in the mode of its appearing. "Being means appearing. Appearing is not something subsequent that sometimes happens to being. Appearing is the very essence of being."[70]

Thus, after a long detour, we have arrived where we started: "the imagining is all appearance and nothing but appearance" (Casey). This means that images are wholes or that they are wholly contained in the way in which they appear, leaving no residual noumenality behind their backs; they are all façade, a bewitching play of illusion in which we are caught so that life may be lived (Jung). In a word, physis qua psyche is imagination. For it is precisely the function of imagination to make internal external and the external internal; to make nature psychical and the psyche natural.

Imagination is the creative power at work not only in our private souls but in the nature as a whole. More precisely, creative imagination, as Coleridge has it, is the threshold between self and not-self, between mind and matter, between conscious

127

and unconscious; it links harmoniously - pneumosomatically - all opposites established by the alienated and alienating reason. Or, as Wordsworth claimed, imagination is "reason in her most exalted mood" (Prelude, xiv, 188) in that it aids reason in arriving at universal ideas (Kant) and, in turn, is giving to these ideas concrete expressions (Goethe). It is the Urpflanze which Goethe saw in the Botanical Gardens of Padua and which Schiller, like Coleridge, when he had lost "inspiration," could no longer see.

To emphasize the essentially creative nature of imagination is equivalent to saying that it is autogenous, productive on its own account or, as Kant held, that it begins of itself and by itself ("self-instituting"). Imagination arises without apparent cause and without any effort on the part of the imaginer; as in Plato, one is seized by "divine frenzy" (Phaedrus, 245). The Romantics of the nineteenth century exaggerated the "madness" aspect of imagination, converting it into Schwärmerei (Kant's term), sentimental enthusiasm. We must insist, however, that the fundamental thesis of Romanticism is sound and must be retained. It is especially important to stress the non-causal character of creative imagination - a feature we do not encounter in the world of perception. Our perceptions typically arise from a nexus of causally connected factors; for example, the shadow I perceive stems from the sun's illumination. In contrast, imaginative experience emerges suddenly and as a single simultaneous totality.

From this it follows that creativity, taken in its unadulterated meaning, is not grounded in anything external to itself. It is its own ground, a groundless ground in that it is impossible to reduce it to anything outside itself without negating it. Creativity is imagination pure and simple, ever and anon producing its own shapes and configurations, never standing still, not even at the "still point of the turning wheel" (Eliot). Its "stillness," such as it is, resembles more the strange stillness of the depths, teeming with florescent, eerie creatures, translucent bodies constantly flowing into one another and yet preserving their own identities.

In some ultimate sense, imagination in its creative dynamis rests on Play, that highest and most absorbing play in which, as Heraclitus says, the child moving counters, possesses "the royal power" (Wheelwright, fr. 24). The childish play-time is the time of imagination, a creative occurence in which change is posited absolutely and, therefore, cannot be adequately expressed by means of the conventional categories of being and becoming. Absolute change is neither being nor becoming but participates in both in that it is absolved from the dead weight of "pure" being, on the one hand, and from the no less deadly airiness of "pure" process, on the other. In the deceptively simple language of Zen Buddhism, the play happens "just so" and is "nothing special." The child plays with gravity; he is transported beyond himself because fundamentally the "royal power" belongs to the play itself. One could also say that the child has reduced - playfully - all things to their imaginal level or to the "poetic basis of mind" (Hillman) which basis is also the groundless ground of nature. In the present context, the soul is the soul of the mind (reason, intellect, spirit) as well as the soul of nature - the anima mundi.

The Court Jester as a Possibility

We must now dwell for a moment on Heidegger's abtruse concept of "possibility." To avoid unnecessary agonizing, it is advisable ot use this term from the very outset together with the adjective "open." "Open possibility" is not a tautological expression. In our context, "open" stands for "radically creative" in contrast to "hopeful" or "it may or may not happen." That which is radically creative must happen because without it nothing else would "happen." Thus, paradoxically, "possibility" will turn out to be something akin to "fate." Heidegger's term will be also helpful in clearing the way for a deeper and more nuanced understanding of the phenomenon of death.

In Western philosophy the concept of "possibility" has been confused with that of "pontentiality." The confusion goes back to Aristotle and was later crystallized into the Scholastic axiom: <u>actus</u> <u>melior</u> <u>ac</u> <u>prius</u> <u>est</u> <u>quam</u> <u>potentia</u> - actuality is better and prior to potentiality.[71] According to this view, possibility is always grounded on the actual constitution of an actual entity. Something is possible only because it is already "potentially" contained in an actually existing thing. For example, I can talk because I have actual organs of speech that can be activated at a certain age. Possibility here means potentiality. That this view is still prevalent among us, witness the glib talk about potential growth, self-actualization, becoming fully functional individual, etc.

The Aristotelian standpoint which is nothing more than a canonization of the common sense, is formed for a world of objects. It takes its cue from things regarded as primary substances endowed with certain qualities and attributes. According to this concretistic fallacy (known also as fallacy of simple location), a thing is located just where it is, confined, so to speak, to its own skin. A thing never "things." Reality consists of substantial things regarded as physical facts, as bits of matter distributed throughout space with various qualities pinned on their surface. Man too is essentially a thing, albeit a spiritual thing or a soul-substance. On this premise, reality is not what we see and experience (the so called secondary qualities of taste, color, odor), but what is measurable and mathematically calculable (the so called primary qualities of number, magnitude, position and motion).

In the modern period the Aristotelian doctrine, elaborated

within a thoroughly Newtonian climate, is continued unchanged in Locke. All potentialities, including the secondary qualities, are to be derived from the mass, arrangement and the mechanical movement of material particles. The world of nature is a material system, a clock work, originally wound up by its Creator and since kept in orderly motion by nothing more than His "general concourse" (Descartes). Man's position in this world is that of puny, irrelevant spectator with a mind which is nothing but the sum of his thinking activities derived from the external world of sensation. E.A. Burtt has described this narrowed vision of the universe - a universe which is seen with the prismatic eye of science, in the following words.

> The gloriously romantic universe of Dante and Milton, that set no bounds to the imagination of man as it played over space and time, had now been swept away. Space was identified with geometry, time with the continuity of number. The world that people had taught themselves living in - a world rich with colour and sound, redolent with fragrance, filled with gladness, love and beauty, speaking everywhere of pur- posive harmony and creative ideals - was crowded now into minute corners in the brains of scattered organic beings. The really important world outside was a world hard, cold, colourless, silent and dead; a world of quantity, a world of mathematically computable motions in mechanical regularity. The world of qualities as immediately perceived by man became just a curious and quite minor effect of that infinite machine beyond.[72]

The basic flaw in the traditional Aristotelianism is that it bars access to the secret of the work of art. As Werner Jaeger points out, "what interests [Aristotle] is the fact, not that something is coming to be, but that something is coming to be; that something fixed and normative is making its way into existence - the form."[73] In this scheme, every change is only a remodeling of the underlying, perduring substance (hypokeimenon). Poiēsis in the sense of "making" or as the generating power produces only that which is pre-given to the

131

artist's soul in the form of an _eidos_ without _hyle_ (matter).[74]
For example, a statue is a modification of the substance "bronze,"
_i.e._, the bronze prefigures its potential of being a statue.
Bronze is the essence, statue - an accident, _i.e._, a mode of the
thing called "bronze." The bronze is never wholly in the statue
or for that matter in a toilet seat, but only accidentally, as an
"after-thought" as it were.

Anticipating Heidegger, we would rather reverse the situation by saying that the bronze is wholly in the statue. In
effect, the bronze is fully bronze only in the form (or in the
image) of a statue. It is the statue as an image that makes
bronze _qua_ bronze possible and not the other way round.
Thus, contrary to the Aristotelian view, we must say that the
statue is prior to the material called bronze. The statue is
indeed the possibilizing power of the bronze in that the latter
acquires its true bronziness in the artwork called "statue." The
artist only uses bronze, like the alchemists use vulgar metals, to
create a new thing and this new thing is ontologically prior to
the stuff out of which it is created.

The traditional distinction between actuality and potentiality
(essence and accidents) has dominated the fate of Western
thought since the times of the Roman Empire and has exercised a
deleterious influence on Western esthetics. Artwork in our
culture is generally considered mimetic to the "real thing," _i.e._,
a re-presentation and re-combination of the materials of sensation
and so only more or less adequate to reality. Artistic images
are after-images, reflecting a "borrowed light" rather than being
"the light by which we see the world."[75] Thus when Plato
decided to locate reality in the realm of immutable Ideas, he and
his followers were bound to censure the "phantasmic" creations
of artists as "mere" images of perishable things and as such
twice removed from their ideal prototypes. Plato, the rationalist,
was applying to art and imagination the epistemological theory of

re-presentation which is based on the metaphysical distinction between actuality and potentiality. W. Bundy, in the only thorough study of imagination in Classical and Medieval thought, has made the pertinent observation that "the association, from the beginning, of imagination with the theory of representation, with the standard of fidelity to the object ... was the most important deterrent to a recognition of the imagination as the noblest creative function."[76]

We owe it to Heidegger to have revolutionized the Aristotelian outlook, encapsulated in the medieval maxim, _actus_ _melior_ _ac_ _prius_ _est_ _quam_ _potentia_, by proposing that "higher than actuality stands possibility."[77] To cut through the maze of conflicting interpretations of this sentence, I would like to suggest that Heidegger's formula is best understood as promoting the primacy of imagination in the life of both man and nature. It is nothing less than an invitation to envision the world of things in their pre-reflexive giveness, in their sheer presence and just-so-isness. For it is on this level - the level that precedes the split between subject and object - that things, instead of being sub-stances or isolated bits of matter, are experienced as images. They are animated, subtle bodies worthy of true imitation because they themselves are members of that Animated Body which to the early Greeks was the world of nature.

To Heidegger, like to the ancient Greeks, nature is _physis_ and _logos_ in one, a Heraclitean conflict of opposites admitting of no final resolution. In this sense nature itself is the possibiliz-ing power par excellence - the dark abyss, the yawning gap and at the same time imaginal and creative ground of everything. With this view of nature Heidegger is in effect returning to Plato the mystagogue. As we saw earlier, the Platonic world of myth is a mixed bag of the combination of contrary forces; it contains a residuum of unexplained brute fact, the "Errant Cause." There is an element of aimlessness and absurdity in our circling that cannot be completely subdued by the upward drive of Reason. Plato's Dimiurge is not an omnipotent God but in some degree restricted by the material at his disposal. In arranging the world he could not persuade Necessity to bring about a flawless product. He could only make the best he could of a not wholly suitable material. The result was not a perfect world but merely "as good as possible."[78]

Thus the World Soul is somewhat "fallen" - not because of a willful and "free" action of its own, but rather because the Demiurge is from the start limited by the pre-existent stuff which contains irrational elements. Demiurge is refreshingly unlike the Jehovah of Genesis who creates a perfect world (valde bonum) out of nothing and, having later realized that he didn't quite succeed, became ill-tempered. Plato's God is essentially an Artist, the Great Imaginer for whom the only attainable "perfection" consists in a combination of light and shade. The Demiurge's work is genuinely creative ("possibilizing") precisely because of this mixture of light and darkness, for what he thus creates is a world of images and imagination. The Great Imaginer images the world. And images, as we have shown, are never "perfect" because their dwelling place is an open region - that possibilizing space of spiritualized matter and materialized spirit from which our notions of mind and matter, being and becoming arise.

It came to me as a surprise that an obscure Iranian Sufist of the seventeenth century by the name of Mullā Sadrā reduplicates almost verbatim Heidegger's dictum concerning the priority of possibility to actuality. According to Sadrā, in the world of archetypal imagination (Malakūt) "virtuality [possibility] is ontologically, and ontically, antecedent to the act." Whereas here, i.e., in the world of empirics "the act is nobler than virtuality because it is its fulfillment," in the "other" world "virtuality is nobler than the act because it is that which produces the act."[79]

What Mullā Sadrā calls "virtuality" is in effect the state of subtle or animated matter. This matter is not extrinsic to the soul or separated from the soul's own act of existing, but is created by the soul itself. In the world of <u>Malakūt</u> everything to which man aspires, is instantaneously present to him. "To picture his desire is itself to experience the real presence of its object."[80] In Heidegger's terms, thought and being are inseparable because they are both rooted in the possibilizing power of <u>physis</u> which, in conjunction with <u>logos</u>, constitutes the imaginal ground of all things. Ontologically speaking, therefore, for something to be possible, that is, to desire something is <u>eo</u> <u>ipso</u> to become what is desired; the desirable is the real. Virtuality, <u>i.e.</u>, the state of our desires (instantaneously) produces the object of desire. To repeat our earlier statement: archetypal imagination posits real <u>imaginal</u> being; it is pregnant with reality.

To say, then, with Heidegger that "higher than actuality stands possibility" means that imagination in its archetypal capacity is a cosmic power subtilizing all life and making the "impossible," <u>not</u> <u>possible</u>, but real and actual. In other words, what is possible for imagination is more real, "higher" and "nobler" than what is actually possible in the so called real life. In this role imagination is like the court jester who sees through the Emperor's clothes. Jesters are tolerated by the kings for the contrast they provide to a life that otherwise would be intolerable in its sheer and uninterrupted pomposity. The court jester is the "possibility" for the kingliness of the king and in that sense higher and nobler than and ontologically prior to the "actual" king. He is the subtle fellow who knows the secret desires of the king and converts them instantaneously into the reality of his own presence.

V: BACK TO IMAGES

NOTES

[1]Watkins, Waking Dreams, p. 99.

[2]Charles T. Tart, PSI, Scientific Studies of the Psychic Realm (New York: E.P. Dutton, 1977), p. 216.

[3]Hillman, Re-Visioning Psychology, p. x.

[4]See Casey, "Imagining, Perceiving, and Thinking," Humanitas, Journal of the Institute of Man, Vol. XIV, No. 2, p. 179.

[5]James Hillman, "Archetypal Psychology," article for the Enciclopedia Italiana--1980, p. 7. Private copy.

[6]Berry, "An Approach to the Dream," p. 61.

[7]Ibid., p. 63.

[8]See Gombrich, Art and Illusion, p. 13, 127.

[9]Ibid., p. 141; cf. p. 127, 139.

[10]Cassirer, The Philosophy of Symbolic Forms 2, p. 25; cf. p. 36.

[11]Ibid., Vol. 3, p. 78.

[12]Quoted in Gombrich, Art and Illusion, p. 94.

[13]It is customary to trace this view to the Greek thinker Xenophanes of Colophon of the middle sixth century who, in his opposition to anthropomorphism, is reported to have said: "If oxen or lions had hands which enabled them to draw and paint pictures as men do, they would portray their gods as having bodies like their own: horses would portray them as horses, and oxen as oxen" (fr. 6, The Presocratics, ed. Philip Wheelwright. The Bobbs-Merrill Co., Inc., 1975, p. 33).

[14]Friedrich Nietzsche, Menschliches allzu Menschliches, Musarions-Ausgabe, Vol. IX. (Munich, 1928).

[15]Kathleen Raine, "What is Man," Lindisfarne Letter 9, p. 32.

[16] See "Le Chef d'Oeuvre Inconnue," *Etudes Philosophiques* XVII (Paris, 1837).

[17] See G.S. Kirk and J.E. Raven, *The Pre-Socratic Philosophers* (Cambridge University Press, 1956), p. 209.

[18] The Romantic attitude toward dreams is comprehensively documented by Albert Beguin in his *L'âme romantique et le rêve* (Paris, Corti, 1960).

[19] Hillman, "Further Notes on Images," *Spring* 1978, p. 170-71.

[20] *Ibid.*, p. 193.

[21] See *Ibid.*, pp. 8-12; cf. pp. 75-79.

[22] Fr. 30. Cf. *CW* 6, par. III.

[23] Hillman, *The Dream and the Underworld*, p. 80.

[24] *Ibid.*, p. 13.

[25] It is generally overlooked that Freud's scientific concepts (such as "unconscious," "id." "death drive," etc.) are rooted in mythical thinking. Thus, as Gügenbühl-Craig once remarked, Freudians cannot properly understand Freud because they take him literally. "The Jungians may be better at understanding Freud because they can read him for his mythology" (quoted in Hillman, *The Dream and the Underworld*, p. 18).

[26] Hillman, *The Dream and the Underworld*, p. 30.

[27] *Ibid.*, p. 54.

[28] *Ibid.*, p. 133.

[29] *Ibid.*, p. 102.

[30] *Ibid.*, p. 61; cf. pp. 99-100.

[31] *Ibid.*, p. 138.

[32] Hillman, *The Myth of Analysis*, p. 184; cf. pp. 185-190.

[33] Hillman, *The Dream and the Underworld*, p. 96.

[34] *Ibid.*, pp. 137, 138, 139.

[35]Gaston Bachelard's main works are: On Poetic Imagination, tr. with an introd. by C. Gaudin (New York: Bobbs-Merrill Co., 1971); The Poetics of Space, tr. from the French by M. Jolas (Boston: Beacon Press, 1969); The Poetics of Reverie, tr. from the French by D. Russell (Boston: Beacon Press, 1971).

[36]Hillman, The Dream and the Underworld, pp. 128, 129.

[37]Letters of Rainer Maria Rilke, 1910-1924, tr. by J.B. Green and M.M.H. Norton (New York: W.W. Norton Co., 1947), pp. 373-74.

[38]Hillman, Suicide and the Soul, p. 76.

[39]Ibid., p. 71.

[40]Hillman, Re-Visioning Psychology, p. 209.

[41]Ibid., p. 209.

[42] Fr. 88 (Diels-Kranz). We are old and young, senex and puer throughout the course of life. See Section 6 of Hillman's "Senex and Puer," Eranos 1967, 36, pp. 334-343. Heraclitus makes the same point by identifying Hades, the god of death, and Dionysus, the god of vitality and life (fr. 15). Cf. Hillman's comment on this identification in The Myth of Analysis, pp. 277-78.

[43]Hillman, The Dream and the Underworld, pp. 277-78.

[44]Bachelard, On Poetic Imagination, pp. 97-98.

[45]Hillman, The Dream and the Underworld, pp. 12, 122.

[46]Ibid., pp. 221-22, note 34. Cf. M. Stein, "Narcissus," Spring 1976, pp. 32-53.

[47]Ibid., p. 202.

[48]See Casey, Imagining, pp. 206, 213, 215; "Toward an Archetypal Psychology," Spring 1974, pp. 16-18; CW 6, par. 711.

[49]CW 8, par. 189.

[50]Henry Corbin, Creative Imagination in the Sufism of Ibn 'Arabi. Bollingen Series XCI (Princeton University Press, 1979), p. 180.

[51]Casey, "Toward an Archetypal Psychology," Spring 1974, p. 21.

[52] Casey, Imagining, pp. 172-73.

[53] Ibid., p. 167.

[54] Ibid., p. 171.

[55] Berry, "An Approach to the Dream," pp. 63-64.

[56] Ibid., p. 68.

[57] Casey, "Comparative Phenomenology of Mental Activity," p. 20.

[58] Heidegger, Being and Time, pp. 89-90.

[59] Casey, Imagining, p. 171.

[60] R.G. Collingwood, The Principles of Art (New York: Oxford University Press, 1958), p. 253.

[61] Casey, Imagining, p. 95.

[62] Ibid., p. 98.

[63] Ibid., p. 97.

[64] See Thomas A. Fay, Heidegger: The Critique of Logic (The Hague: Martinus Nijhoff, 1977), pp. 14-19; 26-35.

[65] Martin Heidegger, Poetry, Language, Thought, tr. by Albert Hofstadter (New York: Harper & Row, 1971), p. 177.

[66] Hillman, The Myth of Analysis, p. 280.

[67] Vincent Vycinas, Earth and Gods; An Introduction to the Philosophy of Martin Heidegger (The Hague: Martinus Nijhoff, 1969), p. 209.

[68] Hillman, The Myth of Analysis, p. 184.

[69] Martin Heidegger, On the Way to Language, tr. by Peter D. Herz (New York: Harper & Row, 1971), p. 163; cf. p. 164, 171, 197.

[70] Martin Heidegger, An Introduction to Metaphysics, tr. by Ralph Manheim (New Haven: Yale University Press, 1959), p. 101.

[71] See Ralph Powell, O.P., "The Late Heidegger's Omission of the Ontic-Ontological Structure of Dasein," in Heidegger and the Path of Thinking, ed. John Sallis (Pittsburgh, Pa.: Duquesne University Press, 1970), pp. 116-137.

[72] E.A. Burtt, The Metaphysical Foundations of Modern Science (London: Routledge and Kegan Paul, 1959), pp. 236-37.

[73] Werner Jaeger, Aristotle, tr. by Richard Robinson (Oxford, 1934), p. 384.

[74] Aristotle, Metaphysis 10 32b; cf. Werner Marx, Heidegger and the Tradition, tr. by Theodore Kisiel and Murray Green (Evanston: Northwestern University Press, 1971), p. 106.

[75] James Hillman, "Silver and the White Earth," Spring 1980, p. 46.

[76] Bundy, "The Theory of Imagination," p. 278.

[77] Heidegger, Being and Time, p. 63.

[78] Plato's Cosmology, tr. by Francis MacDonald Cornford (Indianapolis: The Bobbs-Merrill Co., Inc., 1957), p. 173.

[79] Henry Corbin, Spiritual Body and Celestial Earth. Bollingen Series XCI: 2 (Princeton University Press, 1977), p. 167.

[80] Ibid., p. 166.

Death and Wholeness

The meaning behind Heidegger's recasting of the traditional distinction of potentiality and actuality can be best illustrated by his analysis of human existence in terms of death. In the state of what Heidegger calls the inauthentic mode of existence (das Man, everydayness) death is treated as a future actuality, a something that happens mainly to others; "one dies," we say, or "there is death in the world." The usual strategy is to consider death as an objective event, a fact that befalls us. We fear death either as an imminent or distant accident that, fundamentally speaking, can be avoided. "One dies" always by accident, be it a plane crash, illness or decrepitude. Death for most people in our society is "unnatural."

An authentic awareness of death, according to Heidegger, implies that the possibility of death is an actual constituent of my existence. Man is a being-toward-death or, as the proverb says, as soon as we are born we are old enough to die. Thus the "possibility" of death is not in the same category as the idea of the "not-yet-actual." Rather this "possibility" is an illustration of the essential way in which a human being exists, i.e., as "a being towards possibilities, as a relationship to them, as constantly 'ahead of itself'"[1]

In the classical phrase of Heidegger, "the essence of man lies in his existence."[2] This means that man, unlike a stone lying on the ground in its full weight, exists ex-centrically in the openness of being or, as we would have to say it from the psychological standpoint, in the open space or the mid-world of the soul. Man is essentially a possibility, an extatic tending toward what exceeds him. As Hölderlin, the beloved poet of Heidegger, said, "we are nothing; what we seek is all."[3]

Contrary to the traditional definition, man is not a computation of essence (soul and body) or a zoon logon echon (rational animal) standing at the pinnacle of creation, but transcendence pure and simple. To be a human being is to be a creature of distance, i.e., essentially, constitutionally ex-static. The essence of man lies in his possibilizing thrust toward future, in being out toward possibilities which must be maintained as possibilities without ever becoming fully actualized.

In Homer's mythical Greece the idea that man is not destined to reach the status of a fully realized immortality which is reserved for the gods only, but must forge his own kind of immortality, is exemplified in the story of Odysseus. Unlike the Near Eastern king-hero Gilgamesh who had wandered in search of everlasting life and had returned home only because he had failed to find it, Odysseus rejected the offer of everlasting life made to him by the goddess Calypso. Instead of remaining on a deserted island with the goddess where he could have enjoyed indefinite prolongation of his life, he chose the company of his own wife, Penelope - the mixed bag of happiness and misery that is the lot of the soul. The Greek poet Pindar seems to be pointing in the same direction: "Seek not, my soul, the life of the immortals, but enjoy to the full the resources that are within thy reach."[4]

Farther to the East, the ancient Chinese book of oracles I Ching (Hexagram 60, called Chieh, Limitation) states that limitlessness in life - human and natural - does not exist and is evil. Just as nature has its limitations - the stars have their appointed courses, the tree does not grow beyond a certain height - so human life is only meaningful if it has also its limitations, its right measure. Thus the Hexagram 60 reads that "the superior man creates number and measure, and examines the nature of virtue and correct conduct." It is also noteworthy that in China the symbol of Eros is the rainbow because it connects heaven and - earth, the great principles of Yin and

142

Yang. Rainbow symbolizes (or, as we should say, is) imagination. And so, as we read in the Sumerian poems (not reproduced in the Akkadian epic), it was only when Gilgamesh was on his death bed and had a dream that it was revealed to him that the gods had not destined him to eternal life.[5] Reason (the Apollonian ego) wants eternal life, but only dream images know the foolishness of reason.

What is, then, the reach of the soul? According to Hillman, man exists in the midst of psyche and psyche extends beyond the nature of man: "the soul has inhuman reaches."[6] Heidegger, on his part, has described the epistemological problem of the relationship between subject and object by saying that "Dasein is the Being of this between."[7] Elsewhere he states that "the question concerning man's nature is not a question about man."[8] Or, even more tersely: "the essence of man is nothing human."[9]

What we may gather from these pronouncements is something highly paradoxical: we are truly human only by surpassing our mere humanness, that is, by de-identifying ourselves with the ego-centered consciousness. But what has death and dying to do with this self-transcendence? The answer is: everything. For to conceive death as an actual constituent of life or, in Heidegger's gnomic phrase, as "the possibility of the impossibility of existence,"[10] implies that the elimination or "conquest" of death would be eo ipso a destruction of man as man, that is, of man in his essentially ecstatic nature.

Thus to be a man and to be capable of death is one and the same thing. Death is an opening toward transcendence: we transcend our empirical existence only because we die. We are authentically human because we are mortal, not mortal because we are human. It is not that to be a man is to die, but the other way round: to die is to be a man. By the same token, to die "like a man" is a heroic stance only if it also means a renunciation of super-human heroism.

To most people and philosophers death means either demise, a wasting away or transportation to some other-worldly sphere where death shall be no more. It is seldom realized, however, that both of these hypotheses lead to the cessation of human personality as we claim to know it. For to become food for worms or to be transmogrified into a spiritual being enjoying sempiternal bliss must be profoundly irrelevant to what I am here and now. There is no continuity in either case. Crudely put, somebody else is having a ball at my expense.

The question of personal immortality is a badly posed question creating in its wake a false problem. We are in effect asked to provide guaranties for the continuation and permanence of something which is far from being continuous and permanent to begin with. In other words, we want to preserve and eternalize something we do not have. Hillman has expressed the same idea by saying that the psyche's "existence in 'another life' cannot be proved any more than the existence of the soul in this life can be proved."[11] Man, as we emphasized earlier, is not one but many, and a unified personality is at best a desideratum, not a fact. What is called "the self" is a rendezvous of many people, an empty "place" where many selves come to mingle and depart. As the Polish poet Czeslaw Milosz has said, "our house is open, there are no keys in the doors, and invisible guests come in and out at will" (Bells in Winter, "Ars Poetica").

We wear many masks and the soul that sees through them, particularly the soul that nightly descends into the underworld of dreams, seems to be curiously indifferent to the question of personal survival.[12] It is as if the soul "knows better" because it is better equipped to deal with this question than the "time binding" ego. Mustn't we say, therefore, that the soul is alive - alive all over (self-moving) - precisely because it is a "potentially" dying soul? Jung has expressed this paradox in his Memories as follows:

> The feeling of the infinite ... can be attained only if
> we are bounded to the utmost ... only consciousness
> of our narrow confinement in the self forms the link to
> the limitlessness of the unconscious. In such awareness
> we experience ourselves concurrently as limited and
> eternal, as both the one and the other. In knowing
> ourselves to be unique in our personal combination -
> that is, ultimately limited - we possess also the capacity
> for becoming conscious of the infinite. But only
> then."[13]

Jung is alluding here to the Heraclitean and Plationic idea,
elaborated and amplified in archetypal psychology, that to the
soul, peaks and valleys are equally necessary, that the soul is,
in fact, made up of these ups and downs, and that, deprived of
the one or the other, it courts death. The soul is in love with
the unifying peaks of the mystic and the saint as well as with
the perishable and telluric realities. Yet the soul's most
passionate and enduring love belongs to the circulation between
these two poles and to the chamelionic path of the uroboros.
This must be so because, strictly speaking, there is no other
path. Circulation is the soul's destination/destiny and her most
passionate love is amor fati. To paraphrase a famous saying,
there is no greater love than the love of your "enemy" ...

We must return now to our previous analysis of the phenomenon of death. Following the lead of Heidegger and Hillman, we
stated that death in its vulgar sense is an accident inflicted
upon us from without, something that strikes exogenously as an
outer force. Death must be undergone, suffered or, more
nobly, "accepted" with stoic equanimity. Adopting a lofty tone,
we often speak of death as the fulfillment of life, i.e., as
"actualization" of our "potential" for dying. Yet how often do
we realize that behind such sublime language there is still lurking
the old Aristotelian substance which is essentially indifferent to
its potential manifestation and that, consequently, death is still

something which may or may not happen? But of course we know it "happens." So we have been taught to assume that it can happen only in two possible ways: either as a total cessation ending in putrefaction or as a transition to an otherworldly state of deathlessness. What we seem to have overlooked is that in both cases death, instead of being an essential part of life, is only <u>additive</u> to life. What is added to life in the first case is simply more of the same, assuming, of course, that life, ending in the destruction of our most precious hopes and aspirations, is bound to be no more than a cruel charade, a series of isolated, mechanical happenings during which we manage to stay more or less alive. Thus what "happens" in death is only that a "more" is added to what we already are in life. It's like the old French saying, <u>plus</u> <u>ça</u> <u>change</u> <u>plus</u> <u>c'est</u> <u>la</u> <u>meme</u> <u>chose</u>. When we "pass away," only more "deadness" accrues to the previous state of deadness, ataraxia, boredom, isolation. In this sense death is an event to be dreaded because it is the most uneventful event of our lives, the ultimate bore. Death cancels all eventing; as the ultimate non-event it is utterly meaningless. In our bewilderment we occasionally pronounce it "absurd," especially when "one dies" young or "by accident(!)."

What is added to "life after life," <u>i.e.</u>, to the life in the supraterrestrial realms, is also more of the same, only in the reverse sense. Now there is so much life that one is bound to wonder what a normal person can possibly do with it. If, on the other hand, one is not supposed to be altogether normal in these realms, then, as I already indicated, the continuity between "here" and "there" breaks down and somebody else is doing out there whatever he or she is doing out there. The crucial point in this connection is that to envision after-life in the sense of unalloyed bliss is as distortive of the real nature of death as to "accept" death in the equanimous style of a Stoic or a latter-day humanist. What is denied in both instances is the Platonic

146

"Errant Cause," the pathology of death, its unmitigated horror and awesomeness. For death is not only natural, but also un-natural, not only something to be accepted and reconciled with, but also to be despised and rejected. To what preposterous lengths the fantasy of reconciliation and fulfillment in the "Wonderful World of Death" (the title of a book) can go is shown by writers who speak of "the thrill of death" and who have glorified the after-life trip to the point of making it sound like an amusement-park ride.

Prima facie it seems surprising that Heidegger too has repeatedly stated that death belongs to man's "wholeness." In this he concurs with Rilke whom he quotes to the effect that death is not the opposite of life, but rather its "completion to ... plentitude, to the real, whole, and full sphere and globe of being."[14] Heidegger's own thought, however, is more nuanced. He calls death "the shrine of nothingness" which surrounds and holds everything in unity.[15] "Nothing" or "nothingness," in Heidegger's vocabulary, is not a vague conceptual opposite of Being in its totality or an object of some sort, but the abyss, the yawning gap on which everything rests; it is the Dionysian physis which we identified with the subtilizing power of imagina-tion. Death as "the possibility of the impossibility of existence"[16] or as "the shrine of nothingness" is not nothing-at-all, a pure, complete nihil absolutum, but precisely that which constitutes the background and reality of our experience.

So it is only in this sense that we may speak of death as giving life its fullness. For the kind of "fullness" or "wholeness" we reach in death is not a last perfecting stroke or a subsumption of scattered bits of life. On the contrary, it is a confirmation of man's radical finitude, an enshrining of time's transiency in all forms. From this standpoint, death as a separate event or fact, quite simply, is not. If death is that which gives life its fullness, then patently there is no life without death and no

147

death without life. The integral being of man, therefore, can only be described as life-in-death and death-in-life. In Heidegger's words:

> To die means to be capable of death as death. Only man dies. The animal perishes. Death is the shrine of Nothing, that is, of that which in every respect is never something that merely exists, but which presences, even as the mystery of Being itself.[17]

Here we are once again reminded of Plato who describes Eros as the great daimon midway between gods (immortals) and mortals: "Being midway between the two it fills up the space completely; so that the whole is bound together to itself in one" (Symposium, 202 e). That Eros fills up the space between immortals and mortals means that in our innermost psychic being we are both mortal and immortal; we are addicted to both earthly and heavenly love. In Goethe's Faust it is Mefisto, the "godlike companion" who initiates Faust, the weary scholar, into the world of Eros and leads him into the depths and down to the Mothers. Mefisto is the strange "son of chaos" symbolizing that aspect of the psyche which has preserved a living relationship with nature. Nature, however must not be understood here as the soil beneath our feet, the tangible and empirical earth or the "natural nature" (the Roman tellus and the Greek gē), but rather as chthon, representing the invisible underground, the realm of Hades, who is also the brother of Zeus, the reigning deity of the upperworld. Chthon is Dionysian and, as we saw, the chthonian depths are not without their own logos. This is as much as saying that the psyche participates in both - the world of light and the world of darkness. To be sure, when we die the body returns to the soil (gē), but the psyche will not go with it, for it has a synchronous existence in the underworld of the dark-faced Hades. It is not that the psyche will eventually go there; it is already there. It exists simultaneously in the upperworld of light and ego-consciousness and in the chthonic

148

underworld of quasi-conscious luminousness.

Even more crucially, the underworld is pictured in Greek mythology as a complete counterpart to the upperworld. According to Hillman, "the shadow world in the depths is an exact replica of daily consciousness; only it must be perceived differently."[18] The shadow world of images is accessible only to imagination because it represents a "wholly psychic perspective, where one's entire mode of being has been desubstantiated, killed of natural life." We are "in" it exactly as we are "in" life, as whole persons, but - "devoid of life," i.e., liberated from our entaglements in the literalistic perspectives of the so called real life. "The underworld is a realm of only psyche, a purely psychic world."[19] Joseph Campbell, describing the pictures of animals and men found in the Paleolithic caves of Southern France and Northern Spain (c. 30.000 to 10.000 B.C.) writes:

> It is amazing, how, when one is down in those caves, in the absolute dark, with all sense of direction lost, the light world above is but a memory and, curiously, but a shadow world. The reality is down here. The herds and all the lives up there are secondary: it is from here [i.e., from their images] that they derive, and to here that they will return.[20]

What the mystagogue Campbell and the archetypalist Hillman are saying is that the shadow world is the world of essential images and that we perceive things in our "normal" world only because they are first imagined in the "other world" - "the reality is down here." The shadow is not a more or less faithful reflection or an illusion of the real thing in the sense of Platonic idealism, but, in Hillman's words, "the very stuff of the soul, the interior darkness that pulls downward out of life and keeps one in relentless connection with the underworld."[21]

Time and Eternity

It is often assumed that Plato had provided the essential rationale of the symbolic mode in the Western tradition. The Demiourgos, says the philosopher in Timaeus (37 D.),

> took thought to make, as it were, a moving likeness of eternity; and, at the same time that he ordered the Heaven, he made, of eternity that abides in unity, an everlasting likeness [eikon] moving according to number - that to which we have given the name Time.[22]

Time, according to Plato, is an imperfect sphere, forever yearning toward eternity (the spheric perfection) but never quite making it. Time, therefore, can only be a symbol, i.e., an imitation or re-presentation of eternity, but never a closed and complete sphere of eternity. Note that, in this view, time is not a mere illusion but is related to eternity and it is this relation that justifies the symbolic character of time and of everything that is subjected to it. The lapse of time which haunts man's consciousness is not sheer evanescence and perishing: nature and human productions point beyond themselves and symbolize with a spiritual world of eternal archetypes. In spite of the gap between the spiritual (timeless) and the natural (temporal), the latter is still - even though we do not know how - founded upon the spiritual, and all its forms and all its processes have a counterpart there. The break is not complete and the human condition in this world is best described as a state of exile from the spiritual world to which we are native.

Now I contend that archetypal psychology, starting from its roots in Plato's myth of the soul (not from Plato the rationalist who created the world of eternal Ideas) on the one had, and from Jung's identification of soul with images and imagination, on the other, has developed a position which makes it no longer necessary to perform periodic genuflections before the imposing edifice of a symbolically constructed universe. Hillman's return to images and to the imaginal soul annuls the gap between the eternal and the temporal. Time is no longer a moving likeness of eternity but the time of the soul.

To stress the radical character of this view of time one might suggest that in archetypal psychology, the Timaean cart is put before the horse, implying that eternity derives its reality from time. Already Blake had declared that eternity is in love with the productions of time because without the contributions of time, eternity is sterile. Jung seems to corroborate this by saying that timelessness is nothing to yearn for, since it is merely a state in which the insane live. Psychotic patients "never find their way back from their dreams. For them the hands of the world's clock remain stationary; there is no time, no further development."[23]

I have already referred to Jung's expression "relative eternity" by which he means that "psyche does not exist wholly in time and space." The unconscious psyche may exist in a state of "relative spacelessness and timelessness," i.e., in "a relative non-separation from other psyches, or a oneness with them."[24] Minimally Jung's meaning is that psychic eternity is inseparable from time and temporal existence.

To put this in the context of our previous discussion of death-in-life and life-in-death, it may be said that "immortality," far from being some sort of innate possession, is something that may arise within the cincture of time and mortality, a "something" we create out of a simultaneous acceptance of and rebellion against mortality. In other words, immortality, if the word is to have any meaning at all, must be a product of poiésis, that is, of soul-making. One can only, so to speak, poetisize oneself into "eternal life." And we must add that the product of this "making" is never finished or ever-lasting: like music or a Hamlet on the stage, it lasts only so long as it is being produced.

Jung has avoided writing expressly about life after death,

preferring to "tell stories - mythologize."[25] "When I speak of things after death, I am speaking but of inner promptings, and can go no further than to tell you dreams and myths that relate to this subject."[26] Jung's dream life seems to confirm our contention that eternity needs time or, more specifically, that the "dead," because they lack incarnational experience, show a strong interest in the affairs of the living. It is as if, says Jung, the acts and experiences in time and space, were decisive for the departed ones. In contrast to the traditional view that the dead know far more than we, Jung speculates that the dead know nothing beyond what they knew at the moment of death. It is for this reason that they endeavor to penetrate into life in order to share in the knowledge of men. "I frequently had the feeling that they are standing directly behind us, waiting to hear what answer we give to them, and what answer to destiny."

Jung also accepts the idea of the evolution of the soul after death. A year after his wife's death he awoke one night and knew that he had been with her in the south of France where she had been engaged in studies of the Grail. Jung understood this as meaning that "my wife was continuing after death to work on her further spiritual development."[27] In a like manner, Socrates (in the Apology), speaking in hypothetical terms about the fate of the soul in the beyond, says that the most important thing in the beyond is the continuation of a life of inquiry into the human condition. In Plato's view, the practice of philosophy - "adorning one's soul with the ornaments proper to it" (Phaedo, 114 E) - is the most fitting preparation for death.

Transformation

Speculating on the nature of the post mortem state, Jung writes that he "cannot conceive of any other form of existence except a psychic one ... Psychic existence, and above all the inner images ... supply the material for all mythic speculations about life in the hereafter, and I imagine that life as a continuation in the world of images" (emphasis mine). It is also significant that with increasing age, contemplation, and reflection, the inner images play an ever greater part in man's life. As the Bible says: "Your old men shall dream dreams" (Acts 2: 17; Joel 2: 28). The psyches of the old men have not become wooden or entirely petrified. Rather, "in the old age one begins to let memory images unroll before the mind's eye, and, musing, to recognize oneself in the inner and outer images of the past. This is like preparation for an existence in the hereafter, just as, in Plato's view, philosophy is a preparation for death."[28]

If we now bring together Jung's statement that life after death is a continuation in the world of images and his preference for mythologizing (telling "likely stories") about the hereafter, what we have is that the post mortem state is essentially an imaginal state. In Hillman's terms, it is a "wholly psychic perspective" devoid of a natural life. But, of course, a "wholly psychic" existence is not equivalent to a wholly "spiritual" condition. "Psychic" in our vocabulary stands for the intermediary realm of imagination where both spirit and matter are subtilized. Using the same line of reasoning, we may suggest that in a psychic condition time is eternalized and eternity temporalized.

According to esoteric teachings, the most important consequence of this transformation is that our inner states - emotions, moods, feelings - are no longer purely "subjective" (hidden, suppressed) but produce changes in our demeanor: we are what we mean and we mean what we are. This is only to be expected since the imaginal body cannot possibly behave differently from the images of which it is made up. Moreover, as far as we can gather from the descriptions of those who have "seen," the behavior of the imaginal body is truly ecological: it affects in a decisive manner the constitution of the outer world as well.

Emanuel Swedenborg (1688-1772), known also as the "Plato of the North," points out that what corresponds to time and space in "heaven" is change of inner states: spiritually rich innter states are reflected in an environment that is gorgeous and rich; barren inner states - in barren environment. This is to say that our tendency to see and experience what reflects our wishes - the tendency first to imagine then perceive - is even more accentuated in the "other world" where the character of the spirits is more nearly an extension of their inner experience. Thus "all spirits in the hells ... appear in the form of their evil; for every one is an image of his evil, since with everyone the interiors and exteriors make one, and the interiors are visibly exhibited in the exteriors, which are the face, the body, and the speech, and the gesture. Their quality is therefore known at sight."[29] The same principle applies to the heavenly states. We all create and eventually join the world of our own choices. In this sense life in "the Beyond" would be an essentification of our real (inner) selves, or, in Swedenborg's terminology, of our "ruling love" - the desire of our thoughts when we are unrestrained by any social bonds and considerations.

Like the Buddha, Swedenborg maintains that man builds his own heaven and hell out of the knowledge and experience he obtained here on earth. Every least thing that we have thought, willed, spoken, done or even heard and seen, is engraved in our souls and can never be erased. Physical death in itself, therefore, does not change the human personality. It simply reveals and brings out into the light of open day what we really are in our innermost being.

The Swedenborgian heaven and hell are fully imaginal states inhabited by real people - real as only images can be real, i.e., diaphonous subtle bodies in which the inner and the outer exactly correspond to each other. It is a dream-world peopled by real dream-bodies, a world of shadows containing the seed forms (archetypal images) of our empirical existence. As a Kalahary Bushman once said: "There is a dream dreaming us." It is not only we who imagine our dead relatives and friends in dreams; they too dream and imagine us. We are all dreaming one another's dreams and are parts of a Dream dreaming us. Life and death are not two independent powers but simultaneous and interpenetrating realities; the one does not negate the other. As the grain must die that it may be transformed into new life, so death is a continuous transformation <u>occurring</u> <u>within</u> <u>life</u>.

The idea of the interdependence of the living and the dead is crystallized in the widespread motif of the Community of the Dead. For example, among the Baja of the Middle Sudan and the Nser in the Cameroon, it is held that the dead form a community and that this community is active in the realm of the living. Edgar Herzog, the author of <u>Psyche</u> <u>and</u> <u>Death</u>, sees this motif as a development of the idea that "it is through awareness of death that man comes to feel that he transcends the limits of his earthly existence."[30] It is as if the "untutored savages" of Baja and Nser had prescience of Heidegger when he states that the experience of death is a prerequisite for being fully human. Herzog echoes the Heideggerian and Hillmanian line of thought in the following pregnant passage pointing to the coinherence of life and death.

> Becoming and transformation are tasks imposed on man by Fate, working both from within and without him, and this is something which man becomes aware of at the turning points, the crises of his existence. In so far as man experiences such crises with anxiety and under the image of inescapable death he also experiences himself as one disposed by nature to transcend his existence as it is at any moment and to experience and express previously unknown possibilities.[31]

NOTES

[1]Heidegger, Being and Time, p. 43.

[2]Ibid., p. 67.

[3]Friedrich Hölderlin, Feldauswhal (Stuttgart: Cotta Verlag, 1942), p. 76.

[4]Pindar, Pythian Odes III 186 (183).

[5]See J.B. Pritchard, Ancient Near Eastern Texts (Princeton, 1955), p. 50 ff.

[6]See Hillman, Re-Visioning Psychology, p. 173.

[7]Heidegger, Being and Time, p. 170.

[8]Heidegger, Discourse on Thinking, tr. by John M. Anderson and E. Hans Freund (New York: Harper Colophon Books, 1966), p. 78.

[9]Heidegger, Nietzsche II, p. 377; cf. Being and Time, pp. 89-90.

[10]Heidegger, Being and Time, p. 262.

[11]Hillman, Suicide and the Soul, p. 67.

[12]See CW 8, pars. 809; 380; 377; 645; Hillman, Suicide and the Soul, p. 69.

[13]C.G. Jung, Memories, Dreams, Reflections, p. 325.

[14]Letter of January 6, 1923, in Insel-Almanach 1938, p. 108. Insel Verlag. Quoted in Heidegger's Poetry, Language, Thought, p. 124.

[15]Heidegger, Vorträge (Neske), p. 177.

[16]Heidegger, Being and Time, p. 262.

[17]Heidegger, Poetry, Language, Thought, p. 178.

[18]Hillman, The Dream and the Underworld, p. 55.

[19]Ibid., p. 46; cf. Corbin, Spiritual Body and Celestial Earth, p. 170.

[20] Joseph Campbell, "Joseph Campbell on the Great Goddess," Parabola, Vol. V, no. 4, p. 76.

[21] Hillman, The Dream and the Underworld, p. 56.

[22] Timaeus, 3 D, Cornford, p. 98.

[23] CW 3, par. 356.

[24] C. G. Jung Letters I, p. 256.

[25] C.G. Jung, Memories, Dreams, Reflections, p. 299.

[26] Ibid., p. 304.

[27] Ibid., p. 308, 309.

[28] Ibid., p. 319, 320.

[29] Emanuel Swedenborg, Heaven and its Wonders and Hell. Standard Edition (New York: Swedenborg Foundation, Inc., 1978), N. 553.

[30] Edgar Herzog, Psyche and Death, tr. by David Cox and Eugene Rolfe (New York: G.P. Putnam's Sons, 1967), p. 89.

[31] Ibid., p. 113.

PART TWO

I: PSYCHE AND PARAPSYCHOLOGY

The Rhapsodizing Science

The phenomenon of the subtle body has received the greatest professional attention in parapsychology (the term was coined by Emile Boirac) - a branch of experimental psychology which, since its inception at the beginning of the century, has been dedicated to the establishment of its credentials in the face of an overly skeptical and sometimes hostile scientific community. There is a touch of melancholy in this relentless effort, for, in our opinion, about the only positive results, achieved by psychical research, amount to no more than showing how the question of the subtle body should not be approached. I am saying this in full cognizance of the prodigious energy spent by the parapsychological workers in trying to "prove" the reality of a spiritual world; nor do I disparage their laudable intentions and the occasional genuine insights they have achieved against all the odds. It remains, however, that parapsychology can do no more than its method permits which, in the realm of the soul, is strictly speaking, nothing. Yet it is an instructive "nothing" and so, to use Heidegger's expression, not a nihil absolutuum. In a roundabout and tortuous way the psyche is served even when it eludes the precision instruments of professionals.

The most widely debated notion in parapsychological literature, dealing with the problem of the subtle body, is that of "psychic ether." The respected parapsychologist Hereward Carrington has defined the subtle (or astral) body as "the ethereal counterpart of the physical body, which it resembles and with which it normally coincides. It is thought to be composed of some semi-fluidic or subtle form of matter, invisible to the physical eye."[1] The psychic ether is supposed to be a kind of malleable substance capable of bridging the gap between matter and mind. It would also provide clues to a deeper understanding of such paranormal phenomena as healing by the use of hands, mesmerism, the nature of some types of insanity, dowsing, etc. According to R. Crookall, the psychic ether which he also calls "the vehicle of vitality" or "the etheric body" consists of "semi-physical" matter and must be distinguished from the "soul-body," made of a more subtle "semi-spiritual" substance.

> The vehicle of vitality is more or less closely enmeshed in, or interwoven with, the physical tissues, and therefore is projected, if at all, slowly and with difficulty; the Soul Body, on the other hand, is only partially incarnated and therefore projects easily and quickly. It will be clear that if these conceptions have some correspondence in truth ... then these particular 'doubles' are not, as is considered by some psychiatrists, mere mental images of physical bodies, but objective, though non-physical bodies.

Crookall, however, is not quite satisfied with this statement and goes on to point out that the 'doubles' are not of the same composition:

> Some consist of substance from the vehicle of vitality only (and these show no intelligence or initiative, being mere 'ghosts' of living men); many consist of the Soul Body only, with perhaps, the merest tincture of substance from the vehicle of vitality; some are composite, consisting of the Soul Body plus a significant part of the vehicle of vitality.[2]

Apparently it is only the lack of sufficiently developed tools that prevents Crookall and his colleagues from taking the next step which, I fancy, would consist in trying to measure the exact amount of the respective ingredients in various "doubles." Finally, one would be led to the formulation of certain "laws" according to which these bodies are supposed to behave, enabling the psychical researcher to manipulate their behavior along the lines of the Skinnerian principle of reinforcement of correct responses.

Clearly, parapsychological hypotheses about the subtle body as well as other "paranormal" occurrences (telepathy, clair-voyance, precognition, telekinesis, psychomentry, etc.) are bound up with a determined effort to explain these phenomena in strictly scientific terms and in accordance with the canons of a generally accepted scientific procedure. The commonly used blanket name for all these and other "extra-sensory" occurrences is <u>Psi</u> - coined from the 23d letter of the Greek alphabet to avoid the superstitious which is felt to be associated with the word "psychic." Most of what parapsychology regards as eviden-tial material for <u>post mortem</u> survival, either in the shape of a subtle body or in disembodied form, is derived from two sources: apparitions of or telepathic communications from the dead and mediumistic phenomena, especially the so called "cross-correspon-dence" evidence.[3]

It is not my intention to argue either for or against the claims of parapsychology concerning survival. I am interested solely in the dominant models or the root-metaphors which are at work in this field and which must be regarded as inseparable from the results that are expected to be forthcoming "in the predictable future." In other words, my aim is to describe and to reveal the guiding fantasies or the archetypal motives operating in parapsychology.

According to Hillman, the most persistent and deep-going fantasy of parapsychology is "<u>anti-matter</u> <u>fantansy</u>," manifesting itself "in the upward movement, the transcendence of the categories of matter (time, space and causality), in the immortal-ity drive, in the light, white ghosts without feet, in redemption through love."[4] Parapsychology is engaged in the activity of the Apollonian spirit - the nostalgia of the soul for peaks, ecstasy, sempiternal truth. To this end it has wholeheartedly adopted the methodology of sciences - the same methodology which has emboldened science to deal with <u>all</u> things in the universe as strictly material, measurable and observable entities. I am referring to the Newtonian model of science and its underlying materialistic monism. This method, broadly speaking, consists in devising "the simplest possible working model ... a calculus, preferably a mathematical calculus since that is at once impractical and precise." For this purpose the "subject" must be treated as irrelevant; all emotional, esthetic and moral elements (values) are cast aside: "only those variables are retained which lend themselves to quantitative and to mathematical deduction."[5] The ultimate goal of all scientific pursuit is not to describe or to understand things but to predict and to control them.

Admittedly the scientist must use his imagination to invent "new ideas." Once, however, these ideas are set into motion, the ambiguities, inherent in the initial play of imagination, must be eliminated as far as possible. J. Bronowski, a reputed biologist, has contrasted what he calls the "ascetic and implosive imagination" of science with "the prodigal explosive imagination of poetry." An experiement in science, unlike poetry, does not seek to exploit its ambiguities, but to minimize them.

> This is the paradox of imagination in science, that it has for its aim the impoverishment of imagination. By that outrageous phrase, I mean that the highest flight of scientific imagination is to weed out the proliferation of new ideas. In science, the grand vision is a miserly view, and a rich model of the universe is one which is as poor as possible in hypotheses.[6]

To put it in an even more drastic way, science operates with the speed and resilience of a preying mantis catching a fly: it uses imagination (whenever new discoveries are called for) in order to kill it.

The rigidly mechanistic outlook of modern science, developed during the nineteenth century, and its thorough-going materialistic monism is aptly described by Cyril Burt.

It assumed a single universal container, namely, the three-dimensional Euclidean space, and this was supposed to contain only a single type of substance, namely, matter in shape of indivisible, indestructible, and immutable atomic particles, each characterized by a single property, namely, mass, controlled by a single type of cause, namely, mechanical force operating by contact - all to be verified by a single type of observation, namely, measurements from 'pointer-readings,' with the result expressed by a single type of proposition, namely, a differential equation.

It is from this a priori monistic vantage point that the orthodox science rejects parapsychology, for the very notion of a paranormal process is incompatible with the clear and comprehensive concept of the universe, achieved by some three centuries of scientific inquiry. Scientists are skeptical about some of the conclusions reached by parapsychologists not because they fail to stand up to observational or experimental tests, but rather because these conclusions are flagrantly at variance with what is known of the unity and uniformity of nature. In order to counteract this global argument and to bolster its anti-materialistic outlook, parapsychology has chosen to exploit the discoveries of modern microphysics which allegedly have destroyed the mechanistic view of the universe. In place of solid atoms, rigorously obeying the laws of mechanics, scientists are now confronted with a group of elusive entities, electrons, protons, neutrons and positrons which, we are told, lacking all physical attributes, cannot be observed directly and whose behavior can only be assessed by statistics. We are also advised that matter and energy are identical, that the world of space and time, as we experience them, are illusory and so on.

If, then, argues the parapsychologist, science is on the verge of radically revising the very notion of what is matter and material, why not allow the same latitude to parapsychology when it claims that the phenomena of telepathy, etc., defy the laws of causal determination and de-materialize matter. As J.B. Rhine, the great pioneer of the discipline in the United States, puts it, "it is no great jump from the concept of energy as it now prevails in physical theory to the notion of a special state of energy that is not interceptible by any sense organ."[8] The reference is, of course, to the paradoxical neutrons and positrons which are said to travel momentarily backward in time and to pass through two holes at once - a feat which, as Cyril Burt has said, no ghost has equalled. Maybe so. The crucial question, however, is not whether positrons travel faster than ghosts or vice versa, but the way in which positrons as well as ghosts are approached (or seen) by the scientist and the experimental parapsychologist. As I pointed out a while ago, the basic approach adopted by parapsychology is that of traditional science consisting in controlled observation of and experimentation with nature and in the reduction of the so called secondary qualities (color, temperature, etc.) to quantity. This method cannot change without destroying the very heart of scientific enterprise. As Huston Smith has observed, "it is precisely from the narrowness of that method that its power derives, so that to urge its expansion is like recommending that the dentist's drill be broadened so it can churn a bit of butter on the side."[9] In Theodore Roszak's important book Where the Wasteland Ends, a broadened dentist's drill becomes "rhapsodic intellect" which would change the fundamental sensibility of scientific thought by subordinating it to contemplative encounters with nature where "everything echoes everything else."[10] I am convinced that this is no more than a pious hope. The scientist as scientist cannot change or enhance his organs of perception; he can only succeed in seeing more of the same (smaller and smaller objects with a microscope or faraway objects with a telescope) but never something essentially different. Whether he sees the infinitesimally small or the infinitesimally large, he still sees it as an object because he looks at it in the same quantifying way and with the same prismatic eye.

164

As Goethe knew, "everything factual is already theory," which means that we find what we look for.

Heidegger has shown that the methodology of science is based on a sort of approach or explanatory scheme which is designed to convert whatever is studied into something in space, located "over there" and subsisting separately from and over against us. It makes no difference whether the thing in question is a chair, a man, an atom, a cell, a "sense datum," a "body." For example, we say that a piece of chalk takes up a certain space or encloses a certain space by its surface, in itself, as its interior. But, then, "what does the interior of the chalk look like?" asks Heidegger. Let us see. We break it into two pieces. Are we now at the interior? Obviously not. The pieces of chalk are smaller but what we expected to be the interior turns out to be only an exterior lying further back. We could continue this process of breaking up the chalk until it had become a little pile of powder. Under a microscope we could still break up these tiny grains ad infinitum. "In any case," says Heidegger, "such breaking up never yields anything but what was already there ... whether this piece of chalk is four centimeters or .004 milimeters only makes a difference in how much but not in what (essence)."

According to Heidegger, modern physics and chemistry can never reach beyond the sphere of mechanics. The relations between matter and space are fundamentally the same even after Niels Bohr exhibited his model of the atom (1913).

> What keeps a place occupied, takes up space, must itself be extended. Our question has been what the interior of a physical body looks like, more exactly, the space 'there.' The result is: this interior is always again an exterior for the smaller and smaller particles.

What Heidegger is saying is that the "interior" of nature, if such an "interior" exists, constitutes a boundary across which science, in the strictest sense, cannot penetrate. Science can offer no direct insight into the "inner" life of things and organisms.

A similar conclusion has been reached by C.J. Ducasse, a philosopher who has also contributed to the "discernment of spirits" within the field of parapsychology. Ducasse corroborates Heidegger's contention by pointing out that the subatomic entities - electrons, protons, mesons - of present day theoretical physics are still material even though they are not directly perceptible at all. Their materiality derives from the fact that they are held to be "constituents of publicly perceptible objects - such as stones, water, wood, animal bodies, and so on - which are what the expression 'material world' basically denotes."[12] Furthermore, the essentially material nature of the sub-atomic particles would not be altered even if we assume that some day they will be analyzed into more clearly elementary properties that could account for extra-sensory perception, psychokinesis and other "paranormal" phenomena.

As it turns out, the parapsychological anti-materialism is a hybrid, something in the order of a paranormal materialism or simply the old epiphenomenalism adorned with spiritual trimmings. Moreover, a universe conceived along the lines of such truncated metaphysics would have to be as deterministic as the universe of orthodox materialism. For in psychological terms, it is indifferent whether the determining causes are material or spiritual - they are still "causes." In Ducasse's words, "a psychological robot would be just as much a robot as would a physical one."[13]

The quandary in which parapsychology finds itself is due to divided loyalties. On the one hand, it adheres to a materialistic and mechanistic metaphysics which has remained constant throughout the "revolutionary discoveries" of Niels-Bohr, Heisenberg and Einstein and whose methodology is designed to deal only with what is quantifiable. On the other hand, parapsychology is guided by a fantasy (metaphysics) which assumes the primacy of mind over matter. What we thus have is a clash at the level of metaphysical assumptions - a clash which would be nothing extraordinary in itself were it not for the fact that in our case the conflict is taking place within one and the same discipline. So one witnesses the spectacle of a science - called "parapsychology" - employing methods current in other sciences in order to invalidate the basic assumptions of these sciences. That could be merely hilarious.

What is depressing is that parapsychology, by adopting scientific methodology, has unwittingly allied itself with the ideology of power and a totalized world view known as scientism. The latter has been correctly identified by Roszak as "idolatrous consciousness," i.e., "application of the objective mode of consciousness to the whole of human experience."[14] Scientism is essentially an apotheosis of mind bent on subjugating all things in the universe to the human will, the Promethean drive to predict and to control until, as the She-Ancient in G.B. Shaw's play Back to Methuselah, presages, "the day will come when there will be no people, only thought." To the extent that parapsychology unconsciously shares this vision, it can only end up in the construction of a spiritual robot - a gentle and callous monster, a laboratory saint whose "peace of mind" (that much wonted "peace that passeth understanding") would resemble that of a vampire, the animated corpse.

Soul in Parapsychology

From the perspective of Jungian thought the fatal weakness of parapsychology lies in its failure to recognize the psyche as the middle region between spirit and matter. In an attempt to bypass dualism implicit in the Cartesian mind-body conundrum, parapsychology has opted for mentalistic monism holding that

167

mind or spirit is the only, or at least the most fundamental, reality in man and in the universe as a whole. If, however, one is not unreservedly wedded to some form of "pure" mentalism, it is well nigh impossible to sidestep completely the question of the existence and the role of matter. Specifically, what is the role of the brain in the process of sensory and "extra-sensory" perception?

As I pointed out at the beginning of this inquiry, a number of parapsychologists hold the Bergsonian and Jamesian doctrine (transmission theory) that the brain is an organ, not for generating consciousness, but for transmitting, limiting and directing it. In this view the function of the brain ("the stomach of the soul," V. Nobakov) is mainly to select, decode, classify and abstract the mass of information that constantly bombards the senses, i.e., to make this information meaningful. The brain acts as a filter rather than an originator of thought, transmitting only those aspects of the material environment which are crucial for the survival of the individual. To Bergson, perception is not the real mystery. What is truly mysterious is "not how perception arises, but how it is limited, since it should be the image of the whole, and is in fact reduced to the image of that which interests you."[15]

Aldous Huxley has suggested that on the Bergsonian view "each one of us is potentially Mind at Large," i.e., potentially capable of perceiving everything that is happening anywhere in the universe. It is only because our first business is to survive that "the Mind at Large has to be funneled through the reducing valve of the brain and nervous system."[16]

Attractive as this theory may sound, it still suffers from the dominant spirit fantasy which is at work in the mentalistic paradigm. Expressions like "Mind at Large" (note the capitalization of the first letters!), "perceiving everything everywhere," clearly convey the message that man, if he would only remove certain "valves," is indeed a god-like creature "potentially" (!) capable of freeing himself of the constrictions of time and space. "Mind at Large" really means "more mind": one becomes better and nobler by perceiving more of the same, i.e., by expanding the range of perception. Once again, it is quite indifferent how one perceives, but only what and how much one perceives. The same tendency to replace the quality of perception with the quantity of what is perceived is also present in Bergson when he laments the fact that, instead of perceiving "the image of the whole," we only perceive what interests us. Like Huxley, Bergson fails to realize that "the image of the whole," that is, the universe as a whole, can be perceived in "the grain of sand" and that it is not at all a question of what we see but how we see.

It is at this juncture that parapsychology, in spite of its professed monism - assuming that monism presents a viable "solution" - appears to be wedded to the old ghost of the Cartesian dualism after all. For to hold with the transmission theory that the brain acts in such a way as to transform raw sense data into meaningful messages, can mean only one of two things: either the brain, that small lump of matter, is by some quirk of nature endowed with consciousness, in which case it must possess properties that are possessed by no other material substance; or the "raw sense data," received by the brain, are not raw to begin with, but are already somewhat "conscious" before they enter the brain; in the latter case the brain is merely a passive transmitter of conscious contents that exist, so to speak, everywhere, independently of whether we do or do not occasionally pick them up. In either case the exact role of the brain - be it in transforming or merely in receiving messages - at best remains unaccounted for; at worst, the brain is ultimately reduced to a piece of inert matter. We have thus once again reverted to the all too familiar dilemma of dualism: you cannot have it both ways nor can you have it one way only. Dualism breeds monism and monism feeds on dualism. For these two "isms" are nothing more than manifestations of one and the same tendency - the tendency to reconcile contraries, to reduce the manyfold character of reality to a single explanatory scheme. In the final analysis it is the refusal to accept the human condition in its essential ambiguity and open-endedness.

In contrast to this, we have chosen to stress the reality of the psyche. The psychic perspective requires no "reconciliation" because it says that there is enough space for all views and positions including those of materialism and spiritualism. The only thing the psyche does to these views is to de-substantialize and to relativize them. But dissolution is always followed by transformation because soul as the "third term" is itself a trans-formative agency.

*

Some of our "cousins" parapsychologists, having realized that neither dualism nor monism offers much hope in solving the riddle of para-normal perception, have attempted to introduce new explanatory categories superficially resembling what we call the psyche. For example, Whateley Carrington has proposed that the basic mental agents, responsible for the transmission of extra-sensory information, are "psychons" - individual mental images held together by common associations. H.A.C. Dobbs has suggested the name "psitron" for particles of "imaginary" energy or mass which, travelling with the velocity exceeding that of light and interacting with particles of "real mass" in the recipient's brain, effect telepathic communication. The peak of scientific reserve, bordering on the ludicrous, is surely reached when the psychologist R.H. Thouless and the biochemist B.P. Wieser, having convinced themselves that the word which best expresses

170

the unknown factor is "soul," hasten to rename it by the harmless Hebrew letter Shin.[17]

The basic flaw in these and similar attempts to account for "extra-sensory perception" is that they are based on the old atomistic and sensory psychology advocated by Locke: there is nothing in the intellect that was not before in the senses. As Cyril Burt, one of the most discerning writers in the field, has observed, both those who have adopted the phrase "extra sensory perception" and those who reject it, never explain what other modes of perception they would like to contrast with it.[18] The question which is systematically avoided has to do with the nature of the so called sensory perception itself. Before this question is answered, it is impossible to have any intelligent discussion about para-normal or extra-sensory knowledge.

According to Burt, even in ordinary forms of sense perception, "our cognitive awareness is seldom fixed on the sensory qualities themselves, which vary with distance, illumination, angle of vision; rather it "goes straight to the object or the meaning." This is as much as saying that what we "normally" perceive are not sense data, but images. All perception, including ESP, is, fundamentally speaking, an imaginative process. Thus, "instead of trying to interpret extra-sensory perception as described in the stock text-book, we ought ... to interpret ordinary perception in the light of what we have learned about ESP."[19]

Translated into our terms, ESP would be simply a modified (perhaps sharpened or refined) form, a sub-species of imagination - something like, to paraphrase Wordsworth, imagination in her most exalted mood. Burt ascribes the faculty of paranormal perception (telepathy, precognition, communication with the dead) to what he calls "psychic" or "psychogenic factor" which cannot be reduced to an interplay between brain and consciousness, i.e., to a causal relation. Rather it is a "unique type of

171

relation" resembling "not perception but ... those semi-intuitive glimpses - those flashes of imaginative insight and implicit references that are colloquially termed 'hunches.'"[20]

Insofar as Burt's "psychogenic factor" mediates between matter (brain) and spirit (consciousness), it seems to be similar to what G.N.M. Tyrrell (1879-1952), pioneer in psychical research, termed "mid-level" constituents of our personalities. Tyrrell starts from the assumption that post mortem apparitions are "telepathic hallucinations" which, in contrast to the purely subjective hallucinations of the insane or of drug-takers, correspond in some degree to an external object or event not present in the percipient's vicinity. An apparition, according to Tyrrell, would be a dramatic representation produced jointly by the living (the percipient) and the dead (the agent) at some mid-level between mind and body. What is telepathically transmitted by the agent is a general theme or motif (an outline of a plot) of great emotional intensity. However, before the apparition can occur, this general theme must somehow be specified, made concrete and presented to the percipient - a task which is performed by the two protagonists of the mid-level psyche, "the Producer" and "the Stage Carpenter."[21] In Tyrrell's view, the entire operation is strikingly similar to the dramatization process in dreams. The same dramatic power which is possessed by the dreaming psyche is shown in apparitions, though the apparitional drama, unlike the dream-drama, is a waking hallucination.

Tyrrell also assumes that the apparitional drama is a two-sided collaboration between the mid-levels of the percipient's personality and the mid-levels of the agent's personality since in this region the notion of spatial apartness no longer applies. Thus the theme or the motif is not literally sent across space on the analogy of a wireless message. It is rather that the agent and the percipient participate in a common psychic space. If at this point we are justified in calling for Swedenborg's assistance,

172

we may say that what corresponds to distance in that "celestial" space, are the feelings people have for each other: "They are near to each other who are in similar states, and distant, who are in dissimilar states ... spaces in heaven [read: on the mid-level of the psyche] are merely external states corresponding to internal."[22] We may then take a further step by suggesting that in these imaginal spaces the inner and the outer overlap so completely that the "astral" forms or the dream-bodies who inhabit these spaces, can exist and act independently of the world of empirics; they would be purely psychic images devoid of natural life.

I do not imagine that parapsychologists are prepared to take this step toward what we called "imaginal reduction." As I observed earlier, most of them are working from the premises of a sensationalist psychology which regards images not as autonomous creations of the psyche, but as after-images (results of sensations and perceptions) or as mental constructs ("mental images"). A curious incident reported by Rosalind Heywood, a skeptically minded parapsychologist, may serve to illustrate our point. Once, when she asked a deceased friend - Vivian Usborne - for the evidence concering his post mortem state, the reply was: "I cannot give you evidence ... I can only give you poetic images."[23] Heywood's comment, however, is typical of the prevalent attitudes toward images among her colleagues: "... according to Vivian ... information about conditions different in kind from ours can come at second hand (emphasis mine), by means of [mental] imagery."[24] It would seem that the "dead" have a more "professional" grasp of their own condition than those who have set about to investigate them scientifically.

H.H. Price, a cool-headed and cautious Oxford philosopher, speculates that newly dead individuals may continue, without realizing it, to make mental images resembling their earthly surroundings and that this kind of image-making would be analogous to dreaming. The "other world" would be a world of mental images, a kind of dream-like world in which people would have "image-bodies" (or "psychical" bodies) similar to the old body in appearance but possessed of rather different causal properties. In the image-world, like in the Swedenborgian world of spirits, our desires would have the tendency to fulfil themselves instantaneously. A desire to go to Oxford might be immediately followed by the occurence of a vivid and detailed set of Oxford-like images. "In a dream world Desire is king." To those who dismiss belief in life after death as "mere wish-fulfillment," Price therefore can reply that the post mortem dream world (similar to the Hindu conception of kama-loka, the "world of desires") "would have to be a wish-fulfillment world." As to the nature of the world (celestial, hellish or purgatorial) in which a person in the post mortem state has to live, Price assumes that it would be the outgrowth of his character represented before him in the form of dream-like images. In a sense, therefore, a person gets exactly the sort of world he most intensely and most secretly wants; "and if we ... dislike the image-world our desires create for us - if, when we get what we want, we are horrified to discover what things they were which we wanted - we shall have to set about altering our characters, which might be a very long and painful process."[25] As in Plato and Jung, circulation continues.

Back to Narcissus

Taking Price at his word (except for his use of the term "mental" in conjunction with images), I would like to dwell on an earlier thought, namely, that the soul's journey in the netherworld is "for all practical purposes" endless. It must be endless for the paramount reason that it is impossible to "imagine" a state of affairs in which image-making is itself cancelled. There can be no "still point," no pure, timeless and motionless being, uncontaminated with transiency, unless the necessity to love this ambiguity at the heart of things is accepted as something final and thus "still," "pure," and "timeless" in itself. It would have to be a kind of love that is simultaneously involved in the processes of time and is able to watch this involvement with such an intensity that it can no longer be separated from it. We would be what we love, but we would also love what we are. So we must face again the perennial question: who or what are we?

The answer to this question was suggested by the myth of Narcissus. According to Hillman's interpretation of the myth, what Narcissus is contemplating in the pool, is not his own image or his ego-personality, but the soul which is a much more powerful "entity" than the philosopher's "ghost in the machine." Narcissus sees "the beautiful form of another being."[26] From the archetypal point of view, these "forms" or dream images, far from being merely "mental," as Price and his parapsychological colleagues would have it, are made of a purely psychic stuff - more substantial than dream-images in the Freudian sense (i.e., as residues of the day). They are autonomous bodies, whole and complete in themselves needing no external confirmation or "reinforcement." It is rather our mortal frames, our bags of bones and blood that may require confirmation from their side.

A more intriguing avenue of approach to this subject is available among the primitives, for whom the soul-stuff, as the phenomenologist of religions Gerardus Van der Leeuw has shown, acquires a genuine form only when man sees his own image, for example, in a mirror. The mirror image is a revelation of a numinous power which is attached to the self and yet foreign and superior to it. The dawning of this experience of the soul's otherness is movingly depicted in Wagner's Siegfried music: "I came to the limpid brook,/ And the beasts and the trees/ I saw reflected;/ Sun and clouds too,/ Just as they are,/ Were mirrored quite plain in the stream./ I also could spy/ This face of mine

(<u>Siegfried</u>, Act I, Armour).

In Van der Leeuw's opinion, "the Narcissus experience is essentially numinous, the discovery of one's own powerfulness that is yet strangely foreign, uncontrollable, superior and mysterious."[27] What we seek and find in images are the essences of things, including our own essence, that subtle stuff which is "similar to light winds and fleeting dream" - <u>par</u> <u>levibus</u> <u>ventis</u> <u>volucrique</u> <u>simillima</u> <u>somno</u>. It should not be surprising, therefore, that this kind of experience tends to erase the boundary between life and death. In the realm of images where, as Price said, "the Desire is king," things flow into one another and all desires, especially the desire for life <u>and</u> death, are fulfilled beyond the expectations of the time-binding ego. Here we are not only what we love but we love (narcissistically) what we are - a perilous combination by all accounts. There is danger in looking at one's own image, for the answer, profferred by the image to the question "who am I?" may not coincide with my "self-image." The anthropologist Codrington reports that on the Banks Islands of Melanesia there is a deep hole into which no one ever ventures to look; for should the water in the cave reflect a man's face, he would surely die.[28] Narcissus, to say the least, was a lucky fool. But then again, as Blake in his <u>Proverbs</u> <u>of</u> <u>Hell</u> prophesized, "if the fool would persist in his folly he would become wise."[29]

*

When parapsychologists, particularily those of Price's and Tyrrell's caliber, compare the apparitions of the dead to dream-images, they are undoubtedly pointing in the right direction. What they do not realize, however, is that the figures of our dreams, like other images, are products of a psyche that exists on the boundary between the conscious and the unconscious, the objective and the subjective. On this level, as Jung said, "we are dreaming all the time, although we are not aware of it by day because consciousness is much too clear."[30] That is precisely the crux of the matter. Our consciousness is so "clear" or rather so obdurate in extolling "the despotism of the eye" that pretension to awareness by different kinds of light must be a priori eliminated. The monotheism of consciousness brooks no rivals, no other gods are allowed to share the "mindscape." So we tend to deny or at least to devalue the existence of the oneiric realm and to hush the voices of the dead. As a contemporary literatus has admirably put it: "Light is the jealousy of the sun, shutting out brighter bodies and further suns. But at night, there may be another light revealing world in darkness. Death, I know, is clairvoyant. So is Imagination, which inhabits inner and outer space."[31]

From the psychological perspective enabling us to see, not more, but better, apparitions and "ghosts" do not have to be classed as "paranormal" or "extra-sensory" phenomena. For if we are always both conscious and unconscious, if, in a sense, "we are dreaming all the time," then the so called apparitions, being essentially imaginal creatures, are also in our midst all the time. We do not see them just as we ordinarily do not see the supernatural beauty or, alternatively, the terror of a landscape or of a human face. Our sight is usually riveted either to the "Many" or to the "One," either to the "profane" or to the "holy." Once, however, these supererogatory fabrications are seen through or melted down, in the alchemical mode, to their psychic and subtle essence, they cease to be overwhelming and become part of a Play in which, as Heraclitus said, the "royal power" belongs to the child. And the child - what of it? The child is perennially young and old, playful and grave, idiotic and wise. Yet this is precisely how, not only most human beings, but the ghosts as well are reputed to behave. Thus: please will the real Mr. So-and-So stand up!

Parapsychological speculations about the subtle body, in our opinion, lead into a blind alley; there is nowhere to go beyond what is observable, measurable, quantifiable. Having allied itself with the scientific method which is inseparable from scientific ideology (scientism), parapsychology has fallen victim to its own procedure. It is absurd to claim the superiority of the "spiritual" over the "material," if the "spiritual" is assumed to be amenable to scientific treatment. That way lies methodological schizophrenia and spiritual suicide. In the last resort the mainspring of these pious elucubrations is the scientific-technological drive to subject all things, including the "things" called ghosts, to human control and manipulation. After all, perhaps the ghosts too can be persuaded, by means of the Skinnerian technique, to serve the greater good of a computerized society. Ad majorem scientiae gloriam.

PART TWO

I: PSYCHE AND PARAPSYCHOLOGY

NOTES

[1] Herewart Carrington, The Projection of the Astral Body, p. 15.

[2] Robert Crookall, Ecstasy: the Release of the Soul from the Body (Moradabad, India: Darshana International, 1973), pp. 15, 16.

[3] "Cross-correspondence" stands for alleged messages from "beyond," involving several different mediums and sophisticated information which is said to make sense when fitted together in complicated ways. See Gardner Murphy (with Laura A. Dole), Challenge of Psychic Research (New York: Harper & Row, 1961), Chapter VII.

[4] James Hillman, Loose Ends, Primary Papers in Archetypal Psychology (Zürich: Spring Publications, 1975), p. 134.

[5] Cyril Burt, "Psychology and Parapsychology," in Science and ESP, ed. J.R. Smythies (London: Routledge & Kegan Paul, 1967), p. 100.

[6] J. Bronowski, The Identity of Man. Rev. ed. (New York: American Museum Science Books, 1966), p. 51.

[7] Burt, "Psychology and Parapsychology," p. 101.

[8] J.B. Rhine, "The Science of Nonphysical Nature," in Philosophy and Parapsychology, ed. Jan Ludwig (Buffalo, N.Y.: Prometheus Books, 1978), p. 124.

[9] Huston Smith, Forgotten Truth: the Primordial Tradition (New York: Harper & Row, 1976), p. 11.

[10] Theodore Roszak, Where the Wasteland Ends (New York: Garden City, N.Y.: Doubleday and Co., Inc., 1972), p. 387; cf. p. 380 ff.

[11] Heidegger, What is a Thing?, tr. by W.B. Barton, Jr. and Vera Deutsch (Chicago: Henry Regnery Co., 1967), p. 20.

[12] C.J. Ducasse, "The Philosophical Importance of 'Psychic Phenomena'" in Philosophy and Parapsychology, p. 132; cf. pp. 56-57.

179

[13]Ibid., p. 134.

[14]Roszak, Where the Wasteland Ends, p. 169.

[15]Henri Bergson, Matter and Memory, tr. by Nancy M. Paul and W. Scott Palmer (London: George Allen & Co., Inc., 1913), p. 34.

[16]Aldous Huxley, The Door of Perception and Heaven and Hell (New York: Harper & Row, 1954), pp. 22-24.

[17]See Rosalind Heywood, Beyond the Reach of Sense (New York: E.P. Dutton and Co., Inc., 1974), pp. 185-219.

[18]Burt, "Psychology and Parapsychology," p. 78.

[19]Cyril Burt, "The Implications of Parapsychology for General Psychology," in Parapsychology Today, ed. J.N. Rhine and Robert Brier (Castle Books, 1968), p. 220.

[20]Burt, "Psychology and Parapsychology," p. 118.

[21]See G.N.M. Tyrrell, Apparitions (New York: Pantheon Books, 1973), pp. 88, 95, 104.

[22]Swedenborg, Heaven and its Wonders and Hell, p. 79.

[23]Rosalind Heywood, "Illustion - or What?" in Life After Death, ed. Arnold Toynbee, Arthur Koestler, et al. (New York: McGraw-Hill Book Co, 1976), p. 216.

[24]Ibid., pp. 232-42.

[25]H.H. Price, "Survival and the Idea of 'Another World'," in Language, Metaphysics, and Death, ed. John Donnelly (New York: Fordham University Press, 1978), pp. 10, 191, 193.

[26]Hillman, The Dream and the Underworld, p. 221, note 34.

[27]G. Van der Leeuw, Religion in Essence and Development, Vol. I (New York: Harper & Row, 1963), p. 286.

[28]Ibid., p. 287. Aldous Huxley has observed that objects seen in visionary experiences "do not stand for anything but themselves...; at the limits of the visionary world, we are confronted by facts which, like the facts of external nature, are independent of man, both individually and collectively, and exist in their own right. And their meaning consists precisely in this, that they are intensely themselves and, being themselves,

are manifestations of the essential givenness, the non-human otherness of the universe" (<u>Heaven and Hell</u>, New York, Harper & Brothers, 1956, pp. 13-14).

[29]William Blake, <u>The Marriage of Heaven and Hell</u>, 7, in <u>Writings of William Blake</u>, ed. Geoffrey Keynes 1, 184 (London, 1925). Henceforth referred to by the letter "K", the number of the volume and page.

[30]<u>CW</u> 18, par. 162.

[31]Ihab Hassan, <u>The Right Promethean Fire; Imagination, Science, and Cultural Change</u> (Urbana: University of Illinois Press, 1980), p. 32.

II: SUBTLE BODY IN THE TRADITIONAL THOUGHT

The Dream of Alchemy

To illustrate a way of thinking that envisions man's physical form as a reflection of a more subtle essence, I shall now take a glance at five areas: alchemy, Neoplatonism, Schelling's theology of "corporeality", Blake and the Iranian Sufism. I would like to preface this excursion by briefly describing the idea of subtle body among some of the primitives.

As stated earlier, Jung was fully aware that to the primitive man the psyche appears as a "ghostlike presence which has objective reality." Jung's opinion is amply documented in the writings of anthropologists and historians of religion. Edward B. Tylor, in his pioneering work Religion in Primitive Cultures, reports that the Tongans imagined the human soul to be "the finer or more aeriform part of the body...comparable to the perfume and essence of a flower as related to the more solid vegetable fibre." Having cited other instances of such beliefs among the Greenland seers, the Caribs, the Siamese, etc., Tylor sagaciosly observes that this "lower philosophy" of the savages concerning the "etherality" or "vaporous materiality" of the soul "escapes various difficulties which down to the modern times have perplexed metaphysicians and theologians of the civilized world."[1]

The Australian aborigines represent the soul as having the size of a grain of sand; its dimensions are so reduced that it can pass through the smallest crevices or the finest tissues. From this the French sociologist Emile Durkheim concludes, as if anticipating archetypal psychology, that the form of the soul is "essentially inconsistent and undetermined; it varies from one moment to another with the demands of circumstances..." The substance from which the soul is made, is conceived as being "immaterial to a certain degree." After it has been completely

183

freed from the organism, the soul is thought to lead a life absolutely analogous to the one led in the world; it eats, drinks, hunts, etc. When it flutters among the branches of trees, it causes rustlings and crackings. At the same time, however, the soul--this "infinitely rare and subtle matter"--is believed to be invisible to the vulgar. Only magicians or old men have the faculty of seeing souls. It is only "in virtue of special powers which they owe either to age or to a special training that they perceive things which escape our senses."[2]

Alchemy flourished for the better part of two millenia in the West and has analogies among the Indian and Chinese religions. The alchemical opus--manufacturing gold out of base metals--had absorbed and fascinated some of the most outstanding minds of medieval Europe (12th and 13th centuries). The best among the alchemists have denied that they are dealing with vulgar metals-- with overt boiling, baking, calcination-- and asserted that their elements, apparatuses, and operations, are all invariably "philo-sophic." Their earth is the "philosophic" earth which no man has ever seen; their gold and mercury, their black crow, red lion and golden dragon, are "philosophic." The declared concern of the opus is with the "spirits" which inhabit the gross bodies of these things.

The views of later alchemy are centered on the idea of anima mundi, the demiurge or divine spirit that incubated the chaotic waters of the beginning and remained in matter in a potential state. Man's nature was conceived as a kind of excerpt from this world-soul or as a seed of the universal tree of life. The alchemist's aim was to purify and re-organize man's psychical constitution so as to extract the original divine spirit out of chaos. It was a process of soul-freeing or soul-making. The words "soul" and "spirit" may be used here interchangeably, for in all cases these terms denoted a semi-material pneuma, a sort of subtle body which was also called "volatile" and was identified chemically with oxides and other dissoluble compounds. For example, the famous alchemist Johannes de Rupescia (d. 1375) calls the extracted spirit "le ciel humain," the human sky or heaven.[3]

Among the names most frequently given to this spirit are Mercurius (quicksilver), alchemy's greatest figure, and Hermes, the god of revelation who, as Hermes Trismegistus, was believed to be the archetypal authority on alchemy.[4] Mercurius is the spirit of the world become body within the earth and is described by Mylius, in his Philosophia reformata as an "intermediate substance" - media substantia or anima media natura (soul as intermediate nature).[5] He is also designated as anima nostra, Mercurius noster, corpus nostrum. Note, however, that the nostra here does not mean "our own," but arcane substance and it is the production of this substance, imagined as corpus mysticum or corpus subtile, that is the ultimate goal of alchemy.

The alchemical work is an opus contra naturam. As Hillman explains, it "had to deform nature in order to serve nature. It had to hurt (...) natural nature in order to free animated nature," for " as soon as psyche enters into consideration, the only-natural is not enough...There is evidently in the soul something that wrests it out of the only natural."[6] To Jung, alchemy was the fundamental paradigm and background of his psychology. He was convinced that from the psychological point of view, the physical materials and processes of the opus are symbols for the "rebirth of the (spiritual) light from the darkness of Physis: the healing self-knowledge and the deliverance of the pneumatic body from the corruption of the flesh."[7]

The alchemists wove fantasy and scientific "fact" into a single world. They could not, or perhaps did not, care to interfere with their own imaginative activity. For example, by considering silver as seed of the moon in the earth or copper as seed of Venus and lead as seed of Saturn, they disregarded the distinction between the organic and inorganic kingdoms. To the alchemists, seeds are living forces with encoded intentionality, a capacity to enter into combinations, take on history. "These ore-bodies were not dead matter to be pushed around, but vital seeds, embodiments of soul; not objective facts, but subjective factors." In this way the alchemical view "incorporated into its theoretical premises what modern science is now stating as new: the observer and the observed are not independent of each other."[8] Hillman is referring here to the modern discoveries of microphysics which, as we already observed, are perceived by the contemporary would-be mystics as scientific confirmation of their feelings of unity with the universe and the like. Needless to say, we cannot share this confused thinking. A scientific restoration, let's say, of the concept of anima mundi (supposing it may succeed) would result in nothing more interesting than a Cosmic Robot, and instead of universal animation there would be universal death.

The French philosopher and Orientalist René Guenon has written that modern chemistry and astronomy, insofar as they have issued respectively from alchemy and astrology, are due not to any progress or evolution within the latter, but rather to a process of degeneration. What happened is that the most inferior elements ("the residues") of alchemy and astrology were detached from their spiritual core, became grossly materialized and then served as the starting point for the modern experimental chemistry and astronomy.

Genuine alchemy was essentially a science belonging to the cosmological order which, by virtue of the analogy between the macrocosm and the microcosm, was also believed to be at work in the human sphere. Modern chemistry has not sprung from this kind of alchemy but is rather a corruption and deviation, having its origin among individuals who took the ancient symbols literally and who are sarcastically referred to by the alchemists as "blowers" and "charcoal burners."

Guenon also notes that the "so called restorers of alchemy of whom there is a certain number to be found in the contemporary world, are for their part merely prolonging this very deviation, and their researches are as far removed from traditional alchemy as are those of present day astrologers from ancient astrology."[9] Extending the analogy to the present-day mystics, especially those who imagine that their experiences are confirmed by the latest discoveries in micro and/or macro-physics, we must aver that in reality these individuals are confirming not their feelings and views, but the Weltanschauung of science which, as we saw, is by definition antithetical to the psychical standpoint. But then perhaps we are entering the age of robot-mystics produced by the "residues" of the ancient sciences of alchemy, astrology and psychology. In that event one may derive a fatalistic sort of comfort from the fact that the Tibetan name for Kali Yuga (the age of darkness) is literally "the age of impure residues." Its final phase is likewise described as "the time when impurities grow more and more."

*

According to the sinologue Richard Wilhelm with whom Jung collaborated by writing an important commentary on the ancient Chinese alchemical text "The Secret of the Golden Flower," Confucius held that spirit, far from being something that grows naturally in man, must be acquired in the course of life by strenuous effort. In Wilhelm's words, the spirit

> leads a somewhat precarious existence unless it has been so concentrated in the course of life, that it has already 'built itself a kind of subtle body of a spiritual nature,' made as it were of thoughts and works, a body that gives consciousness a support when it has to leave its former assistant, the body. This psychic body is at first very delicate, so that only the very wisest men can preserve it and find their refuge in it after death.[10]

What we gather from this passage is that "immortality" is the result of a creative effort: a process of crystallization and transformation of the psychic seed which is reborn in the form of a new body, called "diamond body" in Chinese alchemy ("the diamond thunderbolt" or the dorje of Tibetan Buddhism). According to Jung, the new body symbolizes the perfect state where masculine and feminine are united; it corresponds to the corpus incorruptibile of the medieval alchemy, which in turn is identical with the corpus resurrectionis of the Christian tradition.[11]

Wilhelm points out that the physical body itself is quite willing to die when the time is ripe; but there is also an inner aspect of the body that is constantly imagining how death will be before it comes. These fantasies are one of the strongest forces in human life; they have created such buildings as pyramids and at the same time have initiated mass murders of people who held conflicting fantasies about the fate of the soul.

The Chinese alchemists attempted to build up the spiritual body through meditation exercises. The aim was to disengage the energies attached to one's physical body and to endow the seminal power (the psychic kernel or entelechy) with a new body. In one of the many images expressing the necessary concentration, a sage is depicted in deepest meditation with a small child forming in his heart. The small child, according to Wilhelm, represents death already in life. It means "emerging into another order of time, where we can see the whole of life as from another dimension and yet, at the same time we remain energetically connected with our present life in our present order of space and time."[12]

Mercury, the arcane substance of the alchemical opus, appears also in the context of the pan-Indian Kundalini Yoga system, particularly in the so called visuddha chakra. Visuddha is one of the seven centers of the imaginal body, localized in the region of the throat in the form of a lotus with sixteen petals of smoky purple. Within the lotus there is a blue area, in the center of which is a white circle containing an elephant. According to Jung, the visuddha represents "a world of psychical substance" the matter being only a "thin skin around an enormous cosmos of psychic reality." Visuddha means "a full recognition of the psychical essences or substances as the fundamental essences of the world, and not by virtue of speculation but by virtue of fact, as experience."[13]

As the practitioner of Yoga proceeds from the muladhara chakra (impulses, instincts, sex, participation mystique) through svadisthana (the heroic battle with the dragon of unconscious waters, symbolic death and rebirth), manipura (psyche in the abdomen, fiery energies), anahata (the seat of feelings; anemos, wind; whence animus, spirit; increase in volatility), he gradually experiences the autonomous and self-moving character of the psyche until - in the visuddha - he becomes aware of "the world of psychical images only." The ajna and sahasrara chakras are respectively centers of mystical union with God (as in Christianity) - Brahmanic or Nirvanic states which, according to Jung, are "beyond our possible experience"; sahasrara in particular is "merely a philosophical concept with no substance whatever for us."[14] These two chakras would symbolize the fantasy of spirit, a spiritual flight of the soul which is the counterpart of soul's descent to the lower chakras.

What we are witnessing in yogic alchemy is a psychization or subtilization of matter, an alchemical opus in which matter is transformed into imagination and the concrete and literal things and "facts of life" into images. Hillman calls it "an ontological vision with a psychic base in the subtle body of visuddha consciousness and an alchemical base in silver." It is a truly

189

visionary experience "making subtle everything we ever may
have assumed to be concrete body, whether events in the world,
our own flesh, even the elemental minerals in the earth. Alchemy
transmutes the world to the dream..."[15]

An ontology of imagination, if it is ever going to be written,
must assume that all things are determined by psychic images
and that these images are subtle bodies possessing their own
"gleam and ring"; that they are not reflections of the world, but
"the light by which we see the world." But note once again
that this light which shines in the darkness of a crude materialism no less powerfully than in the deceptive fulgurations of an
equally crude spiritualism, is always elusive and ambiguous. It
is not only the light of life but also the light of death, for in
these environs you cannot, as Jung said, pretend to be the only
master in your own house; "there are spooks about that play
havoc with your realities and that is the end of your
monarchy."[16] What is more, these spooks may well be the souls
of the dead or our own souls or the dead souls within our own
souls or the souls of the unborn, hungry for the tree of life.
What I am saying is that in the light of imagination, life and
death are not two separate events or mutually exclusive realities.
There is gradation in being alive and gradation in being dead.
Our ontological status is always that of "more or less." The
light of imagination is a metaphorical light, capable of seeing
"similars in dissimilars" (Aristotle) - ghosts in people, lineaments
of personality in minerals and vegetables, the grin of a cat
(more real than our neighbor's "pussy") in a human face.

Neoplatonic Speculations

The doctrine that mind and body are linked together by a
third factor has a long history in the European thought. It
reaches back from the Cambridge Platonists (Henry More, Ralph
Cudworth) in the seventeenth century to Neoplatonists (Proclus,

Porphyry, Iamblichus, Synesius) in the fourth and fifth centuries. Proclus (c. 4I0-485), the last major Neoplatonist, claims the authority of Aristotle and refers to his theory of starry pneuma which was believed to be the seat of the nutritional and sensitive soul and the physiological condition of fantasia (De gen. anim. 736 b 27 ff). He then combines this starlike pneuma (okhēma pneumaticon or lower pneumatic vehicle) which is permanently attached to the soul and the Platonic concept of soul as separable from its earthly body - a compromise enabling him to hold that the soul is immortal and incorporeal and yet inseparable from the quasi-material pneumatic vehicle.

The synthesis, achieved by Proclus, assumes the existence of two okhēma: I. the higher okhēma, called augoeides (luminous, auroral) is the original body (proton sōma) into which Plato's Demiurge has placed the soul (Tim. 4I E); 2. the okhēma pneumatikon or lower "pneumatic vehicle" (seat of nutritional and irrational soul) is a temporary accretion; it survives the bodily death but is destined to disappear.[17]

Fundamentally, however, the subtle body is one, for the kind of body (higher or lower) we have depends on the transmuting power of imagination. Imagination is the essential stuff of all living, corporeal, and psychic energies. In the words of the platonizing Sūfi master Ahmad,

> Imagination is essential to the soul and consubstantial with it; it is an instrument of the soul, just as the hand is an instrument of the physical body. Even sensory things are known only by means of this organ.[18]

Ahmad is pointing to the ontological status of imagination which we expressed by saying that images are prior to sensation and perception. It is this ontological fact - this union of the universal and the particular in the image - which forbids us to posit hard and fast divisions between various subtle bodies. The transmuting power of imagination is the same power which makes all things, material as well as spiritual, transparent to one another. In the mirror of imagination, "the one and the same ... energy of light is just as much the constituent of the essence of what is qualified as material as it is of the essence of what is qualified as spiritual."[19]

Our ordinary perceptual activities are for the most part governed by fancy (passive or associative imagination); in these states the inner life of things and persons is invisible and what we do is limited to outward appearances. It is only in the realm of archetypal imagination (mundus imaginalis) that the inner is "reduced" to the outer and the outer to the inner. In the archetypal world, writes Corbin, "inner states project visible forms." All imagined forms and figures "are seen and are real 'outside', but they are at the same time attributes and modes of being of man. Their transformation is the transformation of man."[20] Moralistically expressed, on the imaginal level, action is its own reward and the reward is the action itself.

Returning to the Neo-Platonists, we find that in Porphyry's doctrine, the soul as the essence of life cannot be said to change place or be in a place. It can only contract the habits of bodies whose nature is to change place and occupy space. Souls who love the body attract a moist spirit to them and condense it like a cloud. When the spirit is condensed by a superabundance of the moist element, the souls become visible. These souls, says Porphyry, are the apparitions of images of the deceased for "it is probable that, when the soul desires to manifest, it shapes itself, setting its own imagination in movement."[21]

The Neo-Platonic speculation about the soul's peaks and valleys finds concise formulation in Damascius, the last occupant of the kathedra of the Platonic Academy at Alexandria. Speaking of the light of the soul (the augoeides or the vehicle of the manifestation of spirit; the augoeides okhēma of Proclus) as dimmed by its descent into the coarser grades of matter, he writes:

> In heaven, indeed, our radiant (augoeides) portion is full filled with heavenly radiance (auge) - a glory that streams throughout its depths, and lends it a divine strength. But in lower states, losing this [radiance], it is dirtied, as it were, and becomes darker and darker and more material. Heedless it grows, and sinks down towards the earth; yet in its essence it is still the same in number (emphasis mine).[22]

According to ancient physics (which was not divorced from psychology) the downward elements are earthly and moist and the upward, airy and fiery. The moist principle conditions all genesis, generation or birth-and-death - the state of perpetual flux and becoming. It was Heraclitus who first in the Western tradition enunciated this principle: "For the souls to become moist is delight or death" (DK, fr. 77). Death or, for that matter, becoming is not a "fact" that can be "absolved" from life or being. Neither life nor death, neither being nor becoming are absolutes, for "we live their [the souls'] death, and they live our death" (DK, fr. 77). Also: "Immortal mortals, mortal immortals, the one living the death and dying the life of the other" (DK, fr. 62). What Heraclitus is trying to articulate in these proverbs is that the soul occupies a middle position between being and becoming. The soul as the relation between the opposites of life and death, is more fundamental than what is related. The ontological prius of the soul is neither life nor death but their mutual belonging in what Jung calls esse in anima. In the beginning is esse in anima. Thus the soul "dies" when it chooses becoming only just as it "dies" when it chooses being only.

Synesius (c. 365-430) whose treatise On Visions (written c. 404 before he became a Christian) is probably the most detailed Neo-Platonic statement on the subject, writes that the soul (imaginative pneuma) is "precisely the border land between unreason and reason, between body and the bodyless. It is the

193

common frontier of both, and by its means things divine are joined with lowest things." Standing on this "common frontier" the soul is "capable of assuming any form, and an image [or shade] in which last the soul works out its corrections."[23] The pneumatic soul by its natural impulses either rises on high (Plato's "winging" of the soul, Phaedr. 246 D) or, in Heraclitus' words, "becoming dense and moist, it sinks into the depths of earth ... lurking [there] nay, thrust down into the subterranean state" (DK, fr. 118).

It would be difficult to add anything more pertinent to these descriptions of psyche's imaginative propensities, except to exclaim with Synesius: "See how vast a middle state this [soulful] spirit has in which to play the part of citizen!"[24]

Schelling's Theology of Corporeality

The Platonic idea of anima mundi has found, in modern times, a prominent place in the natural philosophy of F.W.J. Schelling. The world-soul, for Schelling, is constituted by the mutual and dynamic relationship between matter and spirit. It is not that first there is matter and spirit as two separate substances which subsequently enter into a hybrid relationship; the original datum, the ontological prius is the relationship or the union itself. Mythologically speaking, the world soul as the tertium quid between matter and spirit, is "in the beginning." Schelling therefore cannot be included, as is customary, among the idealist philosophers of German Romanticism. In what Ernst Benz calls his "theology of corporeality"[25] he left far behind both idealism with its abstract concept of spirit and materialism with its equally abstract concept of matter. Historically, Schelling's belief that there is a continuous and essential bond between the realms of spirit and nature, goes back to Jacob Boehme (1575-1624) and Friedrich Christoph Oetinger (1702-1782), a Swabian theologian and mystic.

194

The notorious Boehmean <u>Ungrund</u> (the abyss or "groundless-ness") is a primal, dark, irrational force, a spirit-body process in which spirituality and corporeality belong together. The cosmic life is conceived by Boehme in a Heraclitean manner, as an impassionate battle, an eternal genesis in which God as creator and nature are correlative.

> The earth has the same qualities and sources as has the depth above the earth, or heaven, and everything belongs together to one body, and that one body is God in his entirety ... the whole divinity is concealed in the earth.[26]

In this view, physical materiality is only a particular form of corporeality. Matter in its present coagulated state arose through a contraction away from the primal ground of being. According to Boehme, the material body of man came into being with the original Fall whereas the paradisiac body of Adam was still of a spiritual-corporeal nature. We find here the echo of the Neo-Platonic tradition holding that our present world of time and space is the result of a progressive detachment - a "descent" from the subtle forms. The corporeal state as a whole has become fixed and can no longer receive directly the imprint of subtle forms. Nevertheless it cannot become completely detached from the subtle state which is its ontological root and by which it is entirely dominated. What has been obfuscated during this progressive solidification of the corporeal states through various terrestrial eras, is the creative character that the relationship between the two states possessed at the origin.[27]

Schelling's philosophy of corporeality is best understood in conjunction with his view of death. In the 32d Lecture of his <u>Philosophy</u> <u>of</u> <u>Revelation</u> Schelling sees death as an "essentifica-tion" or "actuation." Death is not so much a separation as an essentification destroying the contingent and preserving the essential, <u>i.e.</u>, the most truly human. The essentified being of man in whom the physical is preserved, "must be an extremely real being; yes, in truth, it must be far more real than the actual body, which because of the reciprocal exclusion of its parts, can only be a composite and for this reason is merely a fragile and destructible whole."[28]

In Schelling's view, the whole man is essentified in death - a process comparable to the extraction of oil from a plant, the oil being the tincture or the form (essence) of the plant, i.e., its powers of formation and development. Oetinger, in his Biblical Dictionary, says that "to die is only to cast off the things that conceal life, the coarse husk: the driving, living essence is always alive."[29] The separation that occurs at death is not from the inner essence of the body, but from the external and empirical body which is "a tissue of juices, tubes, and fibers and for the most part subject to corruption." But the flesh which is "the temple of the Holy Ghost" is also "an invisible tissue of fibers, tubes, and incorruptible oil."[30]

According to Schelling, life and death are two (different) modes of being, possessed by the whole man during his present life and beyond the grave. He therefore defends the Christian view of resurrection against all "merely rational and sterile doctrines of immortality" and maintains with Oetinger that a spiritual corporeality is already present in our material corporeality. As Benz writes, "in every corporeal thing there is a spiritual-corporeal image that is the nucleus of its essence; this nucleus strives for a higher potency, and this high potency is spiritual corporeality."[31] In Schelling's scheme, the whole universe is carried along in a vast process of endless transformation in which all things strive to fulfill their orginal subtle essence. From the psychological standpoint, it is a movement from literalism toward imagination and metaphorical expression. Schelling's "theology of corporeality" is a "metaphorical ontology" where all is semantic motion,[32] a transformation of coarse matter into dreamlike images, and of the physical body into a metaphorical or dream body.

William Blake: a Modern Shaman

Possibly the most uncompromising and comprehensive vision of subtle embodiment is offered by William Blake. In order to situate this giant of poetic thought more comfortably within the perspective of our inquiry, I should like to approach him by taking as a guide the archaic shaman - a figure of no less formidable proportions than Blake himself and as little understood as the latter.

"Shamanism" as a religious phenomenon in the broadest sense of the term is associated with the prehistorical cultures of hunting-gathering peoples of northern and central Asia, Africa, Oceania, Australia, the Americas, and northern and eastern Europe. Shamans[33] are men whose vocation consists in going up into the sky to meet the gods and in descending to the under-world where they fight the demons of sickness and death. Structurally, shamanism is integrally related to the paradise myth - a time when heaven and earth were not separated and an easy communication was possible between them. All the shamanic myths and rites are centered on quest for the lost time of paradise - a journey that culminates in ecstatic recovery of this primordial condition.

The paradisaic time can be renewed during the shaman's initiation, which usually includes a period of isolation and a certain number of trials and ordeals forcing the novice to undergo symbolic death and resurrection. According to Mircea Eliade, the experience of death means that the shaman shares in the mode of being dead here and now; by seeing spirits, in dream or otherwise, he becomes a dead man and thus transcends the profane conditions of humanity.

> ... if one knows death already here below, if one is
> continually dying countless deaths in order to be
> reborn to something else - to something that does not

belong to the Earth but participates in the sacred - then one is living ... a <u>beginning</u> of <u>immortality</u>, or growing more and more into immortality. It would follow that immortality should not be conceived as a survival <u>post</u> <u>mortem</u>, but rather as a situation one is preparing, in which one is even participating <u>from</u> <u>now</u> <u>on</u> <u>onward</u> and from this present world.[34]

It is through this experience of death and resurrection that the shamanistic ecstasy reveals a world in which "<u>everything</u> <u>is</u> <u>possible</u>; when the dead return to life and the living die only to live again; where one can disappear and reappear instantaneously; where the 'laws of Nature' are abolished; where a certain super-human 'freedom' is exemplified and made dazzlingly <u>present</u>."[35]

So far we have referred to the shaman's ecstasy undertaken "in the spirit" or symbolically. There is, however, a more ancient tradition which regards such journey as a decline and a decadence compared with the primordial status of the shamans. These traditions refer to a time when the shamans were able to travel to the various regions of the "other world" <u>in</u> <u>concreto</u>, i.e., while still continuing to exist in the flesh. <u>In</u> <u>illo</u> <u>tempore</u> the communication with the "dead" was possible not only "in the spirit," but bodily. Eliade relates this idea to the ability of the archaic man to live - as historical being - in eternity, "to achieve an ideal form (the archetype) in the very framework of human existence, to be in time wtihout reaping its disadvantages." The archaic man and the <u>homo</u> <u>religiosus</u> in general "longs for a concrete paradise and believes that such a paradise can be won <u>here</u> on earth, and <u>now</u>, in the present moment."[36]

It is crucial to realize - and here we enter Blake's territory - that the so called "spiritual states" of mysticism in which the senses are transcended, may not represent the most desirable condition allotted to man. Quite the contrary, the "spiritual" state may signify, in Eliade's words, "a fall in compar-ison with the earlier situation, in which ecstasy was not necessary because no separation between body and soul was possible..." This means that "for the primitive ideology present-day mystical experience is inferior to the sensory experience of primordial man."[37]

The assumption underlying the classical mystical experiences and mystical symbolism in general is that the break between the natural or material and the spiritual (mythologically expressed as the Fall) is not complete. In spite of the divorce between these two conditions, the natural world is still in some sense founded upon the spiritual. The point to be emphasized in this connection is that in such a symbolic system natural phenomena are regarded as valueless in themselves; they are significant only insofar as they direct the mystic's attention to something beyond themselves.

Now, in this sense Blake is most emphatically not a mystic. There is nothing in him of the via negativa, the detachment from all phenomena in search of an unnamable God. He is not interested in suppressing sensory experience and losing himself in an undifferentiated Absolute or in a paradise which is unavailable to the bodily senses. Like the ancient shaman, Blake wants to transcend the human condition in concreto, in a sensual and natural manner. "The Nature of my Work," he writes, is Visionary or Imaginative. It is an Endeavour to Restore what the Ancients called the Golden Age."[38] Essentially, what Blake is aiming at is to recapture the ability, extolled by Goethe, to apprehend the universals in the particulars or, expressed in imagistic terms, to perceive the unknowable Jungian archetypes as being fully present in images. Blake's is not a mystical but a mythical vision comparable to that of the primitve, for whom, as Cassirer writes, every new dawn "is a true and original creation - not a periodically recurring natural process following a determinate rule but something absolutely individual and unique. Heraclitus' saying, 'The sun is new each day,' is spoken in a truly mythical spirit."[39]

To achieve this unadulterated vision of the unique and the particular in the regular and the general, Blake suggests that man must acquire the power to visualize independently of sense experience. To say "independently" however is not the same as "apart from." In Northrop Frye's words, the 'visionary' is the man who "has passed through sight into vision, never the man who has avoided seeing, who has not trained himself to see clearly, or who generalizes among his stock of visual memories." What Blake means by "independent visualization" is in effect imagination creating reality. Again Frye: "in the world of sight we see what we have to see; in the world of vision we see what we want to see."[40] We first imagine then see, and if desire is part of imagination, then the world we intensely desire is more real than the world we - in the Lockean manner - passively accept. In Blake's aphoristic style, "If the fool would persist in his folly he would become wise" (K I, 184). So sensory perception cannot and must not be bypassed, but it is blind, fallible and passive without the informing genius of visionary imagination. As Plato wrote in _Theaetetus_ (184 c): "It appears to me, Socrates, that it is more proper to consider the eyes and ears as things through which, rather than things by which, we perceive." According to Blake, by looking through the eye (i.e., imaginatively) and not with it, we shall see "a world in a Grain of Sand/ And a Heaven in Wild Flower" (K 2, 232).

To Blake our senses are framing windows or "narrow chinks in the cavern" which, like Kant's "categories" of time, space and causality, limit the potential infinity of being to finite sense data. If man would cleanse "the doors of perception," he would perceive that what we ordinarily call "things" are only images of a single power of soul, images that can be changed at will by imagination. Imagination is "spiritual perception" - an intuitive power within the senses transcending the "bodily eye" (Wordsworth) only by working through it, toward a deeper sensory participation.

For Blake imagination is actively creative; as such it is not a particular state or faculty but "the Human Existence itself" (E 131). Imagination is reality. Far from being just one of our cognitive powers, valid in the field of artistic creation, scientific discovery and the like, it is our whole power, the total functioning interplay of our capacities. One could also say that imagination is the power which reinforces our common processes of perception and observation and introduces us to a far deeper, far more intimate communion with them. To see clearly and completely this chair, house, lake, mountain, sunrise, is only possible when our sense impression of these objects is raised to and informed by the imaginative power.

In Blake's universe true perception combines the natural and the spiritual. As a man thinks, so does he see. The difference between sensations and spiritual perceptions is one of degree; sensations are dim spiritual perceptions, spiritual perceptions are clear sensations. And it is only in states of spiritual perception (imagination) that we discover the infinite in everything because everything is now transformed into liquefied, translucent bodies which shine with their own internal light.

Blake had vivid personal experience of visions which could be called up at will. He had the capacity to see what empirical psychologists call mental images as, or even more, vividly than ordinary sensory images. These visions, however, were not "eidetic images" or hallucinations; they belonged to a different order of reality - to a world that is "other-worldly" only in that it is not subject to the normative power of everyday dullness - "the sordid" and "slumberous mass." As a patient once told Karl Jaspers, distinguishing ordinary imaginings from the Blakean type of visions, "I feel the figures of my imagination are not in space at all, but remain faint pictures in my brain or behind my eyes, while with these phenomena I experienced a world, but one which had nothing to do with the world of senses."[41] To give another example, Saint Teresa states that she had imaginative visions but never corporeal ones, i.e., not hallucinations.[42]

What Blake means by vision as the product of the entire imagination is most clearly seen in the field of art. Painting a picture or composing a poem is neither an intellectual (mental) nor an emotional (bodily) process; it belongs neither to the "inside" nor the "outside" of the Newtonian universe. To find the "where" of these visionary figures, we must try, with Blake, to see the sun, not as a "round disk of fire somewhat like a Guinea" but as "an Innumerable Company of the Heavenly host crying, 'Holy, Holy, Holy is the Lord God Almighty'" (K 3 162). As Frye observes, it is no use saying to Blake that the company of angels he sees surrounding the sun are not "there." Neither the angels nor the guinea-sun are "in a gaseous blast furnace across ninety million miles of nothing..." "To prove that he sees them Blake will not point to the sky but to, say, the fourteenth plate of the Job series illustrating the text: 'When the morning stars sang together, and all the sons of God shouted from joy.' That is where the angels appear, in a world formed and created by Blake's imagination and entered into by everyone who looks at the picture."[43]

It might be worthwhile at this point to trace Blake's position on imagination to classical antiquity. In fifth century Greece there existed alongside the mimetic theory of art another view which maintained that the work of art is greater than nature in that it confronts the deficiencies of nature's products with a newly created and independent image of beauty. The artist is seen here not as an obedient copyist of nature, but as an independent rival who by his creative ability improves on her necessary imperfections. There is a story - often repeated during the Renaissance - that Zeuxis - the artist who was said to have painted sparrow-deceiving grapes - had requested the five most beautiful virgins from the city of Croton, in order to copy the finest features of each in his picture of Helen. It is also reported that to an Egyptian who sneeringly asked whether Phidias had been in Heaven and seen the gods in their true forms, Apollonius of Tyana gave this memorable answer: "That was done by imagination, which is a better artist than imitation, for imitation can only depict what it saw, but imagination what it has not seen."[44]

This new outlook toward art was raised to the status of dogma in the philosophy of Plotinus. In a passage devoted to Phidias' Zeus, he asserted that the operation of the imagination, the inner vision, were of greater moment than any imitation of reality. Phidias, he claimed, depicted Zeus as he would have appeared should he have chosen to reveal himself to the gaze of humanity. According to the tenets of Plotinus' metaphysics, the image of Zeus that Phidias carried within him was not a representation of Zeus but his very essence.[45]

Returning to Blake, we may now elaborate on the question: where do his angels exist? In a comment on his painting The Bard, from Gray Blake states that

> The Prophets describe what they saw in Vision as real and existing men whom they saw with their imaginative and immortal organs; the Apostles the same; the clearer the organ the more distinct the object. A Spirit and Vision are not, as the modern philosophy supposes, a cloudy vapour or a nothing; they are organized and minutely articulated beyond all that the mortal and perishing nature can produce. He who does not imagine in stronger and better lineaments, and in stronger and better light than his perishing mortal eye can see does not imagine at all. Spirits are organized men (E 532).

What Blake seems to be saying is that imagination as existence or reality itself creates what it imagines. Hence, the angels exist for him who imagines in "stronger and better lineaments," and their "heaven," as in Swedenborg, is not separate from their private being: the outer world corresponds to the creative imagination. But imagination such as this, according to Blake, is limited to the unfallen world. In the present fallen world man's cognitive powers are disjoined: the senses become symptoms of man's descent into mere nature and reason turns into analytic power, the instigator of doubt, the spectre of death, the Satan. We are caught in the tentacles of "a polypus of soft affections, without thought or vision." The forms we see with our organic eye "in this vegetable glass of nature" are feeble replicas of eternal forms, which are plastic and perfectly responsive to the eyes of the soul.[46] It is as the British painter Lucien Freud pointed out: the artist sooner or later must admit that "it is only a picture he is painting" and that the picture will never "spring to life." Even the visionary whose perception is simultaneous with creation in unable to bridge the gulf between Pygmalion's human power that fashioned a statue and the divine power that turned it into a living body. In Frye's words, the sculptor Pygmalion "cannot transform his creature into an object of love; the lover cannot transform his loved one into a creature of the imagination."[47]

Blake would probably agree with this assessment. In the fallen state, we have a limited capacity to transform our lives according to the desires of imagination; our constitutive power, our ability literally to make the world is severly circumscribed. But he would also insist that it is the task of the fallen art to reorganize the "vegetable body," to awaken it to its real potentialities until it regains the clear and precise lineaments of a spiritual body. Only when this task of universal renewal is completed, shall we, in the words of Thomas Frosh, an interpreter of Blake, "enter the images in body, in a new life, and together with other men." At this stage art itself must disappear, for "the goal of art is the moment at which it becomes unnecessary, because the whole of life has taken on the character of art."[48]

Blake's ideas on the "new life" - the Paradise regained - are Heraclitean in character. Paradise is neither a state of supernatural bliss and perfrect rest nor a condition of natural innocence. On the one hand, Blake does not share the prevalent Western conception according to which, in St. Augustine's words, there are no "perverted elements" in Eden and "nothing at all in ourselves ˙or any other, will be in conflict with any of us."[49] On the other hand, he is not interested in a return to the state of natural nature. The natural man exists in the form only of our dirty, fragile, confined bodies. Blake finds it hard to love a Creator who could make our "places of joy & love excremetitious" (K 3, 305). Insofar as man uses as little imagination as possible, he is, as Frye puts it, a "hideous botch" or at best "a speck in a corner of a huge, mysterious, indifferent, lifeless cosmos."[50] Blake wants to retain some version of conflict even in the state of Edenic earth - the concrete Paradise of shaman - for without the clash of opposites there is no life: "Without Contraries is no progression" (E 34). It is only reason that cannot tolerate contradictions and always strives to negate them, whereas spiritual vision rejoices in them. Reason is dualistic and dualism originates in failure to acknowledge the relationship of reciprocal contrary states.

The most disastrous separation brought about by the doubting reason is that of body and soul (or spirit). As a result of this separation, our present bodies are, as Plato has it, a "walking sepulchre" to which we are bound "like an oyster in its shell" (Phaedrus 250). To Blake the material body, this "excrementitious Husk and Covering" (E, 225), is a "false Body: an Incrustation over my Immortal Spirit" (E 141). It is a garment to be shed for a better one: "The Naked Human form divine" (E 514). The word "form" (image) in Blake's sentence is important insofar as it indicates that the body-garment is not to be rejected altogether but only transformed. There is a similar idea in St.

205

Paul's platonizing thought: "It is sown a natural body; it is raised a spiritual body" (I _Cor_. 15:44). St. Augustine, expounding Paul's text, writes: "Just as now the body is called animate, though it is a body and not a soul, so then the body shall be called spiritual, though it shall be a body, not a spirit."[51] Besides St. Paul and the Platonic thought (including that of Swedenborg), Blake's most immediate influences in the portrayal of a risen or spiritual body are Ezekiel, Isaiah, St. John of Patmos, and Milton. If, however, we are to gain a deeper insight into Blake's views on the function of the human body, it is best to overlook as far as possible these extraneous influences and to concentrate on what belongs exclusively to his own visionary experience.

Blake's basic principle is that man has no body distinct from his soul or spirit. The body is the perishable fragment of the soul, the portion of the soul discerned by the five senses. Harold Bloom has formulated the Blakean stance as follows:

> Against the supernaturalist, Blake asserts the reality of the body as being all of the soul that the five senses can perceive. Against the naturalist, he asserts the unreality of the merely given body as against the imaginative body, rising through an increase in sensual fulfillment into a realization of its unfallen potential.[52]

Blake is not anxious to reduce the material to the spiritual or the spiritual to the material; he wants to keep both (eat the cake and have it) in a perfectly balanced relationship not by transcending but by reorganizing the senses through their engagement in the process of poetic work. He intends to keep what we have by radically transforming it.

I would like to suggest that the Blakean metamorphosis of the senses and by implication, of the body, is best understood in terms of what Gaston Bachelard has called "cosmic narcissism."[53] For the sake of contrast, however, we must first briefly dwell on some of the traditional views of narcissism.

206

Most theological and religious writers are inclined to see this phenomenon as a form of self-absorption rooted in the Fall. D.H. Lawrence has described it as follows:

> When Adam after the apple took Eve he didn't do any more than he had done many times before, in act. But in consciousness he did something very different. So did Eve. Each of them kept an eye on what they were doing, they watched what was happening to them. They wanted to KNOW. And that was the birth of sin. Not doing it, but KNOWING about it... Now, they peeped and pried... They watched themselves. And they felt uncomfortable after. They felt self-conscious.[54]

Plotinus and other Neo-Platonists also found in the story of Narcissus an allegory of the Fall. The soul, admiring its image in the water - in a material medium and a flowing, evanescent existence - forsook its spiritual estate and plunged after the outward and unreal image in the pool, only to find itself in a material world of death and decay. It is important to note, however, that both in Plotinus and Blake the fallen soul retains within itself a higher principle, an "inner translucence" by virtue of which it is capable of transmutation. It is only that this inner luminosity cannot be completely effective until freed from physical as well as spiritual dross.[55]

In Blake, too, the narcissism which resulted from the Fall, means self-consciousness: a turning outward from a state of being in which the inner and the outer exist in a dynamic and reciprocal relationship. It is a separation of body and soul and a fall into a world where the disembodied consciousness is forever watching itself and where the body undergoes a process of rigidification, finally completed in the immobility of the corpse. In certain of Blake's drawings, the Fall - the descent into the pit - is headlong; man falls with his head down.

In contrast to this vulgar narcissism, Blake's "spiritual body" is engaged in "cosmic narcissism" which has nothing to do with the contemplation of an external and alienated self-image. For, in Bachelard's vision, the water in which the soul sees its own reflection is not passive matter sluggishly waiting to be stirred, but already living water capable of making its own contribution to what is reflected in it. "A lake," says Bachelard, "is a great tranquil eye. A lake absorbs all the light and makes a world of it. The world is already contemplated, already represented by the lake. The lake, too, can say: 'the world is my representation'." Thus "cosmos, in some way, has a touch of narcissism."[56] The world wants to see itself in man (even after the Fall) as much as man wants to see himself in the world. There is a demiurgic activity outside us, hidden in landscape as well as within our perceptual organs. Bachelard calls it "material imagination," giving life to the elementary correspondence between man and the world; an imagination which "thinks matter, dreams in it, lives in it."[57] One would be hard pressed to find better words for this "substantive mimicry" that is cosmic narcissism than those of Shelley in Prometheus Unbound:

> As a violet's gentle eye
> Gazes on the azure sky
> Until its hue grows like what it beholds.[58]

To Bachelard, Blake is the poet of "absolute imagination," for whom imagination is not the faculty of forming images of reality, but rather "the faculty of forming images which go beyond reality, which sing reality."[59] In Blake's case this means that what is at work in the reorganized relationship among the senses, is synaesthesia - the ability to use the sense of hearing as we presently use sight, to see with the ear. According to Frosh, the effect of synaesthesia is to give us a body in which the distinction between kinds of sensation are not erased, but rather played off one against the other, setting up a rich and mutually heightening interaction. "Blake's risen body is founded not on a return to nonindividuation but on the individuality of minute particulars, and its character, in all respects, is dialectical."[60] Thus when Blake visualized the guinea-sun he could also hear a chorus of angels singing "Holy Holy Holy."

The eternal world and the risen body that lives in Blake's imagination is far more sharply defined and minutely detailed than anything seen by the mortal eye; for "the Infinite alone resides in Definite & Determinate Identity" (E 203). What man sees with his reorganized senses is definite and clear, or, as a Zen Buddhist would say, it is a clear and precise vision. The indefinite replaces the definite, the indeterminate the bound only with the decline of imagination reaching its lowest level in the form of rationalism, personified by Blake as the epistemophagous "idiot questioner," who is always capable of questioning, but never capable of answering. Reason sees only with its organic senses; it is the Spectre of Albion, destroyer of definite form.

Furthermore, there is no contradiction between the definiteness of forms or images and their translucence. In Blake's visionary world, images are both minutely precise and translucent, or rather, they are precise because of their transparency. We must remember that for Blake images are narcissistic: an image is a realization of desire and since the desire (which is the same as imagination) is infinite, it can have no set boundaries. The image must constantly change in tandem with desire.

The English Platonist Thomas Taylor, expounding Proclus, writes: "Very true being ... consists from bound and infinite," whereas corporeal things "rush from the embraces of bound, and hasten into multitude and non-entity." In the same vein Blake states: "Very true being" is "bound and infinite."[61] Frosh suggests that the elemental image of such infinitely flowing form is fire: "the contours of fire are perceived not in single boundary lines but throughout: it is the form which is all line."[62] According to Milton O. Percival, Blake's emphasis on "bound and infinite" as being in some sense characteristic of the ultimate constitution of things is designed, following Plotinus, to preserve "every identity within an all-inclusive unity." In this way "Blake saves his eternal world from the abstract character of the One in Oriental philosophy, and retains for it its determinate character."[63]

We have also found the same idea in Plato for whom Eros, far from being merely a human attitude, called love, is a metaphysical factor holding together the Limit and the Unlimited. Eros is desire and desire, according to Plato, is neither mortal nor immortal, neither divine nor human, but a mixture of being and non-being, i.e., a daimonion. As an intermediary between the two realms, desire is a mixing, a process of bringing together. Blake refines the Platonic scheme by proposing that this process can be effected only by an antecedent endeavor which consists in freeing the soul's original "inner translucence" from "the physical and spiritual dross." The spiritual energies are restored to their true shape not by getting rid of the material but by cleansing and restructuring the material itself. If our desire for the infinite cannot be slaked in the present body, we must remake the body so as to render it responsive, resonant to its desires. Infinite desire presupposes infinite man. In Blake's words, from No Natural Religion, "The desire of Man being Infinite the possession is Infinite and himself Infinite" (E 2).

Thus, once again, there is a perfect correspondence between the desire and fulfillment. But this is possible only because in Blake's thought the infinite is radically immanentized or, if you will, naturalized. It is natural for man, that is, for man in his imaginative body, to experience infinite gratification of infinite desire because in this state there is nothing that is external to his body: what he sees "out there" are images, an infinite proliferation of images which are subtle bodies like his own. So we can say with Blake that "All are men in Eternity, rivers, mountains, cities, villages, all are human." Man "looks out in tree and herbs and fish and bird and beast." The whole cosmos is potentially human. Of course, the cosmic body is not literally corporeal; rather it is like Swedenborg's "Grand Man of the Heavens" or Blake's 'body' of "Jesus the Imagination" of which all human individuals are members. As Swedenborg had insisted, it is neither large nor small, nor of any dimension, being not subject to the Cartesian categories of space and body. We shall also find this Swedenborgian and Blakean conception of the universe in Iranian gnosis, where the question that is consistently asked is not about the essences (whatness) of things, but about the "personality" as, for example, who is the Earth? who are the waters, the plants, the mountains? We live in a fully personified cosmos - not, to be sure, as the nineteenth century anthropologists assumed it to be "personified," but as filled with the soul-stuff (ensouled) from the "beginning." For, as we were compelled to admit with Barfield, Hillman, et al., in the final analysis it is impossible to say who is "souling" whom or what. All that can be said is that "things thing." Imagination imagines. To maintain, therefore, as Blake does, that everything is in a sense human means that the world or reality is artistic or imaginal at its core and that it has a "touch of narcissism."

In this world-picture there are no hidden and remote corners, no spots of unconsciousness. Blake has no use either for the subversive unconscious of Freud or the Jungian unknowable Collective Unconscious. His vision of the regenerated body is radically non-perspectival: it does not compartmentalize experience into discrete segments; it posits no schismatic categories of space in terms of above and below, here and there, before and behind.

The absence of perspective (seeing through the eye, not

211

with it) implies that one is not limited to a single viewpoint; it is a way of seeing that becomes total knowledge. But this is far from saying that man has now been transmogrified into an all-knowing, all-loving, all-powerful being or that in Blake's Eden all is suffused with light and glory. It is precisely because the world of imagination is all-inclusive and so suffers no limitation or division that it includes error and imperfection. According to Blake, there is "a constant falling off from God, angels becoming devils. Every man has a devil in him, and the conflict is eternal between a man's self and God."[64] The devil is none other than reason divorced from imagination. And it is in this capacity that reason produces those monsters which Freud and Jung relegated to the unconscious. For Blake, the reason itself is an "unconscious" monster. If monsters are no longer visible in our world, it is because they cannot be distinguished from our everyday "conscious" reality governed as it is by the "reasonable" daylight rationality. We are no longer conscious of the monstrous and the diabolical because it has been normalized - more or less evenly distributed throughout our institutions and activities. The true unconscious is the "monotheism of consciousness." It has been observed that the demonic may now be so diffused on the terrestrial plane that it has no need or time to appear in single individuals.[65]

The Russian existentialist Leon Chestow wrote that "reason, by its very nature, hates life more than anything else in the world, feeling it instinctively to be its irreconcilable enemy."[66] From this a curious parallel could be drawn between Blake's fallen reason and the Freudian belief that man, lacking the possibility of returning to the quiet of the womb, seeks the quiet of death. Freud's death instinct is of course part of the unconscious, but so is Blake's reason, which, cut off from imagination, acts as a completely destructive force: "This is the Spectre of Man, the Holy Reasoning Power/ And in its Holiness is closed the Abomination of Desolation."[67]

Death for Blake is the reduction of the physical body to inert matter such as rock and sand, the "limit of opacity." To the extent that this condition is appraoched already in life, we are "walking sepulchers," indeed ghosts in a machine that sooner or later must break down. At the other end of the specturm, there is the belief in eternal life of a purely spiritual nature, the visio beatifica of the official theology. Between these two extremes is Blake's middle way - a Western nirvana - the way of a renovated body. The senses with which this body is equipped are akin to our "animal sensing" in that they are sharper, more refined than our usual (literal) sensing. The renovated body is synaesthetic: it senses by means of a "second sense" through the mere sensuous. Such sensing is imagining, for to imagine is to perceive with fullness and clarity, to "see things as they are." Quite simply, to imagine is to see better (not more).

To imagine is to learn to see as the poets and artists see or as Adam saw Eve after a dream - as "so beautiful" (Bachelard). Artistic imagination is creative because it is "creative seeing" (aisthēsis), that is, perceiving the unique by "sticking to the image," to the existence of the image as being ontologically prior to its "essence" or meaning (Heidegger). We may then suggest with Hillman that the Lockean maxim - nothing in the mind that is not first in the senses - can be rehabilitated, for it means that "the mind is primarily aesthetic,"[68] an animal mind and an anima mundi. To a subtle sensing, everything is potentially subtle. So we need not engage in espying "subtle bodies" in paranormal states, take pictures of them or record their voices. As I tried to show earlier, all such "scientific" experiments are fundamentally perverse and intrinsically contradictory. For a subtle body that could be seen by everybody and independently of the way in which it is seen, would no longer be "subtle." Rather it would be a "datum," a "hard fact" and, as such, dead as only literal and rational contraptions can be dead. To Blake death means, not literal dying but solidification and rigidification of the psychical subtle essence which even in the form of a "glorified body" is not averse to anything that the body does, including putrefaction. It all depends on your nose because that's where your ontology is. As Emerson said: "Beware of what you want, for you will get it."

Mundus Imaginalis in Corbin and Sufism

Henry Corbin's main body of writings is devoted to Sufism, Islamic philosophy and Isma'ili Shi'ism - areas in which he has uncovered vistas of thought that had previously been unknown or underestimated. His thinking, nurtured by early interest in Boehme, Swedenborg and Heidegger, extends beyond mere ratiocination to an emphasis on the inner, visionary pursuit of truth. The pivotal figures of this quest are the Persian philosopher and mystic Avicenna (Ibn Sina, 980-1037) and the illuminationist philosopher Suhrawardi, executed for heresy in 1191 - both exemplifying in various degrees the union of discursive reason and imagination.

Corbin's work must be seen as an attempt to correct the fatal orientation of Western metaphysics toward what Bergson calls "the world of solids" - an orientation which begun with the repudiation of Plato's and Avicenna's concept of active intelligence (intellectus agens, poetic intellect) in favor of Latin Averroism and Aristotelian Thomism. From that time philosophical exploration turned toward causal experience and the ratio, reducing the psyche to (empirical) perception and reasoning. Active intelligence which Corbin identifies with archetypal imagination or "agent imagination" was regarded by Western rationalist orthodoxy as heretical or was accorded at best the status of a secondary faculty that "secretes nothing but the imaginary, that is, the unreal, the mystic, the marvelous, the fictive, etc."[69] In the

214

course of this development, the "official philosophy" of the West came to admit only two sources of knowledge: the sense perception providing so-called empirical data and the concepts of understanding which order and govern empirical experience. The active intelligence was denied any noetic function of its own and became the preserve of poets and dreamers. It would not be an exaggeration to say that this trend has been only ascerbated in recent times - in spite of the protestations to the contrary by those who have espoused as their mission to promote "humanistic values," "experience," "involvement," and a host of other allegedly non-rational diversions.

Corbin's (and the Sufist) fundamental position is that the world of archetypes (mundus archetypalis) which is also a mundus imaginalis, is a distinct field of imaginal realities requiring methods and perceptual faculties different from the spiritual and intelligible world on the one hand, and from the empirical world of ordinary sense perception, on the other. The forms and figures of the imaginal realm subsist on an ontological plane above the concrete and opaque density of the material things and below the intelligible world of pure ideas; they are more immaterial than the first and less immaterial than the second.

We thus have a threefold universe (corresponding to our tripartite anthropology): the earthly, human or sensible world (the object of ordinary sensory perception); the intermediary world of archetypal or visionary imagination - known in Sufism as alam mithali or Malakūt, the world of the Soul (the object of imaginative perception); the world of Intellectual Forms, of pure Cherubic intelligences (the object of intelligible knowledge). The function of mundus imaginalis is defined by its median and mediating situation between the intellectual and sensible world. The faculty of perception corresponding to this intermediary world is archetypal imagination, whose "specialty" is to effect a complete and immediate realization of the imagined contents. In

Corbin's words, imagination on the visionary plane "posits real being,"[70] which, as we emphasized earlier, is at the same time "real imaginal being."

In this magical realm there is not and never has been a gap between reality and appearance, for what "appears" or presents itself as an image is from the very outset radically multiperspectival, polysemous and metaphorical. The same must be said of another pair of opposites - being and thinking; in the world of visions being and thought coincide. Thought is creative in the sense that whatever we will or desire tends to be brought about. Of course it is not at all the case that every whim, every fleeting fancy of ours is always in some mechanical way immediately fulfilled; that would be sheer chaos, a madman's world. What is meant by the creative character of thought is that "in the long run," a man is as he thinks. In Heraclitean terms, our character is our destiny. It is only that in states of "true imagination" (the Imaginatio vera of Paracelsus) our "character" is such that there is no wavering between conflicting desires: we desire what we are and we are what we desire.

*

In Sufism the organ which is said to be responsible for the creation of mundus imaginalis is called himma, "creative power of the heart," connoting the notions of meditation, project, intention, desire, force of will, faith. The creativity of himma is ontological in the sense that it produces changes in the so called outside world: the object on which the "heart" concentrates its creative power, its imaginative meditation appears as an outward, extra-psychic reality perceivable by others who have reached an equivalent degree of visionary power. These "objects," however, are not separate from the imaginer's imagination; they are "out there" and yet no other than the person who imagines them.

216

One could say, their "outness" is only an index of the microcosm which is man. It is because man is a syllepsis, a compendium of nature, that his imaginative power is capable of "placing" him exactly where he wants to be. In these realms seeing is not only believing, but also being. In Corbin's terms, the function of archetypal imagination (himma) consists in "initiation to vision." Visions, in contrast to rational demonstrations and sensual perceptions, are "in themselves penetrations into the world they see."[71]

The imaginal world is also called by Islamic authors the "eight clime" (subsisting beyond the seven climes of the sensible world of space) or the "climate of the Soul." It is a concrete spiritual world (the concrete Paradise of the shaman) of apparitional forms, a country of nowhere that can only be reached by going inward - ab extra ad intra - i.e., from the external, literal and exoteric to the hidden, inward and esoteric (ta'wil literally meaning to "reconduct something to its source").[72] In the language of gnosis, it is a movement from macrocosm into microcosm. However, when this journey is completed, the microcosm (the infinitely small) turns out to be a reflection of the macrocosm (the infinitely great). The inner reality now envelopes, surrounds and contains the outer and the visible reality. As a result of this "internalization," the spiritual reality itself is the "place" of all things, meaning that it is not located anywhere in sensory space; in relation to the latter, the "where" of the imaginal reality, "its ubi is an ubique," an ubiquitous place.[73]

The ubiquity of the imaginal space is the very opposite of the quantitative scientific space conceived as an infinite, lifeless, cold void. The quantitative space is the "satanic space" of Blake, the blank, unfeeling stage on which matter plays its aimless, random acts without regard for man. Man, as Pascal has it, is only an accidental reed, liable to be crushed at any moment by the forces of this blind and indifferent universe:

"Cast into the infinite immensity of spaces of which I am ignorant, and which know me not, I am frightened."[74] To be a "thinking reed" may be a special privilege but it also adds to man's essential loneliness in the midst of an unthinking (res extensa) nature. In contrast to the quantitative space of modern cosmologies, the real imaginal space for Corbin is a field of unframed relationships, evoked by myth, dream, and religious vision, in which the figures and events seem free-floating in an environment without clear-cut boundaries. Like the chariot of Ezekiel, the bodies in this qualitative space move through no spatiality external to themselves. Each body has its own world or rather creates its own world in conformity with its "ruling love" (Swedenborg).

It might be possible to understand the structure of imaginal space more adequately by relating it to what Heidegger calls man's essential tendency to remove distance (Ent-fernung), i.e., to bring close, to "situate."[75] Dasein (man) exercises a spatializing function by giving things which he frequently uses their place according to the importance they have in life. The various places of space which arise in this way have no relation to geometric space: their hierarchy is determined by the necessity which they have for the work to be done. Thus what is "nearest" to us is hardly ever that which has the least distance from us, but is rather something that is "within reach" and available to our preoccupied grasp. Heidegger uses the comparison between our "closeness" to a friend approaching us on the sidewalk, and the sidewalk itself. Objectively speaking, the sidewalk is closer to us than the friend; yet we are not aware of our closeness to the sidewalk at all. This observation, trivial in itself, has far-reaching implications. It means that Dasein, instead of being a worldless spirit, is necessarily bound up with existence in space, or, more primordially, he is already in a world. Space, therefore, is neither subjective nor objective, but rather the result of <u>Dasein's</u> spatializaing activity; it is a mode of one's existence in the world. As a de-distancing agent, man carries his own space within himself, a space which he can never cross over himself.

Now once we accept the ontological status of the imaginal world, there is nothing that prevents us from applying to this world the kind of spatializing activity that, in principle, is not different from the one which occurs in the "secular" world of <u>Dasein</u>. Just as man spatializes in his everyday concernful dealing with things, so does he spatialize "in" the <u>mundus imaginalis</u>, in accordance with the directions of his "ruling love." It is only that in the latter case his spatializing is, so to speak, more thorough and consistent than usually; there is no possiblity of falling back into the geometrical space.

In view of the above, it should not be insuperably difficult for us to assert with the Sūfi masters that the imaginal world refers to the archetypal images of <u>individual</u> and <u>singular</u> things; that it possesses extension and dimension, figures and colors. Indeed, everything in this world has shape, size, color and other qualities which the material objects of our world have; it has a scenery like that of the earth, human forms, grotesque or beautiful, senses that know pleasure and pain.

However, these figures, even though they are the exact replicas of everything existing in the sensible world, cannot be perceived by the senses. They are images or essences of sensible corporeal things, having different causal properties from those of the physical world. But this is far from saying that these images are identical to Platonic Ideas or, for that matter, to the unknown and unknowable archetypes of Jung. According to Corbin, the contrast between celestial (subtle) matter and earthly visible matter must not be reduced to a Platonic dualism between idea and matter or between the universal and the particular. For "the state of infirmity, of lesser being and darkness repre-

219

sented by the present condition of the material world, results not from its material condition as such but from the fact that it is the zone invaded by the demonic Contrary Powers, the arena of struggle and also of the prize."[76]

In contrast to the universal and immaterial character of the Platonic Ideas, the beings of the world of archetypal images are conceived by the Sūfi meditators as "particular forms that are separate from matter, but by no means from all material envelopes."[77] They are personal presences, individual and unique, having a corporeality and spatiality of their own, an "immaterial" materiality or what the Cambridge Platonist, Henry More, called spissitudo spiritualis - a kind of spiritual extended-ness. In the median world of epiphanic space, the soul, instead of being bound to spatial coordinates, as in the quantitative space of science, is situative.

Mircea Eliade has described what he calls the sacred or hierophanic space of the archaic religions in terms that corrobor-ate Corbin's interpretation of Sūfi cosmology. According to Eliade, the deepest meaning of sacred space is revealed in the symbolism of "the Center." "The Center" has no geographic implications, but is rather part of what Corbin calls "visionary geography."[78] Every inhabited region may have several centers each of which is called "the center of the world"; it can be associated with sacred trees, rivers, mountains and sanctuaries and is thought to be the meeting point of three cosmic regions: heaven, earth and hell. Eliade believes that the multiplication of such centers betrays the nostalgia to be as often as possible near the archetype. Every man tends, even unconsciously (or, to be exact, imaginatively), toward a "center" where he can find sacredness or "reality." It is "the desire to find oneself always and without effort in the Center of the World, at the heart of reality, and by a short cut and in a natural manner [i.e., in concreto or in a bodily form] to transcend the human condition..."[79]

In the visionary geography of Iranian Sufism the hierophanic space is always and in each case at the center which is none other than the spatializing and situative soul; the soul, by being a spatializing agency, is also a centering power. "Hierophanies take place in the soul, not in things. And it is the event of the soul that situates, qualifies, and sacralizes the space in which it is imagined."[80] The mountain tops of the visionary earth are the mountain tops of the soul. The images of the earth and the images of the soul correspond to one another; as the soul projects the earth, so each physical structure discloses the mode of its psycho-spiritual activity. Put simply: on the visionary plane spirit and nature are reciprocal realities because the substance of the soul is made of the celestial earth and the celestial earth is made of the substance of the soul.

Thus there is far less difference between the "living" and the "dead" than we are accustomed to suppose. In the traditional Sūfi narratives, the question is often asked: "where are the faithful believers post-mortem?" The answer is always the same: "They are in bodies which are in the likeness of their material bodies." The dead exist in the world of archetypal images. They pass through our world, but we do not see them with our bodily eyes. The mundus imaginalis is beyond our world, but it is also invisibly in our world; it is "a description of the outer things which are the apparentiae reales of inner states."[81]

All things in the archetypal world are outer manifestations of man's inner being. "The Paradise of each one is absolutely proper to him. It consists of the man's works and actions, which in the other world will appear to him in the form of houris [voluptuously beautiful young women], castles, and verdant trees."[82] Each man is inside his own paradise or, alternatively, inside his own hell. A Shaikhi saying echoes this fundamental thesis: "The paradise of the faithful gnostic is his very body and the hell of the man without faith or knowledge is likewise his body itself."[83] Hell is essentially a condition of sleep (unconsciousness) in which man is ignorant of the true nature of sensory perceptions. He is passively subjected to them as though they were material, objective and unalterable. It is a complete subservience to data (empirical, historical, etc.) and to the enslaving objectivization of reason, "the idiot questioner."

Another Sūfi *illuminatus*, Shaikh Kirmani points out that man's essential body is fashioned according to the extent of his knowledge, to his capacity to understand, to his spiritual consciousness and moral conduct. The more developed his spirituality, the subtler also will be his essential body. We create for ourselves a dwelling place in proportion to the capacity of our spiritual energy. Just as we create the places of our dreams, so is our environment in the "other" world created by human imagination. Indeed it is only in the imaginal realm that we create the kind of environment that is fully and literally our own (fully human). In Kirami's somber and liberating words, "nobody can ever escape from himself, get out of himself; nobody becomes someone other than himself; nothing becomes other than itself."[84]

According to Swedenborg whose vision of the "other" world is in many respects similar to that of Iranian Sufism, the appearances of things in the world of the dead, are plastic to the states of mind of the spirits. The spirits are not "fixed and dead," but, like images, ever-changing. In an essay on Swedenborg, Yates says: "So heaven and hell are built always anew and in the hell or heaven ... all are surrounded by scenes and circumstances which are the expression of their natures and the creation of their thought."[85]

To use Eliade's conceptual framework, in the world of imagination we are always at the center of the universe, for our center is where the "ruling love" is. As St. Augustine is reported to have said: *amor meus pondus meum* (my love is my gravity). We get what we love, because our love is a space maker, constantly reorganizing and refining the circumstances (environment) of our body. This also means that each soul is not only at the center of the universe, but a universe in itself - a world.

The Sūfi seers have expressed this idea by saying that the subtle body (man as microcosm) is a mode of being which constitutes its own matter. The most frequent comparison used by Suhrawardi is the mode in which images appear and subsist in a mirror. Images are like forms seen in mirror: the mirror is the place of the apparition of images, but the images themselves are "in suspense"; they are neither like material things in a place nor like an accident in its substratum. The expression "in suspense" indicates that the image or the subtle body is "independent of the substratum in which it would be immanent in the manner of an accident (like the color black, for example, subsisting through the black object in which it is immanent)."[86] To convey the full meaning of Suhrawardi's statement, Corbin invites us to imagine the form of a statue in its pure state, liberated from the marble, the wood, or the bronze. Corbin's comparison of the subtle body with the pure form of a statue is certainly helpful, provided we do not confuse the latter with the ideal forms of Plato, relegating the statue itself to "phantasmic" and shadowy piece of artistry (and so twice removed from the ideal form). In our view, the bronze or the wood is wholly in the statue. For it is precisely the artist's task to transform the "material" matter into subtle or spiritual matter in such a way that the former completely disappears or rather, is fulfilled in the latter. It is in this sense that we may say with Suhrawardi that the statue as an image is independent of its substratum, the bronze. The bronze is only used, like the alchemist uses vulgar metals, to create a new thing which, as created, is independent from and ontologically prior to the material substance. Indeed it exists "in suspense" between two worlds, the spiritual and the material, by giving sustenance to both. These subtle bodies, be they artworks or the visionary figures of the mundus imaginalis, are not what we see with our bodily eyes. Rather they themselves are the eyes through which we see the world.

II: THE SUBTLE BODY IN TRADITIONAL THOUGHT

NOTES

[1]Mircea Eliade, From Primitives to Zen (New York: Harper & Row, 1967), pp. 184-85.

[2]Emile Durkheim, The Elementary Forms of Religious Life (New York: The Free Press, 1965), p. 275.

[3]CW II, par. 160.

[4]Hermes Trismegistus was a legendary Egyptian sage who, since the time of Plato has been identified with Thoth. Discovered on the Rosetta Stone as "thrice great" ("megas, megas, megas") he was considered to be the impersonation of the religion, art, learning, and sacerdotal discipline of the Egyptian priesthood. The most authentic group of Trismegistic texts are ascribed to Zosimus (4th century A.D.). See The Divine Pymander and Other Writings of Hermes Trismegistus, tr. from the Original Greek by John Chambers (New York: Samuel Weiser, 1973).

[5]CW 13, pars. 261-262. On the dual nature of Mercurius see 13, par. 267 ff.

[6]Hillman, The Dream and the Underworld, p. 129.

[7]CW 14, par. 104; cf. Memories, Dreams, Reflections, pp. 205, 212, 221.

[8]Hillman, "Silver and the White Earth," p. 23.

[9]Rene Guenon, The Crisis of the Modern World, tr. from the French by Marco Pallis and Richard Nicholson (London: Luzac and Co., Ltd., 1962), p. 45.

[10]Richard Wilhelm, "Wandlung und Dauer." Quoted in "The Beyond," a paper by Barbara Hanna, Copyright 1969 by C.G. Jung Foundation for Analytical Psychology, Inc., New YOrk, N.Y. Cf. Wilhelm's Weisheit des Ostens (Düsseldorf, 1951), p. 28 ff.

[11]See CW 9i, pars. 635-637.

[12]Wilhelm, "Wandlung und Dauer" in Hanna's "The Beyond," p. 81.

[13]C.G. Jung, "Psychological Commentary on Kundalini Yoga: Lectures Three and Four - 1932," Spring 1976, pp. 6, 7.

[14] Ibid., pp. 10, 17.

[15] Hillman, "Silver and the White Earth," p. 45.

[16] Jung, "Psychological Commentary," p. 14.

[17] Proclus, Elements of Theology, p. 320.

[18] "Commentary on the Hikma al-'arshia'" in Corbin, Spiritual Body and Celestial Earth, p. 98.

[19] Corbin, Spiritual Body and Celestial Earth, p. 99.

[20] Ibid., p. 102.

[21] Mead, The Subtle Body, p. 51. According to Synesius, "the whole of the genera of daimons are supplied with their substance by this mode of life. For during the whole of their existence they are of the nature of images and take on the appearances of happenings" (Mead, 71-72).

[22] Ibid., pp. 59-60.

[23] Ibid., pp. 71, 72, 73.

[24] Ibid., p. 78.

[25] Ernst Benz, "Theogony and Transformation in Schelling," in Man and Transformation, Papers from the Eranos Yearbooks. Bollingen Series XXX. 5 (Princeton University Press, 1964), p. 232.

[26] Jacob Boehme, Aurora, selection entitled Earth in Der Schelesische Mystiker, ed. Charles Waldemar (München: W. Goldman Verlag, 1959), p. 63.

[27] See Titus Burckhard, "Cosmology and Modern Science," pp. 147, 159, 160, 164.

[28] F. Schelling, Philosophie der Offenbarung, in S.W., XIV, 207. Tr. by Ernst Benz, "Theogony and Transformation in Schelling," p. 234.

[29] F.C. Oetinger, "Ol," Bibl. Wörterbuch, p. 463 ff.

[30] Ibid., p. 151.

[31] Benz, "Theogony and Transformation in Schelling," p. 242

[32] Hillman, "Silver and the White Earth," p. 45.

[33]"Shaman" is derived from the Tungus shaman, from Sanskrit śramana, "ascetic," śram, "to heat oneself or practice austerities." (Standard Dictionary of Mythology and Legend, Funk and Wagnal, p. 1003. Cf. Mircea Eliade, Shamanism, Archaic Techniques of Ecstasy, tr. from the French by Willard R. Trask. Bollingen Series LXXVI (Princeton University Press, 1964), p. 84 ff.

[34]Eliade, Myths, Dreams, and Mysteries, tr. Philip Mairet (Harper Torchbooks, 1950), pp. 227-28.

[35]Eliade, "Recent Works on Shamanism," p. 180.

[36]Eliade, Patterns in Comparative Religion, tr. Rosemary Sheed (New York: The World Publ. Co., 1958), p. 480.

[37]Eliade, Myths, Dreams, and Mysteries, p. 97.

[38]The Poetry and Prose of William Blake. 4th ed. (Garden City, N.Y.: Doubleday, 1970) copyright @ 1965 by David Erdman and Harold Bloom, p. 545. Henceforth referred to by the letter "E", and the page.

[39]Cassirer, The Philosophy of Symbolic Forms, II, p. 97.

[40]Northrop Frye, Fearful Symmetry, a Study of William Blake (Princeton University Press, 1947), pp. 25, 26.

[41]Karl Jaspers, General Psychopathology (1923), quoted by Mary Warnock, Imagination (Berkley, 1976), p. 168. Jasper's patient also observed that the figures of this imaginal "world" were there in sapce, but "as if they had their own private space peculiar to themselves" (Ibid.).

[42]See Karl Rahner, Visions and Prophecies, tr. by Charles Henkey and Richard Strachan (London, 1963), pp. 32-33.

[43]Frye, Fearful Symmetry, p. 26.

[44]Philostratus, Apollonius of Tyana, Vi, 19 (ed. Kayser, p. 118).

[45]See Erwin Pankowsky, Idea, a Concept in Art and Theory, tr. by Joseph J.S. Peake (New York: Harper & Row, 1968), pp. 9-33; 47 ff.

[46]Blake has inherited the distinction between the fallen and the unfallen world from the Neoplatonic tradition which assumes a supra-mundane and eternal world, a fall and a return. Moreover,

the physical world was conceived as resulting from the interaction of two elemental forces, the one active and formative, th other passive and receptive. On the analogy of sex these forces were often imagined as masculine and feminine; on the analogy of vegetation - as inner and outer. In the language of the Schoolmen, the inner, creative force is natura naturans, whereas the outer, passive creation is natura naturata. The outer vegetative force decays and dies; the life force persists forever.

[47] Frye, Fearful Symmetry, p. 281.

[48] Thomas R. Frosh, The Awakening of Albion; the Renovation of the Body in the Poetry of William Blake (Ithaca: Cornell University Press, 1974), pp. 158, 159.

[49] St. Augustine, City of God XIX, p. 393.

[50] Frye, Fearful Symmetry, p. 40.

[51] St. Augustine, The Enchiridion on Faith, Hope and Love, tr. by J.F. Shaw (New York, 1961), XCI, p. 105.

[52] Harold Bloom, "Dialectic in The Marriage of Heaven and Hell," in English Romantic Poets; Modern Essays in Criticism, ed. Meyer H. Abrams (Oxford University Press, 1960), p. 82.

[53] Bachelard, On Poetic Imagination, p. 79.

[54] Quoted in Frosh, The Awakening of Albion, p. 56.

[55] See Milton Percival, William Blake's Circle of Destiny (New York: Columbia University Press, 1938), pp. 203-204. On Blake's Platonism cf. Kathleen Raine, Blake and Tradition. Bollingen Series XXXV. II. 2 Vols. Also the shorter version Blake and Antiquity (Princeton University Press, 1977).

[56] Bachelard, On Poetic Imagination, p. 77.

[57] Ibid., p. 37; cf. p. 9. Jean-Paul Sartre says: "We must invent the heart of things if we wish one day to discover it," "L'Homme ligoté," in Messages II (1944).

[58] Schelley, Prometheus Unbound (Seattle: University of Washington Press, 1959), p. 293.

[59] Bachelard, On Poetic Imagination, p. 15.

[60] Frosh, The Awakening of Albion, p. 145.

[61]Quoted in Percival, William Blake's Circle of Destiny, p. 81.

[62]Frosh, The Awakening of Albion, p. 130.

[63]Percival, William Blake's Circle of Destiny, p. 81.

[64]Ibid., p. 131.

[65]See Titus Burckhard, "Cosmology and Modern Science," p. 158 note.

[66]Leon Chestow, Potestas Clavium, tr. by Bernard Martin (Ohio University Press, 1968), pp. 10-11.

[67]Quoted in Percival, William Blake's Circle of Destiny, p. 97.

[68]Hillman, "Image-Sense," Spring 1979, p. 143.

[69]Corbin, "Toward a Chart of the Imaginal," in Temenos 1, 1981, p. 23.

[70]Corbin, Creative Imagination in the Sufism of Ibn 'Arabi, p. 180.

[71]Ibid., p. 93.

[72]Ta'wil is that "hermeneutic par excellence" which does not operate on the purely mental plane by the assistance of a formal logic or of dialectic leading from one concept to the next by deduction. It is "theophanic method of discourse" (Ibn 'Arabi) based on the ancient principle "Only the like knows the like." Access to the mundus imaginalis is opened up by generating in oneself a minimum of visionary power.

[73]Corbin, "Mundus Imaginalis or The Imaginary and Imaginal," Spring 1972, p. 5.

[74]Blaise Pascal, Pensées, ed. Brunschvicg, fr. 203.

[75]See Heidegger, Being and Time, Sections 22-24.

[76]Corbin, Cyclical Time in Mazdaism and Ismailism," in Man and Time, Papers from the Eranos Yearbooks 3. Bollingen Series XXX. 3 (Princeton University Press, 1957), p. 118.

[77]Corbin, Spiritual Body and Celestial Earth, p. 174.

229

[78] Ibid., p. 30.

[79] Eliade, Images and Symbols, tr. by Philip Mairet (New York: Sheed and Ward, 1961), p. 55; cf. Patterns of Comparative Religion, p. 367 ff.

[80] Corbin, Spiritual Body and Celestial Earth, p. 23.

[81] Ibid., p. 330 note 16; cf. pp. 255-56.

[82] Ibid., p. 233.

[83] Ibid., p. 102; cf. pp. 187, 227.

[84] Ibid., p. 225.

[85] "On Swedenborg, Mediums and the Desolate Places," Yeats' Appendix to Lady Gregory's Visions and Beliefs, Vol. II (1920), p. 303.

[86] Corbin, Spiritual Body and Celestial Earth, p. 83; cf. p. 127; 80-81; 87-88.

IN PLACE OF CONCLUSION

Art and the Subtle Body

Our aim has been to retrieve the notion of subtle body from its embeddedness in the rigid tenets of an either/or style of thinking (spiritualism or materialism) and to place it where it belongs - in the world of images. At this point it bears repeating that the world of images, though ontologically prior to other "worlds," is not a separate conpartment of being. Images interact with the world of senses (ordinary time and space), they are in it, but not of it. This means that the soul as the third reality possesses an ontological status, not because it stands apart from the physical and material phenomena, but rather because nothing else, including the physical and the material, can exist without the soul. Analogously, subtle bodies are "subtle" not because they are incomparably lighter or more agile than physical bodies, but rather because they are elusive, illusive and meta-phorical, forever escaping the grasp of a literalistic viewpoint. Quite unpretentiously, "subtle" means ungraspable by the tools of scientific method, immeasurable, beyond calculation and rational control.

As it was indicated in our discussion of Blake, the best analogy for subtle states is provided by the dynamics of artistic creation. The central question to be faced here is: what is created in an artwork? Clearly the artist does not create oil pigments or canvas or the structure of tonal vibrations. All these physical realities are given and actual. According to Suzanne Langer, what occurs when an artwork is created out of these elements is that they disappear. In Langer's terminology, which here overlaps with that of Corbin, they are transformed into dynamic apparitions and images (_apparentiae_ _reales_). The given and the actual is transmuted into a "virtual entity"[1] For example, a picture is "an apparition of virtual objects (...) in a

231

virtual space." The virtual space is a piece of purely visual space and the objects which are "in" it exist for vision alone.

This means that the virtual space of a painting is created space. It does not exist apart from the imaginative expression and there is no way of pointing to a meaning beyond its presence. The colors and shapes of visionary space are neither identical with those of actual (normal) space, nor are they "airy nothings"; they exist in their own mode which is that of imagination. If they are an illusion from the standpoint of our normal perception, we must agree with Langer that "illusion in the arts is not pretense, make believe, improvement on nature, or flight from reality; illusion is the 'stuff' of art, the 'stuff' out of which... the unique and often sensuous expressive form is made."[2]

Art is the creation of sheer, self-contained appearances, of shaped apparitions and visions that are real in the same sense in which images are real. In the presence of a picture we neither believe nor disbelieve in the existence of objects that are depicted in it; nor do we compare them with objects in the so called real world. We simply experience. We experience meaning without asking "what does it mean?" because the "content" of an artwork is fully expressed in its "form." The meaning of an artwork is beyond the classical categories of subjectivity and objectivity; it resides in the created qua created.

By analogy the same can be said of the realm of subtle bodies. Like artworks, they too have no meaning apart from what they appear to be; the meaning of a subtle body, like that of an image, is not substantive but adjectival and metaphorical. We are here in a world whose only law is that of movement and mutual interpenetration - a world of total dynamism, pervaded, paradoxically, by the kind of stillness we sometimes experience in states of undivided attention. Typically, such states are beyond the subject-object distinction and by the same token beyond the Cartesian bifurcation of reality in terms of material and spiritual things. Therefore, to say, for example, with the Sūfi visionaries, that the world of subtle bodies is _in_ them or that they constitute their own world, means, quite plainly, that these bodies are neither things nor thoughts but images. The subtle body is an imaginal body, that is, a real _imaginal_ being.

The great paradox of imagination is that, being ontologically _sui generis_, it is nevertheless all-inclusive and all-pervasive. An image is like the Eastern mandala: without a center of its own, it "centers" everything else. Images are essentially egoless, altruistic, non-possessive, god-like. In this respect they are the ideal paradigms of the time and space-bound world of empirical realities.

Consider a shoe. As an ordinary object it is a construction of leather having a particular shape and use. Once however, a picture of shoes is made, we find that the space of this picture and the shoes which are "in" it, are radically different from space of the room in which that new whole of shapes and colored volumes is exhibited. The new space, in Langer's words, is "purely visual space"; "it is nothing but a vision."[3] A picture of shoes is an apparition and the shoes in the picture are a celestial pair of shoes.

We may amplify this description by referrring to Heidegger's famous interpretation of Van Gogh's _Les Souliers_. As contemplated by Heidegger, a pair of peasant shoes, painted in somber, heavy monochromatic browns are placed in an indefinite space; they

> stand out, and their dignity is precisely in having been worn into the state they are in. In standing out they hide part of the earth, which yields its harvest only to those not allergic to hard work. The crushing weight of the human body against the hard surface of the earth has produced these shoes."[4]

Heidegger's point is that, in Van Gogh's painting, shoes are, so to speak, essentialized, saying in effect: look at what a pair of shoes can be! We must be careful, however, not to slip at this point into platonizing the picture of the shoes as the ideal proto-type of concrete shoes. What we see in the painting is not an idea of shoes but a concrete prototype, a pair of dream shoes that are more real than the materials (oil, pigment, etc.) out of which they are made. In Sūfi terms, they are apparitional shoes worn by celestial peasants laboring on a celestial earth.

What all this amounts to is that reality imitates art. To put it in Heideggerian cum archetypal language, the experience of artwork discloses the thingness of a thing in its imaginal con-figuration. Things receive their space of possibility, that is to say, their apriority, their ontological status, through the works of art (aisthēsis). This must be so because the work of art creates an autonomous and self-sufficient world in which a thing, such as a pair of peasant shoes, may stand in its own being and shine in its own light. In artistic experience - Heidegger calls it "poetic dwelling" - "the world appears in such a way that one looks upon it as for the first time."[5] Hans-Georg Gadamer has described this experience in the following words:

> The tones that constitute a musical masterwork are tones in a more real sense than all other sounds and tones. The colors of a painting are colors in a more genuine sense than even the nature's wealth of colors. The temple column manifests the stone-like character of its being more genuinely in rising upward and support-ing the temple than it did as an unhewn block of stone.[6]

It is the privilege of art to reveal nature in her pristine, archetypal dynamism - a process which is similar to the opus of alchemy where the natural nature (natura naturata) is deformed in order to liberate animated nature (natura naturans), i.e., nature in her imaginal aspectivity. The alchemical opus reduces nature to the prima materia, a state of coincidence in which, as Patricia Berry writes, "there is no opposite, no other principle," because it "contains in its radicality its own internal opposition."[7]

The symbol of coincidentia oppositorum should not be understood in the sense of an abstract unity or reconciliation of opposites. There is a world of difference between the latter and the "coincidence" which is polar and dynamic. For polarity is not a mere balance or compromise, but a living and generative interpenetration. Polar opposites, unlike logical opposites which are banally contradictory, generate each other and this co-generation is also the birth of a new reality. In a polar situation, each quality or character is present in the other. Hence they can be distinguished, but not separated. It is also for this reason that the power to apprehend polar opposition is not given to logic-chopping but belongs to imagination.

The new reality (Jung's "new level of being") revealed in art (as in the alchemical conjunctio) is the imaginal "gold" at the heart of things, the "double" of every individual event, thing and person. The double, however, is not a (celestial) duplicate, but the concrete essence of a thing, just as the colors of a painting express the essential colors. As Barfield has observed, "we admire not what we see but what Carot or Turner, or the illustrator of our favorite fairy-stories, saw, in the landscape."[8]

One cannot overemphasize, however, that these essential images (or concrete essences) are not the Platonic Ideas. Like the apparitional figures of mundus imaginalis in Sufism, they are particular forms that cannot be completely separated from matter. They are things of this world in the subtle state and therefore impenetrable by our sensory organs. The "eight clime" of the Sūfi gnosis is a real place, fully accessible to imagination: There are heavens and earths, animals, plants, minerals, cities, towns and forests. The physical things of our terrestrial earth are reflections of the celestial earth, the world of the soul. Or again, as Corbin, in another variation of this theme, observes, the celestial earth and all things belonging to it, represent, as it were, the phenomenon of the earth in its absolute state, i.e.,

"absolved from the empirical appearance displayed to the
senses... Here all reality exists in a state of Images and these
Images are a priori or archetypal."[9] In other words, it is a
realm of absolute or pure psychic activity. Or, if you prefer,
the mundus archetypus is a world composed of absolute matter,
that is , free from the determinations that are peculiar to the
dense and corruptible matter of the sublunar world. Absolute
matter is a kind of pre-material or primal matter which is fully
transparent to its own forms. Like things in an artwork, it is
pure apparition, a purely visionary thing, an image pure and
simple.

It is also significant that the traveler in the ubiquitous
soul-space is said to be unable to indicate the road to others .
He can only describe where he has been, but he cannot show
the road to anyone who does not share the "mentality" of the
traveler himself. Roads can be shown only because there is a
distance between the traveler and his destination whereas in the
celestial landscape, as Swedenborg said, "all progressions ...
are effected by the changes in the state of the interiors,"[10]
i.e., by the "ruling love" of the traveler. The soul itself spatializes, converting geographical destination into her destiny. The
soul is not only a space-maker, but also a time-maker.

Time of the Soul

The space of the soul is inseparable from the time of the
soul. By moving in the imaginal space, the soul creates its own
time - an imaginal time which is distinct but not separate from
the physical time of astronomical computations. The time of the
soul may be compared to movement in music. It is felt or experienced time possessing a sort of voluminousness, complexity and
variability that makes it impossible to posit real beginning (creatio

ex nihilo) and end (final resolution). A musical creation, like any other artwork, is made of the stuff of imagination: a combination of the same and different, limited and unlimited, the time of life and the time of death.

I would like to suggest that the temporality peculiar to the soul in her uroboric itineration has the paradoxical character of what I previously called "finite infinitude." By saying this I am only harking back to Plato for whom time is the realizaiton of eternity through limitation and in the last analysis through mortality. We found the same idea in Jung: "The feeling for the infinite...can be attained only if we are bounded to the utmost..."

What I mean by "finite infinitude" is something like immortality minus everlastingness or static perfection. "Eternal life," as it is conceived by theologians who are governed by spirit fantasy, is like a perfect painting in which there is nothing to be seen. In contrast to this, we may give some thought to what the Harvard philosopher W. E. Hocking calls "immortability," by which he means "the conditional possibitity of survival."[11] The soul is not endowed with immortality as something fixed, degreeless, and given to it irrespectively of its secret desires.

> Immortality may be 'put on'; one may also put on mortality. The soul may resolve to take the present, partial scene of things as final, and may by determined action upon that hypothesis make it true for its own experience.[12]

I would like to illustrate these thoughts by referring to the concluding line of T. S. Eliot's Burnt Norton: "Only through time time is conquered." Also relevant is the opening coda to Little Gidding:

> We shall not cease from exploration
> But the end of all our exploration
> Will be to arrive where we started
> And know the place for the first time.

We must try to relate the last line from the Little Gidding to the line from <u>Burnt</u> <u>Norton</u>. What we then get is that time is "conquered" by knowing " the place for the first time." Even though I resent the word "conquered" because it carries the undertones of triumphalism peculiar to the Apollonian spirit - the only member in the psyche's household who consistently refuses to die - the sense of Eliot seems to be that "the first time" is necessarily an "always." Now, since there is <u>always</u> a <u>first</u> time (note the paradox of "always" and "first"), it follows that what we bombastically call the search for meaning must take place in the lived instant without throwing furtive glances toward the past or the future. For it is precisely in the present instant - an infinitesimal hairline between past and future - that time and eternity meet.

Instants or the "eternal nows" are, as the mystics claim, the stuff out of which the real time is made. In this sense, instants are like images: individual monadic wholes without pre-established order or sequence. Hillman has written that "imagistic view eternalizes...it's not that images are eternal (...); but rather that images, like paintings, have all their parts going on concurrently, simultaneously... and so the image is always going on, eternally present."[13] Patricia Berry, in her ground-breaking discussion of dreams, points out that "the dream as Image makes no causal statements. Events occur in relation to each other, but these events are connective, as in painting or sculpture, without being causal." In a dream "all events affect and simultaneously constellate each other."[14]

An excellent illustration of the non-sequential character of time is found in the Zen tradition:

> When the wood becomes ashes it never returns to being firewood. But we should not take the view that what is latterly ashes was formerly firewood. What we should understand is that firewood stays at the position of firewood. There are former and later stages. We do not consider... that Winter <u>becomes</u> Spring or that

Spring <u>becomes</u> Summer.[15]

According to Zen, all action occurs in an infinite present, in a "now" that is not causally connected with the "before" or "after." There is no attempt to construct a sequence: all events occur not in a continuous and linear progression, but simultaneously.

In an equally sharp contrast with the Western obsession with the idea of linearity and historical development is the total present-centeredness which the anthropologist Dorothy Lee found to be the main trait of time experience among the Trobriand Islanders.[16] When these people describe the maturation of a plant, they see the ripe plant called "taytu," as <u>remaining</u> a ripe yam. When an overripe yam appears, it is a different entity, not causally or sequentially connected with the ripe yam and is given another name, "yowana." According to Lee, what we consider a causal connection between events, is to the Trobrianders an ingredient in a multidimensional pattern. The following brief exchange between a Sūfi and a scholar sums up the linear and the non-linear views of time.

"What is Fate?" Nasrudin was asked by a scholar.
"An endless succession of intertwined events, each influencing the other."
"That is hardly a satisfactory answer. I believe in cause and effect."
"Very well," said the Mulla, "look at that." He pointed to a procession passing the street.
"That man is being hanged. Is that because someone gave him a silver piece and enabled him to by the knife with which he committed the murder; or because someone saw him do it; or because nobody stopped him?"[17]

In the esoteric tradition (in which we include Avicenna and Sufism) an instant of time has no past and future because these two tenses are present in the instant's now. Each instant is an individual entity that differs from other individual entities not only numerically, <u>i.e.</u>, as one individual thing among others of the same species, but as "specific individuality," an individuality

239

that is itself its own species.[18] The present instant may well be the "result" of past occurences as well as of my future anticipations and in that sense there is a connection between the present, past and future. But this connection is not strictly causal in that what happens now can never be traced to a single cause. This means that the cause of an event is not really outside and separable from the event itself, but is identical with it. What we have here is "polar causality" as distinct from "mechanical causality."[19] There are many, indeed, innumerable "causes," an inextricable conglomeration of factors which, precisely because they are innumerable, can never amount to a satisfactory explanation of a momentary situation. There are correspondences, connections between events, but no single explanatory cause. As the Easterner, describing the law of karma would say: there is action, but no agent of action. Karma seems to be utterly "impersonal": "the acts of one are acts of the whole, and the acts of the whole react on the littlest part."[20]

What we seem to be witnessing here is ecology on a cosmic scale, a "hidden harmony" where the "littlest" part is precisely the instant - a simultaneous constellation of all the other parts. An instant is thus the most radically finite "entity" - evanescent to the point of being nothing. But, paradoxically, it is at the very bottom of its finitude and no-thingness that lies what Wordsworth called "premonitions of immortality." To paraphrase the archetypal psychologist R. Lopez-Pedraza, we must stick to the instant for in the last resort there is nothing else to stick to. Instants, like images, are wholes, microcosms reflecting macrocosm. They are worlds whose mode of being constitutes their own matter.

Now the time, created by the soul, consists of such instant-worlds. And it lasts only while it is created. In every creative act of the soul "we know the place for the first time" (Eliot) and the "first time" is also an "always." In such a context what we call "immortality" of the soul would be nothing more grandiose than the soul, making time from instant to instant within its imaginal orb - "making it" indefinitely, but not necessarily infinitely. The soul is "immortable" because it is changing from instant to instant and because, while it is thus changing, it may choose different "speeds" or, in extremis, it may elect not to change at all and thus "die." What I am suggesting is also consonant with the process of transmigration, usually described in terms of transmission of a flame from one combustible aggregate to another. If we light one candle from another, the communicated flame is one and the same, in the sense of an observed continuity, but the candle is not the same.

The karmic concept of change entails total disappearance as well as appearance, discontinuity as well as continuity. There is no sharp boundary line between life and death. Put within the context of archetypal psychology, what disappears are the empirical bodies, what continues are the imaginal bodies. These bodies - in their ante as well as post mortem states are flamelike in their continuous changes of contour, fully dynamic, ab-solved from the weight of dead matter, but not from all materiality. Hence their flaming may be upward- or downward- or sideward-directed; the heat which the flames carry may be heavenly or hellish or purgatorial; but it is the same heat and the same flame.

Thus what continues throughout the realms of life and the realms of death is the imaginal body, a compendium and a reflection of the universal in the concrete. This dreamlike entity is forever new because it continuously recreates itself. Every instant it is itself and the other; indeed, its self-sameness consists precisely in being responsive to the other, i.e., in being essentially ex-static. It is by being generative of what it is not.

One could, therefore, propose that our continuation beyond the grave is best described in terms of continuous creativity -

as a transformative process in which the agent of the transformation is born anew and dies from instant to instant. So there is an "I" but it is an "I" which lasts only for an instant, an instantaneous (imaginal) "I" perduringly flowing into and out of other "I's" (human as well as non-human). But, remember, these instants and a posteriori the instantaneous "I's" (subtle bodies) are also "eternities," eternal nows. They are instantaneous eternalizing apparitions. We must, therefore correct our previous statement: "There is change but no agent of the change" by saying that "there is change and there is an agent behind the change, but this agent is radically finite in that it lasts only for an instant." At the same time, however, precisely because its life-span is infinitesimal, it is also eternal. The agent (the soul) is infinitely finite.

*

Our notion of the imaginal body owes little if anything to the classical (Aristotelian) view of man as a composition of body and spirit, a view which, as we already pointed out, was formed for the world of things. For the sake of clarity let us reiterate that traditionally spirit or intellect (nous) constitutes what is highest, most powerful and most worthy in the essence of man. It is the seat of his creativity, but - and this is the crux of the problem - the creativity of the nous is confined to a remodeling or compounding of a substrate (hypokeimenon) which as such is already present and perduring. For example, an architect produces only the house that is pre-given in his soul in the form of an image (eidos). His producing is not really "creating" at all, but an imitating (mimesis) - fortunately never successfully! - of a perfect essence.

This is not, however, how the artist himself envisions his work. To him, a genuine artwork is not only a new creation but

242

a recurrent creation; he cannot afford to succeed in producing a perfect image for just as it would be impossible to live in a perfect house so there is nothing to see in a perfect image. Art creates a world that is self-explanatory; this means that an artwork must continually, repeatedly invent its own meaning and thus can never be regarded as finished.

If, on this analogy, we imagine the subtle body in the so called post mortem states, we might say that in these realms artistic activity is concentrated not on creating works that subsist apart from the human body and are exhibited in the museums, but on the body itself. Man in the "Beyond" is, without remainder, his own maker; he is what he fails to be in life: an autogenous, wholly spontaneous agent - the absolute artist engaged in "cosmic narcissism" in that he is his own museum and his own spectator. In Blake's lapidary phrase, "The Imagination is the Human Existence itself." But, of course, even in these cosmic surroundings, the spontaneity and freedom of imagination is not immune from "error." One may err (I am now speaking ontologically and not phenomenologically) and do "the evil thing" just as spontaneously as one may be pursuing the "straight path." It all depends on your "ruling love." But this is the price which imagination exacts from those who fall in love with it. The only reward one may expect for giving up the pretense of being the master in one's own house is freedom - freedom not to do what we want, but to want what we (spontaneously) do.

*

Shaman, Dionysus and Tantrika

In conclusion I should like to place the complex notion of the dream body within the context of three psycho-mythological topics: shamanism, the figure of Dionysus and Tantric Buddhism.

243

We have already seen that the essential feature of the primordial shaman is that he can ascend to the celestial regions without negating the senses, i.e., not only in spirit, but bodily, in concreto. What we did not mention was that the precondition for such flight is a feminization of the male shaman.[21] The neophyte must undergo a transformation in the course of which he relinquishes his former male behavior and adopts the female role. In this way he becomes "a soft man being," i.e., an androgyne whose essential mission is to be an intermediary between the cosmological planes of earth and sky. It has been remarked that the effort to incorporate this paradox involves the shaman in "the constant practice of transformation, as if moving from one point of view to another provides the experiential ground of understanding, of wisdom of true perspective."[22]

The figure that in Greek mythology corresponds to the "soft man being" of shamanism is Dionysus Zagreus. In contrast to the Dionysus of classical scholarship which has stressed the irrational, intoxicated and instinctual aspects of this god, Jung prefers to see him in the state of Zagreus, the suffering and dismembered god "whose divine substance is distributed throughout the whole of nature."[23] Elsewhere he conceives dismemberment in a Neo-Platonic fashion: "the divine powers imprisoned in the body are nothing other than Dionysus dispersed in matter."[24] Hillman, elaborating on Jung, understands the dismemberment as referring to a psychological process that involves a "bodily experience" - an experience which would result in the abandonment of "central control" and at the same time in "the resurrection of the natural light of archetypal consciousness distributed in each of the organs."[25] What is intended here is a spiritualization of all parts of the body: the mythological dismemberment is homologized to a psychological awakening of the whole man, an initiation into the archetypal consciousness of the imaginal body.

Jung, as I explained in the preceding pages, had discovered what he called the fundamental dissociability of the psyche and its multiple consciousness (luminosities). It was a decisive move designed to dethrone the ego and consciousness (reason) from its hegemonic position in the totality of psychic life. What the Dionysian experience should do for us is to decentralize, so to speak, across the board by redistributing the soul throughout the body and by activating the psychic life of the whole organism; for it is only in this way that real renovation or "resurrection" of what Blake called "the worm of sixty winters" and "seventy inches long" may occur. In Hillman's words, the Dionysian experience "disconnects the body's habits at the animal-vegetable level, releasing a subtler appreciation of the members and organs as psychic representations."[26]

Dionysus was also known as Lysios, the loosener. The word is cognate with lysis meaning "loosening, setting free, dissolution, breaking bonds and laws." In this capacity Dionysus is psychologically related not only to the soft and androgynous being of the shaman, but also to the Tantrika, the practitioner of Tantra who aims at awakening Kundalini - the unconscious life force or psychic energy and spreading it throughout the body. Tantra[27] (Hindu and Buddhist) is a religious experience which is said to be most appropriate to life in kali-yuga, the present age of enlightened darkness. Starting from the actual "occultation of the spirit in the flesh," the tantrika strives to realize freedom and immortality in the body itself. Like the shaman and the Blakean man, he wants to make the best of both worlds.

The basic principle, underlying this experience is that enlightenment must be attained by the same means which have caused perdition, occultation and bondage. "By what we fall, by that we shall rise." According to Lama Govinda, Tantra uses the elements of our present personality as the raw material to be converted into a work of art, the completely realized human

245

being. In this way "the inner and the outer worlds are transformed and unified in the realization that the basic qualities of
human individuality binding us to our worldly existence (samsara)
are at the same time the means of liberation and of enlightenment."[28] A Tibetan Tantric text expresses this idea as follows:

> How can there be bliss in the absence of the psycho-
> organism?
> Bliss encompasses a sentient being.
> In the same way as the fragrance of a flower
> Cannot be experienced in the absence of a flower,
> Bliss is without meaning
> In the absence of psycho-organismal patterns.[29]

The Tantric view that there is no true spirituality without
an embodied existence is a variation on our theme that "eternity"
or "immortality" can only be realized in time. Time and the
time-bound human body are the vehicle for the attainment of
(relative) timelessness. In Govinda's words: "Transiency is as
necessary to immortality (or to the experience of eternity), as
the body is to the soul, or as matter is to the mind."[30] Goethe
has encapsulated this dialectical relationship between time and
eternity in the aphorism: "If you want to approach the Infinite/
Examine the finite on every side" (Willst Du ins Unendliche
schreiten/ Gehe im Endlichen nach allen Seiten).

So it is futile to set arbitrary limits to the beginning or to
the end of life. Reality is composed of many parts, many begin-
nings and many ends, all playing against one another in a tension
of mutually supplementing opposites. Life and death are not
facts of nature or history and for that reason they happen, not
in nature or history, but in imagination. Essentially they are
mythical events which always begin in illo tempore, i.e., in
every "now" fully and imaginatively lived and that includes
dying as well.

Rilke is one of his Letters states: "Nothing that is real can
pass away." But then he adds: "I believe that many people are

246

not real. Many people and many things."[31] I would have no quarrel with these lines if they could be modified by prefixing to the word "real" the qualifying "psychologically" or "imaginally," saying "nothing imaginally real can pass away." For it may well be that "death" in all its forms is due to the lack or exhaustion of imagination. There is imagination not only in life but also in death and its absence in the latter must be nothing short of a "second death." But the secret word that unlocks the entrance to the isthmus between life _and_ death and thus to both an imaginative life and an imaginative death, is transformation. Again it is Rilke who has put it best: "...it is our task to imprint this provisional, perishable earth so deeply in ourselves that its reality shall rise in us again 'invisibly'."[32]

IN PLACE OF CONCLUSION

NOTES

[1] Suzanne K. Langer, Problems of Art (New York: Charles Scribner's Sons, 1957), p. 6.

[2] Ibid., p. 34.

[3] Ibid., p. 28.

[4] I owe this paraphrase of Heidegger to E. F. Kaelin, "Notes Toward an Understanding of Heidegger's Aesthetics," in Phenomenology and Existentialism, eds. Edward N. Lee and Maurice Mandelbaum (Baltimore: The John Hopkins Press, 1967), p. 79. Cf. Heidegger's Holzwege, p. 25.

[5] Heidegger, Hebel der Haufreund (Pfullingen: Neske, 1965), p. 19.

[6] Hans-Georg Gadamer, Philosophical Hermeneutics, tr. by David E. Linge (University of California Press, 1967), p. 223.

[7] Patricia Berry, "On Reduction," Spring 1973, p, 80.

[8] Owen Barfield, Poetic Diction, a Study in Meaning. 3d. ed. (Middletown, Conn.: Wesleyan University Press, 1973), p. 182.

[9] Corbin, Spiritual Body and Celestial Earth, p. 82.

[10] Swedenborg, Heaven and Its Wonders and Hell, N 193.

[11] W. E. Hocking, Thoughts on Death (New York: Harper & Brothers, 1937), p. 108.

[12] Ibid., p. 219.

[13] Hillman, "Further Notes on Images," Spring 1978, p. 161.

[14] Berry, "An Approach to the Dream," pp. 75, 76.

[15] Dogen, quoted in Alan Watts, The Way of Zen (New York: American Library, 1957), p. 123.

[16] See Dorothy Lee, "Codification of Reality: Linear and Nonlinear," Psychosomatic Medicine, Vol. 12, no. 2 (March-April 1950).

[17] Quoted in Robert E. Ornstein, The Psychology of Consciousness (San Francisco: W. H. Freeman and Co., 1972), p. 75.

[18] Corbin, Avicenna and the Visionary Recital, tr. from the French by Willard R. Trask (Irving, Texas: Spring Publications, 1980), p. 47; cf. pp. 78, 80, 81, 83.

[19] Owen Barfield, What Coleridge Thought, p. 248 note 3.

[20] Christmas Humphreys, Karma and Rebirth (London: John Murray, 1976). p. 39.

[21] See Waldemar Bogoras, The Chuckchee. Jesup Borth Pacific Expedition, Vol. 7 (American Museum of Natural History Memoirs, Vol. II, 1904), pp. 450-51.

[22] Joan Halifax, Shamanic Voices, A Survey of Visionary Narratives (New York: E. P. Dutton, 1979), p. 28.

[23] CW II, par. 378.

[24] CW 9ii, p. 158 n.

[25] Hillman, "Dionysus in Jung's Writings," Spring 1972, p. 201.

[26] Ibid., p. 203.

[27] See Eliade, Myths, Dreams and Mysteries, pp. 144-46; Arthur Avalon, The Serpent Power (New York: Dover Publications, 1974). pp. 287, 290, 297.

[28] Lama Anagarika Govinda, Creative Meditation and Multi-Dimensional Consciousness (Wheaton, Ill.: The Theosophical Pub. House, 1976), p. 43.

[29] br Tag - gnys (Hevajra - mula), fol. 7b. quoted by H.V. Gunther, Tibetan Buddhism in Western Perspective (Emeryville, Calif.: Dharma Press, 1977), p. 90.

[30] Govinda, Creative Meditation, p. 288.

[31] Letters of Rainer Maria Rilke, 1892-1910, tr, by Jane Bannard Green and M. D. Herter Norton (New York: The Norton & Co., 1948), p. 145.

[32] Letters of Rainer Maria Rilke, 1910-1926, p. 374.

BIBLIOGRAPHY

Avens, Roberts. Imagination Is Reality; Western Nirvana in Jung, Hillman, Barfield & Cassier. Spring Publications, Inc., 1980.

Bachelard, Gaston. On Poetic Imagination and Revery. Trans. Colette Gaudin. Indianapolis: The Bobbs-Merrill Co., 1971.

Barfield, Owen. The Rediscovery of Meaning and Other Essays. Middletown, Conn.: Wesleyan University Press, 1973.

Berry, Patricia. "On Reduction," Spring 1973.

_____. "An Approach to the Dream," Spring 1974.

Casey, Edward S. Imagining; A Phenomenological Study. Bloomington: Indiana University Press, 1976.

Cassirer, Ernst. The Philosophy of Symbolic Forms. 3 vols. Trans. Ralph Manheim. New Haven: Yale University Press, 1955-1957.

Corbin, Henry. Spritual Body and Celestial Earth. Bollingen Series XCI: 2. Trans. from the French by Nancy Pearson. Princeton University Press, 1977.

_____. Creative Imagination in the Sufism of Ibn Arabi. Bollingen Series XCI. Trans. from the French by Ralph Manheim. Princeton University Press, 1969.

_____. Avicenna and the Visionary Recital. Trans. from the French by Willard R. Trask. Spring Publications, Inc., 1980.

Crookal, Robert. Ecstasy; The Release of the Soul from the Body. Morradabad, India: Darshana International, 1973.

Dodds, E. R. Proclus; The Elements of Theology. A Revised Text with Translation, Introduction and Commentary. Oxford: Clarendon Press, 1963.

Eliade, Mircea. Myths, Dreams and Mysteries. Trans. Philip Mairet, New York: Harper & Row, 1957.

Friedländer, Paul. Plato I. Bollingen Series LIV. Princeton University Press, 1969.

Heidegger, Martin. Poetry, Language, Thought. Trans. Albert Hofstadter. New York: G. P. Putnam's Sons, 1967.

Hillman, James. The Myth of Analysis; Three Essays in Archetypal Psychology. New York: Harper & Row, 1972.

_____. Re-Visioning Psychology. New York: Harper & Row, 1975.

_____. Suicide and Soul. Zürich: Spring Publications, 1964.

_____. Loose Ends; Primary Papers in Archetypal Psychology.

_____. The Dream and the Underworld. New York: Harper & Row, 1979.

_____. "An Inquiry Into Image," Spring 1977.

_____. "Further Notes on Image, " Spring 1978.

_____. "Image-Sense," Spring 1979.

Jung, C. G. The Collected Works of C. G. Jung. 20 vols. Trans. R. F. C. Hull. Bollingen Series XX. Princeton University Press, 1957-1979.

_____. Memories, Dreams, Reflections. Recorded and ed. by Aniela Jaffé. Trans. from the German by Richard and Clara Winston. Vintage Books, 1961.

Mead, G. R. S. The Doctrine of the Subtle Body in Western Tradition. London: Stuart & Watkins, 1967.

Miller, David L. THe New Polytheism. Prefatory Letter by Henry Corbin. Appendix by James Hillman. Spring Publications, 1981.

The Poetry and Prose of William Blake. 4th ed. Garden City, N. Y.: Doubleday. Copyright 1965 by David Erdman and Harold Bloom.

Price, H. H. "Survival and the Idea of 'Another World'," in Language, Metaphysics, and Death, ed. John Donnelly. New York: Fordham University Press, 1978.

Raine, Kathleen. Blake and Tradition. 2 Vols. Princeton University Press, 1968.

Rhode, E. Psyche. Trans, W. B. Hills. 8th ed. London, 1925.

Swedenborg, Emanuel. Heaven and Hell. Trans. George F. Dole. New York: Swedenborg Foundation, Inc., 1979.

Tyrrell, G. N. M. Apparitions. New York: Pantheon Books, 1973.